I Give You My Word

FRANÇOISE GIROUD

I Give You My Word

Translated from the French
by Richard Seaver

Illustrated with photographs

HOUGHTON MIFFLIN COMPANY BOSTON 1974

FIRST PRINTING   V

First American Edition
Copyright © 1974 by Houghton Mifflin Company
All rights reserved. No part of this work may
be reproduced or transmitted in any form by any
means, electronic or mechanical, including
photocopying and recording, or by any information
storage or retrieval system, without permission
in writing from the publisher.

Library of Congress Cataloging in Publication Data
Giroud, Françoise.   I give you my word.
Translation of Si je mens . . . Conversations avec
    Claude Glayman.
1. Giroud, Françoise. I. Glayman, Claude. II. Title.
PN5183.G55A313   1974   070.4'092'4   74–8791
ISBN 0–395–17219–5

Printed in the United States of America

Originally published in French under the title *Si Je Mens* . . .
Copyright © 1972 by Société Express-Union and
Editions Stock.

Foreword

THIS BOOK came into being under rather unusual circumstances. I edit the French weekly magazine, *L'Express,* which is more than enough to keep me busy. A book? Where would I find time? And why?

"That's just the point," a journalist named Claude Glayman said to me one day, with a publisher standing at his elbow. "Since you won't take the time to write, let me interview you, ask you the questions I and other people have been wondering about you. For a long time you've been on the balcony of history. How does one get there? What does one see from that vantage point?

"We'll tape-record our conversations. And then we'll see what we've come up with."

I didn't know Claude Glayman. He is young and likable. The book he had in mind about me was meant to inaugurate a whole new series for his publisher. He had taken the trouble to read hundreds, thousands of articles I had written . . . I accepted.

After about thirty hours of interviewing, I found myself with some 600 pages of typed transcriptions. Unpublishable pages. Private words, stripped of the voice that uttered them, are not of a nature to be turned into black and white on the printed page. So then what? Tear them up? Difficult. I didn't have the courage. I had fallen into the trap that had been set for me. In these 600 pages there was "something." I tried to make them readable without depriving them of that "something" which, in my eyes, was the sole justification for publishing them: the freedom of voice with respect to everything and everybody and, in the final analysis, with respect to myself.

F. G.

Illustrations
following page 134

Françoise Giroud with her older sister and their mother, 1917
André Gide, 1930 (*L'Express — Photo Allégret*)
Françoise at seventeen, 1933
On a movie set as script girl, 1934
With other members of the cast and crew of *Courrier-Sud,*
    1935
Françoise, 1937
In Paris during the Occupation, 1943
As editor of *Elle,* with publisher Hélène Lazareff and members of the staff, 1950
Françoise's mother and Françoise's daughter,Caroline, 1951
Maurice Thorez, 1953 (*AGIP*)
With Jean-Jacques Servan-Schreiber and François Mauriac at *L'Express,* 1954
Albert Camus, 1955 (*Tele-Photo*)
Former premier Pierre Mendès-France and Socialist Party leader Guy Mollet, 1956 (*Lattes*)
François Mauriac and Jean-Paul Sartre, 1957 (*Intercontinental*)

On a reporting trip to the Soviet Union, 1960 (*Michelangelo Durazzo*)

Jacques Boetsch, 1970 (*L'Express — Christian Taillandier*)

Jean Monnet and Bertrand de Jouvenal with Françoise, 1973

During a recent editorial staff meeting at L'Express (*L'Express — J. R. Roustan*)

In her Paris apartment with daughter, Caroline, 1973 (*Gerard Bousquet*)

With François Mitterrand, 1973 (*Ch. Simonpietri-Gamma*)

In her office at L'Express, 1973 (*L'Express — J. R. Roustan*)

With France's new president, Giscard d'Estaing, shortly before his 1974 election (*L'Express — J. P. Guillaume*)

With Jérémie, her second grandson, 1973

I Give You My Word

I

— WHAT KIND of childhood did you have?
— A strange one.
— Strange? Why?
— It's hard to explain. And anyway, I'm not sure I want
to. Childhood is something so close, so special . . . It's
something you ought to keep to yourself. The way you keep
back tears.
— But can't you give me a few landmarks . . . some
points of reference for later on?
— My father was an absence more than anything else, and
a myth. An absence first of all because of the war, then because of a mission the French government sent him on to the
United States. And after that because of an illness which at
the time was incurable, and later killed him. The illness went
on for years, and during that period I never saw him. I
adored him. At home, they used to talk about him as a hero
who had given his all for France — which was considered
the least any well-bred soul could do for his country . . .
"well-bred soul . . ." Where is that from? Corneille? It's
a line from Corneille my mother used to read to me when I
was four or five . . . "For souls well-bred, worth waits but

for the crown of years . . ." Quite a catechism! And then there was Péguy, too: "Blessèd be the ripened grain, blessèd the harvested wheat; and blessèd those who have died in a just war . . ."

My mother was . . . *the* mother, the mother we all dream of having: beautiful, good-natured, tender, with a sharp sense of the ridiculous. And with an inner strength that was unshakable. Really extraordinary. She played a very important role not only in my own life — which is natural — but in the lives of everyone she came in contact with. And that was true even in her waning years. People used to come to see her the way they go to a spring for water . . . As far back as I can remember, and up until the last days of her life, our house was always a very special place.

What else? A grandmother who was as arrogant as she was unbending, a woman who lived on lamb chops, played bridge, and every afternoon pressed someone into service for an hour to brush her hair. I also had an English governess until I was six or seven, who taught me that one should never raise one's voice, talk about oneself, or bring up personal subjects . . . which is not going to make our conversations any easier.

In any case, after my father's death I watched the world of my childhood disintegrate. Everything was sold off, little by little. The knickknacks, the rugs, the books, the piano. A Bechstein grand piano, of which I was very fond. Maybe that's why I don't have any sense of ownership. The only thing I feel nostalgic about are the gardens, those big, lush gardens. The governess went too, of course, along with the maid, the cook, one floor of the duplex apartment, the jewelry, the silverware . . .

My mother, who was a jack-of-all-trades and therefore master of none, squandered the vestiges of her inheritance on several of those absurd businesses just made for "ladies-in-distress."

The private residence transformed into a hotel where the owner just can't bring herself to make the customers pay . . . the high-fashion boutique so undercapitalized that the capital is all used up before you open the doors . . . I'm an expert on the subject of debts! Not to mention pawnshops! "God will take care of us," my mother used to say with simple faith, and off she would go again on some new tack. The family, who would have liked to see her fit neatly into the "poor cousin" category, looked on askance. The widow — there was one in every middle-class family . . . Their apartments were spacious enough. They took them in and made lady-companions out of them. If these poor cousins had children, the children were made to feel their "difference," as long as they were poor. But my mother was the proverbial mule and refused to give in and play the "poor cousin" game. My sister and I were shipped off to boarding school. A school which was always paid late, of course. That's an education in itself, being a little girl in a prim and proper boarding school where your tuition is always in arrears. I learned a lot there, and I never forgot it.

My sister reacted by falling ill. My method of coping was to make sure and always be first. First in everything, impertinently first! "The brazen little imp!" the headmistress used to say. But I had an incredible memory, so studies were easy for me. I kept telling myself I'd take up law . . . I had an uncle who was a lawyer. And I greatly admired the most famous lawyer of the period, César Campinchi, who had been very close to my father. Or maybe medicine. One of my grandfathers had been a doctor. He'd been the official physician for the Sultan of Constantinople, who had made him a pasha. A colonel and a pasha. If I had a calling, that was it: not to be a pasha, of course, but a doctor. But seven years of study after the baccalaureate, or even eight! And who was going to pay for it? Then, one day a little darker than the others, just before I turned fifteen, I realized that all that was pure fantasy, a pipe dream, and that the only thing for me to do was go out and find a job. Earn my living. Bring money into the house instead of being a drain on my mother's remaining resources. So I went out and got a job. So much for childhood.

— And your mother let you?

— Listen, to finish with this period of my life once and for all, there's something I should explain. Throughout my childhood I had kept hearing my mother say, "Ah, if only there were a man to help us!" But there wasn't any man — probably because she didn't want there to be any. The image of my father, his noble acts, his memory, his myth had to remain inviolate. Who could have taken his place? The image we had of him, from the stories my mother told my sister and me, was truly that of a knight who had without a moment's hesitation set out to cut off the head of the dragon.

What choice did I really have, then? Objective truth is one thing. The truth as I saw and experienced it is this: a young, beautiful but terribly harassed woman — my mother — was forever faithful to the memory of the hero — my father — struck down in the course of a noble battle, and it was up to me, since he never had the son he desired, to try and carry on in his place, to go out and look for dragons! Therefore, I went for them. Or, more prosaically, I wanted not only to earn my own living but also to save my mother from the sorry straits she found herself in.

I think she understood. She used to say that I had a cross on my forehead, a cross that she alone could see; she called it the sign of destiny. "Destiny" was a big word. But I'm forever grateful to her for having spared me the usual maternal ambitions — especially in those days when all that mothers wanted for their daughters was an advantageous match. No one ever talked to me about a "good marriage." I never had to fight against any preconceived future, or submit to it. That's an extraordinary stroke of luck.

I should add that my mother was no ordinary person, assuming of course there are ordinary people, which I don't for a minute believe. A few days before she died, in 1959, she said to me: "What bothers me most is that I'll never know the outcome of the Algerian War. It's going to last a long time. I won't be able to hold out till it's over. Unless Jean-Jacques comes up with something. Ah, why can't that young man be at least a little pro–De Gaulle?"

The "Jean-Jacques" she was referring to was Jean-Jacques Servan-Schreiber, who later became a *député* from Lorraine and President of the Radical Party. She adored him. A few years earlier there had been a pointed exchange between them. At least it seems so in retrospect. It was just after the fall of Dienbienphu and the Laniel government, in 1954. It seemed virtually certain that René Coty, the French President, would call on Mendès-France to form a new cabinet. Naturally, Jean-Jacques thought of nothing else. He was only thirty at the time, but politics had already become his sole consuming interest.

One Sunday he invited himself over for lunch. "Mendès-France is certain to be called on to form a new cabinet," he said. "I have an idea for him about Indochina. Before I submit it to him this afternoon, I'd like to know what you think of it." This was his idea: tell Ho Chi Minh that he had the following choice — either agree within the week to begin peace negotiations, or Mendès-France would call for full mobilization, after which he and his cabinet would resign.

My mother, whose passion for politics was virtually as great as Jean-Jacques', heard him out, then said to him: "A week. You're always too much in a hurry, my dear Jean-Jacques. A week is too short. Give them a month." "A month? Do you really think so?" "I not only think so; I'm sure. But it's a good idea, an excellent idea."

And that was the origin of the now-famous "gamble," which led to Mendès' remark about Servan-Schreiber: "Even if he never does anything else in his political life, he saved an entire generation of St.-Cyr cadets from being killed." Not to mention the Indochinese! I don't know whether Jean-Jacques still remembers. That goes back a long way, doesn't it?

Anyway, with that in mind it doesn't seem so absurd for an elderly lady, a few years later, to hope that Jean-Jacques might "come up with something" for Algeria before she died, as it was her right to regret sincerely that he wasn't pro–De Gaulle, since by then De Gaulle was in power and she, like all the elderly ladies of France, loved him.

What was more, from childhood on she had been too involved in politics, too privy to the intimacies of the political process, to be unaware of the part played by private conversations, the weight of individuals, the importance of secret diplomacy, the role of this or that person, whose name is often forgotten by history, in making important decisions. I've seen enough personally to have my own ideas on the subject generally referred to as "influence," or on a politician's "inner circle."

As is true in private life, one finds only what one is looking for. A man involved in political struggle only accepts the influence that suits him, as he puts up with the inner circle that befits him — that is, essentially people who buttress his ego and his ideas, who therefore help strengthen him, build him up in his own eyes, give him more confidence in himself.

At the most basic level, this is the very function of courtesans. But it takes an extraordinarily gifted and subtle courtesan to know precisely where the anxieties of the person courted lie . . . and how great or small they are, and how to allay them. One rarely finds anxieties by consciously looking for them; it is by responding to them, often unconsciously, that one discovers them.

Anyone in a position of power or authority will only respond to that influence which is noncompetitive, no matter what area is involved. As soon as there is any kind of rivalry, even veiled, the influence vanishes. The other person — the one trying to influence — has to be dismissed, or even crushed.

Some prominent or powerful men derive their ego-satisfaction from beautiful women, others from social status superior to their own, from a wife or mistress, from their colleagues, while still others find it in the deference or admiration paid them by young people, especially when their own children, if they have any, refuse to give it to them. There are others who find it purely and simply in the devotion of which they are the object, the extraordinary and often touching devotion you find around all politically powerful men. The make-up of these "inner circles" would make a fascinating study.

I find myself talking to you about these matters because of my mother, because it was she who showed me that the ways of man are mysterious, decisive, irrational, that one must always try to clarify them, never to be taken in by them. Her assessment of others was remarkable, especially since she had not had the slightest theoretical basis for her opinions.

But I sometimes think that it was a lesson I learned too well, that I carried it too far; I think I might have liked to be taken in occasionally, to delude myself. To understand is sometimes a strength, but more often it's a weakness. There are times when I find myself watching my opponents or enemies the way one might look at the works of a watch.

You can't hate or despise a watch because it was badly put together, or because someone stepped on it.

This is a feeling that goes back very far with me, one I experienced for the first time at the lycée when a little girl named Albertine threw a stone right in my face. It broke one of my teeth. The teacher got very excited and upset and said that she was going to really punish that awful Albertine whose conduct, in fact, she could never fathom. And I said to her, "But, Madame, it's because she's a red head."

The reason seemed obvious to me. And it wasn't Albertine's fault if she had red hair. And if it wasn't her "fault," then I might prefer never to see her again, but I couldn't have cared less about revenge or punishment.

I'm not at all sure that this attitude stems from as lofty a sentiment as it might appear on the surface, but that's a whole other story.

— Let's get back to the factual aspects of your own story. You weren't yet fifteen, and you had a job. What kind of work were you doing?

— My mother's disappointments left me with an intense hatred — which I still retain to this day — for amateurism. I wanted a trade, a real trade, that I could master quickly. The decision I made that day is the only act in my life of which I am unequivocally satisfied, because it was the result of a measured judgment, a decision made completely on my own. I needed five hundred francs to pay the tuition for the Remington School. I borrowed them from an old, homosexual cousin . . . I didn't know at the time he was a homosexual, but I had sensed that, in my mother's sternly rigid family, I was dealing with a pariah. And one can always come to terms with pariahs.

I got my five hundred francs. And, a month later, I was the proud owner of a diploma guaranteeing that I could take dictation at the rate of 120 words a minute.

In that school I also learned something far more complicated than stenography. I learned the existence of a world of which I had been completely unaware. A world where the only things the girls read were movie magazines or the latest scandals in the daily tabloid. They were no less deprived than I was; on the contrary. Nor were they any less intelligent or quick. They were much more experienced than I in the things that make fifteen-year-old girls giggle together. But they were immured in a kind of closed universe where nothing I was familiar with or could relate to had penetrated: books; music; politics, of course; the Poincaré franc; the cartel of the Left; and even a certain kind of film, the "art" films that were shown in the very active ciné clubs of the time — forbidden Soviet films such as *Potemkin;* all that was as strange to them as the notion of social class was to me. At first I didn't understand anything about such distinctions. Nor can I claim that even after a time I understood. But something did happen there which left its mark on my life. At the school, we were the same and we were not the same. Today it's difficult to conceive of, perhaps even impossible. First of all because now there is a much broader and more heightened "social consciousness." And also because differences of language, clothing, and even life-style have become much less distinct. Television, the ten-cent stores, and the automobile have left their imprint.

At the time . . . the Remington School was located in a building not far from the office of one of my uncles. One day as I was coming out of school I saw his car, a dark blue Citroën. "Look, there's my uncle's car," I said.

The girls I was with — one was the daughter of a café owner, the other a daughter of a floorwalker at the Bon Marché department store — looked at me as though Cinderella's fairy godmother had just passed by.

We were no longer the same. And yet, I was also not the

"same" as the young ladies who took tennis or music lessons, or learned needlework while I was learning stenography.

I fitted in nowhere. And I was in the process of losing my identity. But that too is another story. What I wanted to say was that, at the Remington School, I experienced the privilege of what today is called the "cultural environment" of a child, which occurs when a child assimilates any new experience. How come it has taken so long to discover it?

The biologist François Jacob maintains that even in purely scientific areas discoveries occur only when they are ready to be received. For decades people skirt them, approach them, closer and closer. They see, but they stop on the edge of perception. And then one day something clicks, someone understands what he's seeing. Generally a man alone. That lead over the rest of the pack is what is called genius. The genius of a Galileo, of a Freud!

The more these "seers" disturb the mental images by which their contemporaries live, the more they undermine their security by introducing a kind of chaos into the prevailing thought of the time, clearly the more they will be poorly received, or even rejected and persecuted. That's only normal. The world isn't flat, it's round; it's turning, turning, it's a spinning globe! How upsetting! Your child isn't a delightful, innocent baby but a polymorphous pervert. What a disturbing idea! What could they teach us today that would be as disquieting and, in the final analysis, as unbearable? Lots of things, certainly, lots of things, but simply to conceive of them would require a little of that creative imagination, which is so rare even in very circumscribed and modest areas.

The ideas are there, concealed behind the door; they will loom into view tomorrow or in twenty years, and by then it is possible that your brain cells and mine — mine before yours, since I'm older — will have become so rigid that our minds will no longer be able to assimilate a new idea, nor even a new arrangement of old ideas.

On the level of societies, in any case, it is obvious that great revelations can occur only when they are about to become tolerable, when they can be assimilated.

It is possible that this discovery — which is not overwhelming but nonetheless important — of the part played by cultural environment, was accepted the day when television came into being and became part and parcel of every household, that is, when the technical means of reducing cultural differences was born and made the notion that they should be reduced acceptable. I have a strong inkling that forty years ago the idea had not crossed anyone's mind. Equality was thought of in those days in terms of obligatory education: secondary schooling had only just been made free.

— In 1931, to drop out of school before age fifteen in order to become a stenographer must have caused a few repercussions, I would imagine, at least within your family circle . . .

— They were upset, yes. They found me pigheaded; it was not the first time. I very roundly condemned — too roundly when I look back on it today — the attitude of my uncles. But I had only one desire: to deliver my mother from their yoke, never have to depend on them again for the rest of my life, never have to see them again, forget they ever existed. To live several lives, you have to die several deaths. Let's say that that was my first death.

 II

— So there you are with your diploma. What's your next step?"

— I start looking at the want ads in the newspapers. I don't want to be "recommended" for some job, find a position through "connections." I need to be free and clear of any taint of "connections." A bookshop has placed an ad for a clerk who can also type and take dictation . . . I like books. The shop in question deals in rare and out-of-print books. I put on lipstick and high heels to try and look older, and apply in person. I say I'm eighteen. It works.

Today it wouldn't work. Medical exams; social security; obligatory declaration to the authorities . . . But at that time there was none of that.

— And what did you do in that bookshop?

— I took care of the mail. Bibliophiles carry on a lot of correspondence. And compiled the catalogue . . . When the bookseller was away I waited on customers. And I read . . . I was lucky I didn't end up working for a wineseller, no?

I read every book in the shop . . . I was pleased and proud to earn 500 francs a month. My sister, who was a sales-girl in a department store, earned only 300 francs and didn't

have the right to sit down. I was fairly well treated. For that
time, of course. It was another period altogether, so dif-
ferent . . .
— You had a "good" boss?
— There aren't any good bosses.
— Did you work in that bookshop very long?
— I don't remember. Seven, eight months . . .
— Did you expect to stay on there?
— Quite honestly, I don't believe I gave it any thought
. . . For three people to make ends meet with the equivalent
of what would be in terms of today's money, 1000 to 1200
francs [$220–280] a month is not conducive to theoretical
reflection . . . We had — at long last! — rented an apartment in a section that was in keeping with our actual means,
and taken to living within our budget. Two rooms and a
kitchen, which my mother had managed to turn into something charming, as she always did. The only problem was
to get to it you had to cross a rat-infested court yard. I was
afraid. My mother refused to allow anyone to be afraid —
on that point she was adamant — nor would she allow this
kind of minor unpleasantness to assume false proportions and
cloud one's perspective of the essentials.

Life, then, was pleasant enough because she wanted it to
be, because we were a closely knit family and the house was
always filled with friends, as it was filled with music emanating from a little phonograph which you had to wind up —
a gift someone had once given my sister in exchange for her
advice on how to decorate an apartment. We had two records. One was "Roses of Picardy" . . . My sister was
radiant, surrounded by friends . . . She had a sense of fes-
tivity, of gaiety, which I have always lacked . . . I was
rather the touchy one, sensitive, like someone afraid of opening a fresh scar . . . I kept thinking that my mother had
nothing and that I wanted everything for her. One day when

she was down on her knees scrubbing the floor I saw her hands . . . They had become all red and cracked . . . There were no "gentle, hand-softening" products in those days. I kept thinking that I had to give her back her hands. But how?

— Did the fact of being put into contact with the written word, in that bookshop, give you any desire to go on in that direction?

— Not really. I have always been fascinated by the written word, because of my father. Did I mention that in 1908 he had founded a political paper? I still have the first issue. My father wrote a great deal; basically political texts, though. How could I have presumed to follow in his footsteps?

— Did you know then that you were beautiful?

— People told me I was, but I was never really aware of it. To be brutally frank, it was a capital I never exploited. You have to have a talent for it. I didn't have it.

— What made you leave that bookshop?

— Because the film director Marc Allégret happened in one day . . . He had known me when I was a little girl. He went and bought me some pastries, then set out explaining to me that I was wasting my time there, and he ended with: "Come and work with me. Movies are the wave of the future, you'll see." So I went to work for him. And the movies *were* magic. Fabulous magic. Unstable, too. We were employed on a weekly basis; from one day to the next you could be out of work.

— You didn't have even a moment's hesitation?

— Who would have hesitated? No, not for a moment. But I remember precisely the immediate feeling I had at the time that it was, for me, a fateful moment. It was Friday, May 13, 1932 . . . I met Marc in his apartment, where he was working with a scriptwriter. He lived in the apartment next to André Gide's on the rue Vaneau, the apartment of

Les Faux-Monnayeurs. I got into the elevator . . . It had a wood smell, a very special wood smell that I swear I could recognize anywhere. I put my finger on the button for the top floor and let a full second elapse before I pressed it . . . A second during which I had the impression that I was holding myself in the palm of my hand, like a pair of dice I was going to throw.

— Are you a gambler?

— With my life, yes. On the eve of my twentieth birthday I gambled on a husband, tossing a coin: heads or tails . . . He lost . . . Luck, always luck. With cards, chips, no, I don't gamble.

— Did you meet Gide?

— Not that day, no. I met his library. That was where Marc worked when Gide wasn't there . . . It was a big, ill-proportioned room with an interior staircase laden with books, a room wrapped around a long piano. I always want to touch pianos and dogs, and since they know it they respond to me very nicely . . . I met Gide a little later. The first time I met him he took me to see *La Dame de chez Maxim's,* a movie directed by Alexander Korda starring Florelle. I was amazed. That film destroyed a few of my preconceived ideas, and at fifteen — as at seventy-five, too — people have preconceived ideas.

— In the final analysis, great men are very ordinary . . .

— Ah, he wasn't ordinary, not at all! Besides, I think you're wrong. I never knew any great men who were ordinary. They, like everyone, are caught up in the commonplace aspects of existence, and they have, more or less, the simplicity to let the world see this side of their lives. But the intimate, even the racy anecdote — and God knows I know more than my share of them about a lot of men of high station! — reveals a great deal less about what a great man actually is than it does about the person who observed him.

When you look low, you see low. Therefore I'll refrain from telling you any. No, I take it back; I'll tell you one about Gide, because it's such a superb witticism. One day when we were seated on the terrace of the Café de Flore someone came up to Gide and asked for his autograph, which he gave. The waiter said to him: "Ah, Monsieur Gide, how annoying it must be sometimes to be famous!" To which Gide replied: "You're wrong . . . What's so annoying is to be famous and realize the number of people who don't recognize you!"

— He was very famous?

— He was indeed, but not the way people are today . . . One day he asked me to go to the post office and send a telegram for him. The telegram was addressed to Paul Valéry, and the wording was ordinary enough, something to the effect: "Expecting you Monday afternoon at five." But I nonetheless carried this telegram as though it were the Holy Sacrament itself, fully convinced that I would make a big impression on the lady at the post office. And would you believe it, I made no impression at all! Gide, Valéry . . . The two names meant nothing to her. Imagine today a telegram signed by Sartre sent to Malraux. Who in France, thanks to the transistor and television, doesn't know those two names, even if they're not quite sure who they are? Who hasn't seen their faces? Actually, it's a very artificial familiarity which destroys part of the mystery, and therefore the prestige. But anyway, it does exist. Forty years ago, we were still living in a compartmentalized society.

— Did Gide have any direct influence on you, as he did on so many other young people of the time?

— Direct? . . . Yes, but how can I explain it properly? . . . I was so young when I knew him, he and so many other famous people — Malraux, for example, with whom Gide invited me to lunch one day. "Come, I'm going to introduce you to a young man who's far more interesting than

his books," he said. My very youth prevented me from having the so-called normal reactions. What I mean is, I wasn't
the girl fawning in the presence of the famous author, or
famous whatever, trying to make a good impression, but
rather someone solemn, the way children so often are, quietly
solemn, completely unaware of what separated us, aside from
the age factor, and sometimes capable of unexpected out-
bursts of spontaneity. And they, in exchange, tended to be
more patient and understanding with me than they would
have if I had been ten years older. It may well be that Gide,
without knowing it, determined for a long time thereafter
both the nature and the basic healthiness of my relations with
anyone or anything famous.

But that, obviously, was nothing compared to the influence
of his books . . . *Les Nourritures Terrestres* may be un-
readable today, for all I know, but at the time it was devastating!

— In what way?

— The courage to "become your own truth" . . . Such a
simple little thing! "The overwhelming obligation to be
happy . . ." "Families, I loathe you; Nathanaël, take off on
your own, I'll teach you passion. A painful existence,
Nathanaël, rather than a peaceful life . . ." A painful existence! . . . *That* was radical confrontation! More radical
that Sartre's is today.

— But less political.

— Not at all! You think Gide's *Retour de l'U.R.S.S.*
isn't political? And his *Voyage au Congo?* And what is
more political than exalting a sexuality which is assumed
even unto its deviations? In 1940, Pétain explained that
France had lost the war because of Gide, the corruptor of
youth.

— But what was your own personal reaction to reading
Les Nourritures Terrestres?

— I don't remember. And I don't want to make anything up. I could very easily describe for you today a Gide "reconstituted" from what I read, learned, or understood since. But that is precisely what I want to avoid. We've agreed to be subjective, let's stick to our plan, and the subjectivity of a fifteen-year-old girl is narrow indeed. All I can remember is the feeling of shock, the shock you receive from ideas that surprise you, that are different from what you expect.

— You didn't believe in God?

— I was more or less confused. At thirteen, I wanted with all my heart to be Protestant, and I preparing for it with the pastor of Epinay. I was in boarding school. They wouldn't let me. And yet it was my own decision to make. Many things from that experience have remained with me to this date. But not faith in God.

What a disaster for France the Revocation of the Edict of Nantes was, when you think about it! That horrible Madame de Maintenon, and Bossuet too: together they really did a fine job! Although here too one should be careful not to heap all the blame on the entourage. If Louis XIV hadn't deserved Madame de Maintenon, he wouldn't have had her. If he hadn't wanted to crush the Reformation he could just as well have listened to Colbert instead of sending him to his grave by bickering with him about the cost of the Versailles gates . . . Poor Colbert took to his bed and never got up.

Michelet says that Madame de Maintenon made Louis XIV evil and violent by trying to convert him, because after she had delivered one of her moralizing sermons to him she would pack him off to sleep with the queen, which bored him terribly. "He no longer had any pleasure with women," says Michelet. So he began to drink, drink like a fish. All of which, according to Michelet, explains his aggressive political behavior during the last decade of his reign, and his war on the Protestants. He would have been far better off continuing to father royal bastards. What a gift he gave to England, Holland, to Germany! What a material loss for France! How many were there who managed to emigrate? Three hundred thousand, three hundred and fifty, from a population of about twenty million? That must be about right . . . But that included among the most intelligent, the most active, the most conscientious . . .

— The managers, in short?

— Oh, the way you use that word! With that marvelous French contempt for industry, commerce, finance, business, for all those areas where the Protestants concentrated their efforts, as opposed to tilling the land, as do those people who feel either personally threatened or feel their goods and possessions endangered and want to be able to retreat quickly . . . Do you know what they took with them, those people who managed to flee the persecution? Aside from their silver and themselves, they took with them the art of weaving silk and woolen goods, which henceforth ceased to be the sole province of the French, and the art of hat-making, and the art of cutlery . . . But the real disaster was that they took with them something even more important: Protestantism, that is, the substitution of civil authority for religious authority; it was the liberals departing; the denial of any authority higher than individual reason; the intelligence of the persecuted who are forced by circumstances to be intelligent; an entirely different attitude toward money.

That well-known reactionary, Balzac, says that Protestantism doubts, examines, and kills beliefs. That it represents, therefore, the death of art and love. It is, in any case, the death of dogmatism. The result? The only countries where there are strong Communist Parties are Catholic countries.

— I imagine that Gide also swept religion aside in *Les Nourritures Terrestres* . . .

— He swept everything aside. "Don't hope, Nathanaël, to find God anywhere but everywhere . . ."

— What was Gide's relationship with the cinema?

— Intimate, as far as I know. I think he even wrote the dialogues for the film Allégret adapted from the Conrad novel, *Under Western Eyes.*

— And what about you? What were you doing in the cinema?

— I was a script girl . . . And I discovered a mad, mad world . . . Really crazy. What was — and still is — so seductive about the cinema was the crew. Thirty, forty people join together for a few weeks, a few months, live together, travel together, work together, love one another, grow jealous, help one another, become fast friends. And then, once the film is over, the crew breaks up . . . It's the end of a liaison. And then you start in all over again, with other people, in other places. And between films you stay in your room or apartment with your eyes glued to the door, waiting for the *pneumatique* to arrive that will summon you to this or that producer's. Anyway, that was the way it used to be . . . Today, I don't know. All that revolving around those pathetic, burlesque characters known as "stars" . . . The first film I worked on was *Fanny,* the Pagnol play, with Raimu and Pierre Fresnay.

— Were they already well known?

— Very. Fresnay had just been involved in a major scandal, having stolen Sacha Guitry's wife away from him, and was completely radiant, bathing in the glory of the romantic exploit. Raimu was simply an extraordinary actor. Pagnol was at the pinnacle of his glory, played everywhere in the world. And the prestige, the mystery, the mythology which enveloped the whole film world, and especially the stars, have no real equivalent today.

When stars begin to reveal themselves without make-up

and advertise automobiles or appliances, they cease to be supernatural creatures. Bardot is the last of the lot, together with Burton and Taylor . . . But even there, it's not the same.

Mount Olympus is no longer peopled by the movie world. — Why? Because there are no longer any movie giants? — I suspect it's rather because there are no longer any showmen, those entertainers who were adored but kept at arm's length, the way Gypsies are in the villages. By integrating themselves into society, they have, as they say of unmarked police cars, made themselves ordinary. At the time when they were still lionized the way Molière was, they had to reciprocate and act accordingly . . . Then they were the object of every folly and felt themselves obliged to munch diamonds on caviar canapés. Now, movie stars do their own shopping and sign petitions to change the abortion laws. How do you expect them to still titillate the imagination?

Today, movie stars are creators, those who have something to say . . . The technical aspects have been completely mastered. In the early days, in France, it hadn't yet been. The soundtrack especially was often abominable. It was a beautiful, brand-new profession, and it was fun because it was in the hands of pioneers, of adventurers. When I think that I might have spent my youth sitting in some insurance-company office, I feel like counting my blessings.

— You wouldn't have stayed there?

— No, I probably wouldn't have. But anyway, it's easy to say that in retrospect. Things are never so simple that people can pretend to control or direct events. I have had enough experience in directing my life with determination to know that there are many times when I was "directed." You can reach for the brass ring, but it has to be available to you. The cinema was available to me.

This said, I must add that I did not take to the cinema like a fish to water. I had the reputation of being both a snob and a Communist. A snob because I had always had trouble employing the familiar *tu* form of address, and in the movie world easy familiarity was in fashion. You have to have seen and worked with the film production managers of the time to believe them. Real slave drivers. I was involved in a few incidents — noisy ones. And besides, I was, after all, a snob in some ways for the simple reason that I was a "displaced person" on the geographical map of society.

A Communist after the major strikes of '36 . . . I already related that episode a few years ago in *L'Express,* as part of an investigative report. I was the script girl for an Allégret film. The working conditions at the time were poor. We had to be at the studio — which was always out in the suburbs — at eight o'clock in the morning, and we were sometimes still there at midnight, without any overtime.

One morning I arrive at the Billancourt studio. The gates are closed. The workers have decided to emulate the factory workers and strike the studio itself. On the sidewalk technicians and employees are arguing. If the shooting is stopped, we won't be paid at the end of the week. I won't be paid. One technician, who is furious, is grumbling: "The dumb bastards! They'll only be happy when they've destroyed everything! What about us? What'll we buy food with next week?" He opens the door of a car and says to me: "Come on, I'll drive you back to Paris. There's no point wasting your time here, maybe getting into real trouble when the cops come to clear these idiots out . . ." But I don't feel like getting in the car. I have no desire whatsoever. I see that two camps are forming. In one of the camps is the production assistant, and also lots of people I know who have been thrown into a panic by the elections. The camp of those who are afraid. Afraid of the workers. If I were afraid I would leave. But I'm not going to pretend. Besides, I know the workers, who are milling there in a group behind the closed gates; I've known them all for a long time. We've shared hundreds and hundreds of hours of work. I can't be afraid of them. It's not their side that will do me any harm. Instead of getting into the car, I walk over to the gates because I have to, physically I have to go over to them, physically I have to choose between the two camps. This choice in no way resembles that of today's young radicals, the children of the middle class. I made it neither out of a murky sense of generosity nor as a result of any political analysis. Humble among the humbled, I go over and join the camp where I think I have the best chance of finding a little human warmth. As for the other camp, my eyes have been opened. One of the stagehands spots me and calls to me through the gates: "Could you run an errand for me? Go tell my wife what's going on and ask her to bring us something to eat." I answer that I will. My choice is made. The car left without me, and the next day, the production assistant came up to me and said: "I would never have thought you were a Communist, the way you behave . . ."

All that was very idealistic, of course, idealistic in the Marxist sense of the term, and did not stem from any political awareness on my part.

— Did you stay in films for a long time?

— For a long time, yes. A lifetime, it seems to me. You know that the younger you are the more slowly time seems to pass. I was a script girl until about 1937, as I recall, and then a production assistant, the first female assistant. It was a male profession. Then I wrote some adaptations. And finally, dialogues.

— What are the important films you worked on?

— Important for whom? You never know what is important when you're working on a film . . . What matters is not the films themselves but the people you meet because of the films.

— What? The handsome male lead?

— No, that's not the kind I was referring to. In fact, I worked on at least ten films starring Fernandel, a comic actor who could hardly be considered "handsome." The encounters I meant were something altogether different . . . Everyone has had that experience in his or her life . . . the man, or men — or women — who opened a door for you onto some new aspect of the world, or sometimes revealed something you didn't know before about yourself.

— Were there many such people?

— I never thought to count them. But I have the feeling that there are a lot of them, yes, and I haven't given up hope that there are still more to come! The movies gave me Saint-Exupéry, Jean Renoir, Jacques Becker, Louis Jouvet . . . You're too young to have seen Jouvet in the flesh. But you know what he was? A cross between Peter Brook and Laurence Olivier.

— What does "gave me" mean?

— It means just that: "gave." I didn't have to go out of my way to meet them, they just happened to be there, in this film or that, and for a brief moment in time we traveled together along the same path.

— Did Saint-Exupéry make any films?

— He wrote the script and was present at the shooting of *Courrier-Sud,* a film adapted from his novel.

— Tell me about him.

— He was a romantic. A guardian angel . . . Physically he resembled a shaggy bear; he struck you as being bigger than his plane, a little red Caudron. He never seemed to feel the cold. Wings suited him perfectly. Encamped at the Lutétia Hotel, always broke, saying: "One should be able to work out a system whereby, for only a week, one belonged to one of the two hundred families." (He was referring to the two hundred families who were reputed to control the entire fortune of France.) "Just long enough to reconstitute one's wardrobe."

Courrier-Sud was shot for the most part in southern Morocco. As you know, it's the story of a pilot whose plane crashes in the desert. Just as the crew and actors were ready to depart for location, the producer realized that there were forty men who would be spending a month in the depths of Morocco. And only one woman. I was that one woman, if the term really applied. I was eighteen. He decided that he couldn't take that responsibility. At which point Saint-Exupéry, the knight in shining armor, arrived and said: "Let her come with us. I'll look out for her." And off I went to join the others at Mogador. That was the first time I flew on a regular, scheduled airline. I had to take the train to Toulouse, and from there I flew to Casablanca. I was the only passenger on the plane. Not only was I alone, but I was terrified because the flight pattern took us over Spain. When we landed in Barcelona we could hear the sound of shooting on all sides. The civil war was in full swing.

I never think of the past, unless I'm obliged to the way you're making me do right now. I don't like to reminisce. I don't remember who it was who said: "Beautiful memories are like lost jewels." As for bad ones . . . But the memory of that early flight came back to me suddenly last year, after thirty-five years, when by a strange coincidence I flew the same route. Paris-Toulouse, overnight at a hotel in Toulouse, then a plane across the Mediterranean. But this time it was aboard the Concorde, inaugurating the route to Dakar. Another kind of adventure.

And there, on that still unfinished plane, I felt almost physically the full weight of those intervening years. Not like the weight of age, not the weight on my own shoulders, but the intensity, the richness, the commotion and tumult, and the horror too, the full, enormous scope of the ruptures and wounds and upheavals with which those thirty-five years had been filled.

A beautiful plane, the Concorde. Slim. You have the feeling you're traveling inside a cigar — but a beautiful cigar. What a pity it is so unsalable. Which brings us right back again to the Revocation of the Edict of Nantes. Commercial viability? How can one even talk about anything so vulgar?

Everyone involved in the Concorde project — be it building it or selling it — is really in love with that winged creature, and one can understand how they feel. They become incensed when anyone even suggests that the public funds used to finance the project were misspent, due to a miscalculation of basic priorities — priorities for which they of course do not bear the responsibility. They react as though someone had said to them: "Your child is beautiful, but how much does he bring in?" The very notion of profit is judged base and contemptible when weighed against the notion of prestige, the prestige that France and England are supposed to derive from the joint effort.

When Harold Wilson came to power in 1964, he did his best, within the framework of his financial retrenchment program, to scuttle the project. But the French reaction was so strong — and legitimately so, since the program was undertaken jointly — that he had to back off.

This priority given to prestige in the appropriation of public funds, that is taxes that you and I pay, is especially interesting when one realizes that nothing prevents a country from having both prestige and profits. Look at Marcel Dassault, the plane manufacturer, who ought to know: he is purported to be the richest man in France. But it isn't he who's building the Concorde! No, he builds *Mirages, Mercures, Mystères* — all those planes that sell.

The Concorde is subsidized by you and me. We're the little Egyptian workers of *that* pyramid. And all the French with us.

When a few years back the Maine-Montparnasse apartment complex was built, at the same time as the new Montparnasse train station — all on city property — there was an agreement made among the parties involved which called for the construction of a garden for the children to walk and play in. Today there is still no garden. The City of Paris has to provide the funds. The City Council now finds that it's too expensive.

There are hundreds — thousands — of such examples. Sometimes I feel like making badges for the children to wear, badges which would read: "I'm playing in the street because I'm helping pay for the Concorde." Or, for suburbanites packed like sardines into their trains: "I can't sit down because I'm helping pay for the Concorde."

And the Concorde is only part of it, although the sums spent on it are astronomical. But it is the symbol of a policy and a concept of a policy — or rather, of a nonpolicy. That is perhaps what is most maddening. Everything happens as though the gears meshed and turned without anyone being able to say: "I'm responsible for it." Is it a lack of overall plan, of will, or the impossibility of formulating any plan, of exercising any will in a nation where various bottlenecks pile up one on top of the other?

If that's what it is, one fine day in the not too distant future we'll be witnessing one of those fearsome social crises that occur in France every now and then.

We were speaking of Saint-Exupéry; he would have loved the Concorde, obviously . . . The image of Saint-Exupéry has not withstood the passage of time very well, I fear, despite the posthumous success of his books. They've made him out to be some kind of boy scout, slightly foolish . . . Which is absurd. That offends me not only because I really liked him, but also because there is nothing more stupid than judging people outside of their historical context. Lamartine, dear, gentle Lamartine, Lamartine the liberal earned a great deal of money from the slave trade of the times. So did Voltaire. It seemed perfectly normal to them. It is likely that today Lamartine would not seek or accept income derived from exploiting immigrant labor!

Saint-Exupéry was a man born into the wrong period. He hadn't even reached, much less assimilated, bourgeois values. He lived according to a system of aristocratic values which placed honor at the top of the scale and situated it in terms of individual accomplishment, which is basically French . . . He was a Frenchman from another time, a time so far back in history that it's hard even to conceive of it today. Time cannot be calculated in terms of years. There are people who can live — who once could live — by the same values, which for some were aristocratic, for a great many others bourgeois, and in such a situation nothing changes substantially except the surface of things.

Change, real change, is one that affects concepts, alters your way of thinking, your view of the world and your place in it. With the single exception of physical pain, everything is imaginary. And even there Diderot relates — I can't remember exactly where — how certain fanatics are able to undergo the most painful operations by subjecting themselves to a kind of self-hypnosis. What I am trying to say is that, between Saint-Exupéry's vision in 1935 and that of his equivalent today we can't even speak of evolution, however rapid; we can only speak of rupture, of a break in continuity, not only on the human level, but also in terms of a class which has virtually disappeared . . . The only word I can think of to describe what World War II, and the fifteen years that followed, destroyed and what they engendered is "mutation." We were mutants — and by "we" I'm referring to those of us who were, say, twenty or so during the war and survived it. I mean we who, calmly and imperturably, went to visit that exposition in Paris, in Vincennes, called The Colonial Exposition. With its black women on platforms. I sometimes wonder what it is we're doing today with the same kind of oblivious ease that, in another thirty years, will strike people as just as horrendous. To try and speculate on that subject would be a worthwhile project for some futurologist.

 III

— A LITTLE WHILE AGO you mentioned Jean Renoir. When did you meet him?

— In '36, as I remember. Or perhaps at the end of '35. In any case, I spent the better part of '36 revolving in his orbit.

I was out of work. I was taken on to type a film script, which was then still being written, called *La Grande Illusion*. I believe it was adapted from some book, but I have no idea who the author was. Charles Spaak had done an initial treatment. Then Renoir had reworked the script, both its plot and dialogues, at least a dozen times, especially after he had persuaded Eric von Stroheim to play in it. We were already on location in Alsace when Stroheim joined the cast. In French the term "director" is "metteur en scène," which means literally "he who stages"; with Stroheim I saw for the first time a director, in the English sense of the term; it is a term which can be applied to the management of any enterprise or undertaking. Even to building a dam! All the elements were there: the overall perspective, the attention to detail, the authority, the ability to inculcate affection and, above all, yes, above everything else, the art of using men, of bringing out the best in them and, in doing so, making them happy.

Renoir had patience and serenity, the gift of being interested in other people, no matter who they were, and honest-to-god modesty too, that innate modesty you find only in men who do not feel constantly compelled to prove their virility. Needless to say, they are few and far between. He was the first French director to have the honor, and I use the term advisedly, of counting Eric von Stroheim among his cast. Stroheim who was washed up in Hollywood; Stroheim the magnificent; Stroheim, the man who had made *Les Rapaces* [*Greed*]. He was not an easy bird, not to mention that he spoke not a word of French. Renoir spoke German with him; Jacques Becker, who was Renoir's first assistant, spoke English. Renoir handled Stroheim with consummate intelligence, letting him compose his own character, his costume — do you remember the orthopedic back brace that he wore? — his text, his set, the black sheets, the geranium . . . without, nonetheless, letting go of his hand. On the contrary . . . You had to be a master to accept this master, and integrate him into your plans . . . The proof of Renoir's mastery is that subsequently no one was ever able to bring out von Stroheim's genius in the same way.

Looking back, I realize I have even greater respect for Renoir now than I did at the time. For me, he remains the example of what the act of directing means, or should mean. He had the ability to solicit everyone's opinion, to mobilize every talent and resource. All of which would of course be worthless if the results were flops.

My personal debt to Renoir is to have ignited the first dim light for me in the tunnel I found myself in. True, I was earning my living, but in fact I was barely scraping along, and to what end? With Renoir, everything fell into place, assumed a sense, and *La Grande Illusion* in particular!

— What, really, was your contribution to the film?

— A minor one, aside from my position as script girl; I contributed a bit of dialogue here, a scene there, a few ideas I passed on, all of which, of course, were taken and integrated by Renoir himself. But he was the first person to really look at me seriously, take me for what I was. Until then I had been considered a kind of pet, a touching object, or the object of various other sentiments, because of my youth — but twenty is no longer fifteen. But is it ever possib'e for a young, desirable — and poor — girl to be taken seriously by a man? I doubt it. It's almost as though she should be flattered by his desire, as though she ought to curtsy and say thank you, kind sir, for desiring me. You're ugly, married perhaps, never free on Sunday, and in the evening, you know, it's very difficult; or free as a bird but dull as dishwater, dreaming only of sitting in your slippers by the kitchen stove, and you'll see, my mother will love you; or else big, fat, won't you get in and go for a spin with me in my Packard? And if a girl doesn't say thank you? An ungrateful wench, a gold digger. And if she does? A whore.

What I got from Renoir was the revelation of my possibilities, the realization that I was a person still in the process of evolving, full of potential. And the realization that life is full of possibilities, that anything can happen to you at any time. When actresses were sent to him on someone's recommendation, he used to say: "Tell them to come back after they've had a case of the syph or the clap. What do you think acting is all about?" All things being equal, Renoir thought, symbolically, that I ought to experience a dose of the clap. He would say to me: "You have gifts. Start off by ruining them." But the point is, he gave me courage. And besides, working on La Grande Illusion gave me the opportunity of forming a friendship, a real friendship with Jacques Becker, one that lasted for both of us, through each of our personal trials and tribulations, till the end of his life. After the war, he was the one who gave me my first chance to write dialogues for a film. In 1946 we made *Antoine et Antoinette* together. Later we shared a passion for motors. I would have loved to be a mechanic for Ferrari . . . I've experienced the pleasure of taking a few carburetors apart in my time!

— Do you still?

— No. I don't think I'd know how any longer . . . and besides, today they've taken all the fun out of cars.

— These men you were talking about earlier, did they have a feeling of who they were, of their importance, of being what we know them to be today?

— Gide did, surely. Malraux? I don't know, because I don't know what he thinks he is. It's quite possible he thinks his writing is secondary and considers his political contribution the only thing that really counts . . . But in the course of that luncheon he was already in the realm of high abstraction. Completely different from Renoir. Renoir was much more down to earth. He was a sensualist, an artist, not an intellectual. He was the son of Renoir, which is not bad for a start. And besides, before *La Grande Illusion* he had already made *La Chienne,* and that remarkable film, *Le Crime de Monsieur Lange,* whose soundtrack, unfortunately, is so bad you can hardly hear it. And *Les Bas-fonds* . . .

— In what way did these people feel they were important? Because they were powerful or influential? Because what they were doing was beautiful? Because they thought they were contributing something to the world, to France?

— Could you answer that question if someone asked you the same thing about your own contemporaries? People's image of themselves and the image others have of them is extremely mysterious . . . Let's simply say that they were all aware of what they were worth in their own areas —

Saint-Exupéry in the world of aviation — that they wanted to participate in the world's tumult rather than spending their lives on the sidelines, that they saw themselves as being among the actors — or if you prefer, the agents — of history. Today we feel as though we are passengers on a wildly pitching galley, where everything is all mixed together: writers, mass media, art, love, politics . . . We have the feeling that life used to be much more peaceful.

Life has never been peaceful. I suspect that the basic difference is simply the feeling that people have — or do not have — that they can plan ahead over a relatively long period, that is, of the relative stability of institutions in the broadest sense of the term. But what is this feeling based on? Instead of propounding theories, let me try to find a text I think will surprise you, unless you already know it. It should be here in my library. Erb: does the name mean anything to you? He's a nineteenth-century neurologist.

Here is what he wrote in 1895 — remember that date — in a study about the increasing problem of nervous disorders in the modern, civilized world:

> The extraordinary conquests in modern times, the discoveries and inventions in every area, the constant progress in the face of growing competition can only be made at the cost of an enormous intellectual effort and can only continue to be made if this same effort is applied. The degree of productivity that the struggle for life demands has grown considerably greater; he can only meet those demands by utilizing all the intellectual powers at his command; at the same time the needs, and the aspirations, of the individual have increased in all mileux; a taste for the finer things of life has permeated to layers of the population which had never known them before; discontent, greed and the breakdown of religion have reached an ever greater proportion of the population; the enormous growth in population, the universal network of telegram and telephone

have completely transformed the means of communication; everything takes place in an atmosphere of speed and frenzy, with night being used for travel and days for business; even vacation travel tends to tax the nervous system; the major political, industrial, and financial crises have a way of communicating their excitement to a much larger segment of the population than in the past; an interest in politics has become completely commonplace; political, religious, and moral struggles, party activities, the fervor of elections, the fact that associations increase at a frightening speed: all this overheats the brain, impels the mind to ever greater efforts, impinges further on times formerly devoted to rest and relaxation, and to sleep; life in big cities has become more and more sophisticated and restless. Peoples' nerves are on edge, and they try to relax by searching for ever more exciting pleasures and stimulations, which only tend to fatigue them even more; modern literature deals first and foremost with the most thorny problems, problems which stir the passions and preach sensuality, the taste for pleasure, and contempt for every ideal and ethical value; it offers to the reader's mind pathological cases, the problems of sexual psychopaths, revolutionary problems, and others besides.

By assailing us with strong doses of an obtrusive and boisterous music, the world over-stimulates and enervates us; stage shows excite and capture all our senses; even the graphic arts choose to deal with what is disgusting and hateful, what arouses, and have no hesitation about depicting for us in gruesome detail everything most shocking and horrible that life has to offer.

This over-all description already shows us a whole series of dangers inherent in modern culture; anyone who wishes can complete the picture by adding any number of details out of his own experience . . .

That's a text people should always carry around in their pocket, to show anyone who starts to talk to them about the good old days when life was peaceful . . . In any case, if it was, people remained woefully unaware of it.

The "peaceful" time we're referring to is that of the rise and triumph of Fascism, after the fearsome financial panic of '29. It is that of the Spanish Civil War, the Popular Front, as in Russia it was the period of that great, stirring, and often misunderstood adventure which for many represented the hope of the world . . . The men we were talking about, for example, were without exception fascinated by Soviet Communism.

— And what about you?

— Me? I fit rather neatly into the contemptuous definition that Lenin gave of Leftists: "Those petty bourgeois who are so terribly upset by the horrors of capitalism . . ." I was disgusted, shaking with disgust, but with no outlet through which to articulate it politically. I was, out of a combination of background, heredity, temperament, contagion, and God knows what else, on the side of the "poor and downtrodden." But it all stemmed from feeling rather than from any analysis of the historic role of the proletariat.

One evening in 1936 Renoir took me to hear Maurice Thorez.* I was spellbound. It was Jean Gabin with dialectics. Twenty years later I saw him again, when I interviewed him. He was one of those people who truly had charisma. I don't remember the exact year, though I think it was '55, but I do remember the exact date — July 4 — because of a rather funny incident.

Jean-Jacques Servan-Schreiber, our friend Simon Nora, who was a high-ranking member of Mendès-France's brain trust, and I were waiting for Thorez at Jean-Jacques' apartment. Our meeting was scheduled for early afternoon. Jean-Jacques had already had several talks with Thorez at party headquarters. All three of us were standing on Jean-Jacques'

* Long-time head of the French Communist Party. — *Translator.*

balcony watching for Thorez to arrive. A black car arrived and stopped. The chauffeur got out and opened the door. We saw him helping Thorez out of the car — he had a serious physical handicap — and just as he did we heard a band start playing martial music. "I don't believe it," Simon Nora exclaimed. "You don't mean to tell me he brings his own music with him wherever he goes!" It seemed absurd, but to all appearances that was what was happening.

It was a few moments before we realized that, by a strange coincidence, Thorez's car had arrived at the very minute when, a few blocks away, a band had started playing before a statue of George Washington to celebrate the American Fourth of July.

There were two people with him, one of whom was a union leader. Thorez was a very changed man from the one I had seen twenty years before. His right arm was paralyzed and he had only slight use of his right leg. His face, too, had a tense, frozen look about it. But his blue eyes were as bright as ever, and he still emanated an aura of strength and power. He was distinguished looking, with that innate distinction you find in true "sons of the people."

He also had his "Pinay side,"* if you see what I mean. A stubborn Frenchman. But with a much more highly developed mind. In any case, Thorez analyzed the then current situation very shrewdly and intelligently. We had a very long conversation, ranging over a wide variety of subjects none of which would probably seem very meaningful in today's framework. What was interesting was to talk to him

* Antoine Pinay, a conservative-minded politician, who was French Premier for a time in the fifties and was very popular with thrifty Frenchmen, since he stood for anti-inflation and fiscal responsibility. When De Gaulle returned to power in 1958, he chose Pinay as his Minister of Finance, to help make devaluation more easily acceptable. Later, Pinay resigned with a great deal of sound and fury because he was in disagreement with De Gaulle's policies. — *Translator.*

face to face. It was very hot that day, and when I served the drinks I took off my jacket, and I never put it back on. That led to another rather funny incident that occurred right after our guests had left.

In Jean-Jacques' mind, the sheer blouse I was wearing was completely incompatible with Communist sobriety. Simon Nora shared that august opinion. They were both upset with me. I had, it appeared, been provocative, albeit unwittingly. What were the Communists going to think of me, of us all?

The next day I received, on letterhead stationery of the Communist Party union headquarters, one of the warmest declarations I have ever received via letter.

Looking back, what delights me most about that story is the youth and inexperience of my two would-be censors who had already assumed what the reaction of the other persons would be, and their effort to deify politics, to try to make it somehow inviolate, untainted by human contact.

I went to Thorez's funeral in 1964. A year before he had already officially passed on the leadership of the party to Waldeck Rochet. The word was that, in order to resolve the conflict between the liberal tendency in the party and the hard-liners, Thorez had given the key post to Waldeck but had literally surrounded him with new men of Stalinist orientation. In this way he retained the unofficial post of arbiter within the party. Today, Waldeck is gone. And who arbitrates between what and what? . . .

What is so remarkable — and to me horrible — is that passivity on the part of the party faithful, who applauded Thorez in '36 when he shouted: "Catholics, workers, employees, artisans, peasants: we offer you our outstretched hands, because you are our brothers and because you are confronted and overwhelmed with the same concerns that we are."

Back in 1924 these same militants were applauding this

declaration: "All the talk about a marriage between Communists and Socialists is completely incompatible with the Bolshevist concept of things. We have no desire to join forces with any social-democracy. You don't marry fire and water!"

And then in '39 they were applauding the German-Soviet pact. That, at least, was a hard pill to swallow. But they swallowed it nonetheless. And since then, good God! What haven't they swallowed?

*Perinde ac cadaver.** That's the epitome of everything I loathe. No matter what church it is. Or what dogma.

In '36 the Communist pressures on the film industry were considerable. But I found it impossible for me to make the concrete commitment. There's no way to become a naturalized worker. A certain lucidity, which often paralyzed me from taking actions and sometimes kept me from succeeding in a given venture, also at times kept me from making errors.

In one sense, though, you were right in saying that life was more "peaceful" in those days, in that all this commotion, all these cries and demonstrations — they went on incessantly, and were much more violent than they are today — occurred within the context of a great nation which had proved its mettle on the field of battle and emerged victorious, which felt sure of its position as the leading nation of the world, whose roots went deep into a soil judged to be solid and unshakable, behind fortifications believed to be impregnable — the Maginot Line — a nation which was both the crucible and protector of the most cultivated, refined, and successful civilization on the face of the earth, the

---

* *Perinde ac cadaver:* literally, "like a corpse." It was the expression used by Ignatius de Loyola to describe to the Jesuits the kind of discipline and blind obedience expected of them by their superiors. — *Author's Note.*

only one where art, literature, dance, elegance — and by clear implication the appreciation of fine food — were truly understood and appreciated. All of which had to help foster a certain feeling of security and power.

— Did you have that feeling?

— I did. And I assure you I was not alone! I think it was in a letter that Engels wrote in 1840, 1842, in which he relates that in Paris he saw European civilization in all its crowning glory . . . That it was a city where all the nerve endings of European history converged, a city from which, at regular intervals, electric charges emanated that made the whole world tremble. I can't swear I'm giving it to you verbatim, but that's the gist of it. The point is, in the thirties people still believed it. France was a lighthouse built on a rock, if you'll excuse the awful image. The rock was made of cardboard, as 1940 was to show, but no one in his wildest imagination could even conceive of such a collapse. It was . . . I was going to say arrogance, but it wasn't arrogance. Simply a kind of French certainty of its own impregnable superiority; I can't even begin to describe it for you. It simply can't be communicated.

— And this certainty was widespread?

— I could tell you that I have no idea. But what ensued showed, alas, that it was indeed!

— Wasn't it a purely Parisian feeling?

— On the contrary. Paris has always been both more unruly and more skeptical.

— But wasn't it a feeling generally shared in all the countries of the West?

— No, I don't think so. It was specifically French. At the time I had never been to England, but the English have always been merchants, therefore of necessity aware of the world abroad, even if in their hearts they despised it. France was still a nation of farmers and artisans, exporting relatively little, with a paucity of youth because children were not in fashion . . . I use that expression advisedly. Procreation and fertility have their cycles of being in and out of fashion, for reasons which have never been properly explained. The French were Malthusians, and especially ignorant of the mechanics of economics — and I mean really ignorant. The French economist Alfred Sauvy has written some enlightening pages on the subject. The population was relatively old, and therefore more conservative than dynamic, looking back on that glorious military past whose praises it was forever singing. On another level, no artist or performer — be he a painter, pianist, singer, or dancer — could lay any claim to fame until he had "made" it in Paris. There were no pretty women except in Paris. The title of a famous book of the time was *Dieu est-il Français?*

Don't think I'm embellishing. I didn't have a happy childhood, and I wouldn't want to relive it for anything in the world. Believe me, it's not a question of reminiscing about the "good old days" . . . far from it. I don't have to fake anything to dredge up intact all that blind faith in the grandeur, the generosity, the oneness and invincibility of France, the country of the arts, of the rights of man — and of champagne. And I hesitate to say it, but in a way that faith helped people to live.

— Didn't you have any contacts with the Surrealists?

— No, none.

— And you didn't try to have any?

— No. I didn't "try" anything. Who knows, I might not have taken to them. As people grow older they have little or no difficulty looking back and seeing themselves as young revolutionaries, when in fact they were simply slugs, who perhaps participated in a demonstration or two in their pimply adolescence. I never had acne, and I have no memory of being a slug. But neither was I a revolutionary when I was twenty. In those days, in fact, it was the youth of the far right who were the most active and vociferous — and the most hateful, with their lead-weighted canes . . . I had one of them in my own family, so I had a chance to witness the breed close up. He took part in all kinds of rightist movements. In the thirties he was in the *Cagoule,* which plotted to bring down the Republic. Later, during the Occupation, he joined *La Milice,* working for the Germans. The whole gamut. In those days the right was much less subtle than it is today. It was smug and self-assured, without the slightest trace of bad conscience.

Actually, there were two "rights." First, there was the monied right, the one that never goes down into the street to demonstrate but discreetly finances the Socialist parties "just in case." It still exists. Check and see who is not included in the latest program for nationalization promulgated by the Socialists and Communists. It's an amusing and instructive little game . . . And the second right is, or rather was, the mad right, the hallucinating right who thought the devil had returned in the person of Léon Blum.

— And for you, who was Léon Blum?

— A gentleman who bounced me on his knees when I was four and sang me some child's ditty in a high-pitched voice . . .

— What did the Popular Front represent for you? Did you believe in the straight-line progression toward "good"?

— Not toward good, because I was not of a religious bent, but toward a "better world." And what a "better world" it was too. An extraordinary explosion of joy! The first paid holidays, the first vacations: I wonder what the French could be given tomorrow that would rival that unprecedented feeling of betterment. I don't know whether you've seen the documentary film Henri de Turenne made called *36* . . .

Do you remember how the workers looked back then? They were small, puny, poorly clothed . . . Their children — or rather their grandchildren, since we're talking about forty years later — simply do not seem to belong to the same race. They appear to have emerged from a long darkness. There was nothing very original about being against poverty and hunger, being for the pleasures of life.

Why is it that in France things happen only through violent explosions after a long period of tense stagnation? That explains the extraordinary resistance to change that culminates in a wrenching, or even breaking of the social fabric. Back in those days, was it simply the negative weight of demography? Perhaps. I don't know. I don't know what makes history.

— Are you saying that in the twenties and thirties society was stagnant?

— Yes, stagnant with undercurrents of unrest. Rigid. Frozen. Today people complain, and rightly so, of the indiscriminate urbanization going on, the anarchical construction. Someone my age may have spent his entire youth without ever seeing a building going up . . . People lived in apartments for thirty years without ever repainting them.

And yet at the same time it's true that the world back then was less heavy, there was more simple gaiety, fewer basic uncertainties.

— Had you heard of Freud?

— Heard of him, yes, but no more than that.

— And in the circles you traveled in?

— I doubt it very seriously. Gide, who was aware of everything, studiously ignored him.

— Might this not explain, at least in part, that gaiety, that lack of uncertainties?

— Perhaps. I never thought of that. There's no doubt

that the popularization of a kind of watered-down psycho-analysis can produce some strange results. And the atom bomb too!

— Would you say that people's emotional life, their sexual life, occurred more naturally then?

— Naturally! What a way to put it! Eroticism wasn't invented in 1950! In fact, I have a feeling we're in the process of uninventing it.

— Is it a subject that interests you?

— I was on the verge of replying, "Happily"! But in those days we talked about love, and we made love, but we didn't talk about how to make it. That's really a phenomenon of contemporary times, that widespread dissemination of rather ponderous literature dealing with the technical aspects of what transpires when a male organ encounters a female's. But I fail to see any relationship between this kind of information, which is doubtlessly useful to circulate, and eroticism, which takes place in one's head.

What's been happening today is not an explosion of eroticism; it's the presence, the omnipresence of sexuality, which is not new, since it has always been all-powerful, but now is acknowledged and even shouted from the rooftops.

Eroticism — that is, what makes a man or a woman the noninterchangeable object of someone else's desire — has nothing to do with the mechanics of sexuality which, in times past, the experienced imparted by practical demonstrations to those younger and less knowledgeable than they. And I might add, from the viewpoint of pure efficiency, that might well be the better method.

What a bore for a girl to discover her body through the stuttering efforts of a boy her own age! Even if he's done his homework on the techniques. And probably the reverse is also true, though the consequences are doubtless less serious. Or it may well be that today the young people are dealing with the matter better than ever, and that there are no problems. I really don't know. I hope so, for their sake, especially for those girls who strike me as still completely unliberated. Centuries of repressed sexuality cannot be repaired with a few years of the pill.

It would be funny, I think, if all of a sudden the primitive woman were to re-emerge, the woman who had to be subjugated, muzzled, humiliated, imprisoned in one way or another so that men could have the strength to do something other than make what is called love and could concentrate on creating civilizations. In Polynesia, women are still these extraordinary "man-eaters" — any man. They set out to do their marketing, meet a man along the way, and it's, "Bang, grrr, thank you sir!" The women are delighted.

Fleshly delights, in the real, civilized sense of the term, are not just around the corner, if in fact they ever come to be. But simple fleshly pleasures ought nonetheless to be within the realm of possibility for more than the privileged few.

If I go on about this much longer, I'll surely raise more than a few eyebrows. Or perhaps not, I'm not sure. I don't know. Where are we in France on this whole subject? When you think that sometime back in the late twenties Victor Margueritte was stripped of the Legion of Honor for having published *La Garçonne* [*The Flapper*], a work that today would read like a Sunday School story . . . Or that Léon Blum was considered depraved when his book *Du mariage* dared to suggest that people ought to experiment a bit before getting married . . .

Those were the days when dirty jokes were the height of fashion, and when adultery was the basic subject of every vaudeville act, every play — tragedy or comedy — when the Minister of Education was known to possess the finest collection of pornographic books in France, and when orgies were the order of the day in the Bois de Boulogne. Names were named . . . Apparently the practice still goes on, but it is now no longer confined to the bourgeoisie. Ah, my friend, what has the world come to when even the orgy itself is no longer what it used to be!

If my joke's in poor taste, it's because I find myself deeply irritated by a kind of elitism in the whole area of debauchery — a subject which in itself interests me not at all. Yet we all know that eighteenth-century France was one of the most dissolute societies of all time, the aristocracy especially, where libertine practices were rampant. Later the upper-middle class had its own unfettered fling. But throughout, the men were meticulous in making a clear-cut distinction between their wives — duty, maternity, goodliness, and innocence, migraine headaches — and women — pleasure, whores, mystery, the nether world . . .

In other words, it was as though they had come to terms with the cohabitation of . . . let us say for the sake of simplification, of the Angel and the Beast in them, but that they refused to tolerate a like accommodation in women. It was as though men needed an angel for the Angel in them, and a beast for the Beast. All of which is simply a way of denying women all their truth and complexity, their human ambivalence.

And what is the net result of such an attitude today? First, an increased intellectual refinement, the cerebration of an ever greater number of people leading them to a constantly wider search for eroticism in the real sense of the term, to the cerebration of sexuality.

The upshot of all this is that eroticism becomes less and less the exclusive province of the upper class, particularly of the men, who saw nothing wrong in indulging in it with women reserved for that purpose, but who now begin to scream in protest when they realize or suspect that it is a game no longer limited to their own kind.

What we are also witnessing is that women are beginning to escape from that artificial division of Angel and Beast. And that, I suspect, is something very new indeed in that it transcends the boundaries of the happy few.

But actually I have to admit that I know very little about what was happening in this area prior to the war. In this area and many others. No one can give a fair account of any given period, and if you push me on in this direction, I'll end up telling you absurdities. Each of us has only his two eyes to see with, that is an angle of . . . how many degrees? Ninety? Today, in our profession as journalists, we find ourselves at the center, as it were, of a nervous system. As a result, we pick up a great many things, even if we don't go into them very deeply . . . We learn how to become, if you like, a seismograph.

Before the war I was not in this privileged situation; and since I was "atypical" to boot, the respect for information that I acquired forces me to put you on your guard and ask you to keep insisting that I confine what I say to subjective testimony. All I'm trying to do is to give it to you raw, and not any warmed-over reminiscences.

 IV

— Do you remember the Spanish Civil War?

— Yes, very well. If I had been a boy, I think I would have gone to Spain and joined the fight. I think.

— Did you know Spain?

— I had gone there, but I can't really say I knew it.

— Did you have the impression that what was going on there would, in the long run, be a threat to France?

— No, not really. The awful thing about it was France's indifference, her silence . . . I have a bitter memory of that.

— Did you ever hear Hitler on the radio?

— Yes, and I saw him in the newsreels of the time. And I also heard a lot about him because among the refugees who began to flock to France there were a goodly number from the German film industry who did their best to find some position, no matter what, in French films. Their stories were ominous . . . It's strange, but I remember very clearly one conversation, where Louis Jouvet was present, in which one of the refugees told us about how he had fled . . . He talked about Dachau, he described what was going on in Berlin. And we kept saying over and over: "That's terrible, that's terrible." But it seemed to us more distant than Hanoi does today, more foreign. It was, in the literal sense of the term, unimaginable, therefore unreal . . . It seemed unthinkable that the plague could reach us.

— But what did you think of Hitler? That he was mad? Hysterical?

— Simply that he was a Fascist. Like all the children of my generation, or almost all, I was brought up to hate Germany . . . A universal, indiscriminate hate . . . At an age when children are learning nursery rhymes, I was being taught *Sambre et Meuse* and *Ils n'auront pas l'Alsace et Lorraine* . . . Germany was the land of the Boches, the Krauts. So I didn't have to force myself to hate Hitler: he was only a new variation of German degradation.

After World War II, I had enormous difficulty overcoming that ridiculous hatred of an entire people. But I wanted to with all my might, and I ultimately succeeded. But even as late as 1952, seven years after the war, I went to some Congress for Europe at Aix-la-Chapelle with Jean-Jacques Servan-Schreiber. It was the first time I had been back on German soil. The train arrived at night . . . on the station platform there were uniformed employees. They were shouting, in German obviously, *"Schnell! Raus!"* Lord knows what . . . I don't know what came over me, but I climbed back on the train. Fortunately, the stopover was long enough so that I had time to get hold of myself . . . But it was a reflex with very deep roots.

— Do you remember Munich?

— Indeed I do. Very well!

— What what were your feelings at the time?

— Shame.

— Why?

— Because of Czechoslovakia's base cowardice . . . One of my mother's cousins, whose son was of draft age, went to applaud Daladier and took part in a collection to raise money to buy Chamberlain a country house. I called her every name in the book.

— Didn't you think, nonetheless, that Daladier had extricated himself from a very ticklish situation?

— Not in the least. I thought that he had yielded to extortion, and one of my hard and fast principles is that one should never give in to blackmail. Never. It's a principle on which I have never compromised, a principle the validity of which I had a chance to verify once again recently. On that point I'm inflexible. As for the rest, I'm talking to you of someone who no longer exists, of whom I can speak as though I were talking about some little sister who had died and about whom I can be excessively lenient.

— What you mean is, since it was extortion, it could not end there.

— Precisely.

— Did you suspect then that there would be a war?

— I was sure there would . . . And if I, who was young and ignorant, knew it, how could the others not realize it just as clearly?

One might have understood Munich if it were thought of as a tactic to gain time, to prepare. But Munich as a victory for peace! . . . Especially when Hitler had made no effort to hide his intentions. They were printed in black and white in *Mein Kampf*. The first German edition was translated into French by Colonel Chappat, whose son married my sister. He was a classmate of Albert Lebrun, the last President of the Third Republic. The man who cried. He cried at the drop of a hat. Chappat took him a copy of the French translation of *Mein Kampf* and strongly advised him to read it. Either he didn't read it, which is appalling, or he did — which is even worse.

— What were you doing at that time?

— In September of '38? I was an assistant director. I was

working on the script of a film whose title, as I recall, was *Les Otages.* Rather prophetic!

— And the war: what did it mean to you?

— If I were to tell you the truth . . . I think I have to, because it can help to understand certain things today. The truth is that I said to myself: "War is that enormity they've dinned into my ears all these years. Now it's going to be interesting to see it firsthand.

— What aspect interested you? The heroism?

— No, not at all. I didn't for a moment foresee how it would turn out; and for the most part war was not a woman's concern. It was . . . curiosity. Wanting to know what it was like. When, in May of '68 and afterward, I heard adults exclaiming, "But these children are crazy! They're going to destroy everything. If they only knew!" I was reminded of when I was twenty. Yes, if they only knew, but the problem is they don't. And they want to know. When young people keep hearing endless tales about the war and the Resistance, even about the Algerian War, they don't say to themselves, "How lucky I am not to have been involved in any of that!" They say: "And what about me? What's my adventure going to be?" I know that what I'm telling you is shocking, and I also know that, today, I have the deepest horror of war. But I look back, and sometimes it frightens me. I remember that the day I heard the announcement on the radio of the Soviet-German pact I was at my mother's house, and her comment was, "This time war is really coming . . ." To which I replied: "At last, I'm going to see what war really is . . ." and she slapped me. It's the one and only time in my life she slapped me . . . I deserved it.

— Basically, I understand your feeling. But why does anyone feel that way?

— Out of a desire for change, for adventure, for action . . . A need to prove oneself.

— And a predilection to violence?

— Not in my case.

— Did any of your friends and colleagues express similar sentiments at the time?

— Oh, no! Not at all. Maybe some of my peers might have, but I didn't see many of them. They tended not to verbalize. Young people, as we know them today, did not exist. And the others were not very warlike. Nor was I, as a matter of fact. I didn't want a war, far from it, but when it arrived I saw it as a kind of dark glitter.

— Because you still had that confidence in the superiority of France? In the belief that France was invincible?

— Invincible. It was a matter of three months. That seems ludicrous in the light of what happened. But that was the thought in everyone's mind at the time. Yet a week later the French army was in full retreat! It makes you dizzy, doesn't it? Sometimes I say to myself, "And what about right now? What are the shifting sands we are mistaking for solid foundations today? What are the monumental errors of judgment, the mistakes and blunders that we are blind to? . . . Is there someone who, on another plane, is at this very moment crying in the wilderness the way De Gaulle did in the years prior to '40 about armored tanks?"

But that brings up the whole problem of information, both the refusal to give it and the refusal to receive it, and in particular the question as it applies to France. I assume we'll have a chance to talk about that later.

— I'm sure we will. But let's pause for a moment here before going on to another period, because 1940 represents the end of something. I'd like to go back and try to find the seeds which were sown in the preceding years. From '32 to '40, did you ever have any desire to try your hand at journalism?

— No, the thought never crossed my mind. I had low

periods when I found myself growing impatient about a certain mediocrity. I mean my own. I thought that my aim was not exceeding my grasp. But the variety of the film industry always gave me the feeling — sometimes justified, sometimes not — that my situation might improve. A different producer, a new director, a trip, an interesting project, and my entire outlook on life could change.

— But did you have any particular goal in mind?

— I was searching . . . I was searching for a cause. But the notion of "commitment" which has since become so widespread was nonexistent then. There was Malraux, I know — to change experience into awareness. That was something else. He fought first, and wrote about it afterward. Committed literature, committed movies, committed songs are a very recent phenomenon. Go back and read Sartre's *Qu'est-ce que la litterature?*, his manifesto published after the war. That was the first salvo. But even Sartre, before the war . . .

I had settled my mother into a reasonably peaceful life; my sister was married and lived in the provinces. I was available. So much so, in fact, that I began to pay some attention to my own personal life. In 1940! I really knew how to choose my moments!

— Did you think about marriage? Children?

— About marriage the way you wait for Christmas, or the way you have chicken pox or the mumps, as something you ought to have? No, never. As for children, that was something you didn't give much thought to in those days. And I gave it even less thought than most. I was the child. Not intellectually, but psychically. I might even say that I wasn't yet in a position to love, only to be loved. And indeed, in March or April of 1940 I thought I would be happy becoming the wife of a man who wanted to marry me. How can I describe that last spring in Paris, its beauty, its glory, its gentleness, and, yes, its unconsciousness too . . . How could anyone make any plans, talk about love, have dinner in the Bois, look for an apartment? . . .

I'm going to tell you what happened because it's the kind of experience that ought to be turned into awareness. The only duty the freedom I enjoy imposes on me is to use it to tell the truth. Still, it's not pleasant.

Had the Germans arrived in Paris two weeks later, I would have been married. Instead of which, after those hectic days, those weeks we all know about during which the national tragedy invaded and overwhelmed all our personal destinies, I wound up alone three hundred miles from Paris in a tiny room — which in itself was a miracle — and pregnant. For two months I dragged myself to one, two, three doctors, begging them to help me. During that period I had cut my hand, and it had become infected. Penicillin did not yet exist. I was shaking with fever. In this country which had just experienced the Apocalypse, a country literally in a state of shock and stupor, with three million of its sons prisoners of war, I could not find a single doctor to listen to me. They were all scared to death. Some took it on themselves to insult me. To hear them talk it was me, with my loose ways, who had lost the war. I tried everything. During the war there were hundreds of thousands of abortions performed under the most abominable conditions, which shattered the health of hundreds of thousands of women. Even these abominable methods failed me, and in 1941 I gave birth to a little boy, who was born with rickets because I was in such a frightful physical state myself.

Since he was born out of wedlock, the authorities refused to give me all the normal ration tickets, from wool to clothe him to milk to feed him. He suffered every indignity from every quarter. And I might add, so did I. The day he was baptized the priest went out of his way to call me "mademoiselle." I returned the compliment by calling him "monsieur." He wasn't going to get any "father" from me . . .

When he was four, he looked like a child of two. Nothing ever entirely makes up for the misfortunes of those early years. Everything came hard for him, very hard . . . One should never be the child of a mother who has had a difficult pregnancy and wept over the birth of her child. Nothing ever makes up for that. Nothing.

Worse, in the midst of this whole impossible situation, I began by doing everything wrong. Out of ignorance. Thinking I was doing what was best, doing my duty. It seems to me that today people know a little more, but does everyone? And as life is indeed a tale full of sound and fury told by an idiot, when my boy had finally reached maturity, after a long, thorny path that we traveled together, he died.* So much for that.

If you don't mind, let's go back to where we left off.

* Françoise Giroud's son was killed in a skiing accident in 1972. — *Translator.*

V

I THINK we were talking about sowing seeds, and you wanted to know if during this time I had any thoughts of becoming a journalist. The answer is no. Actually, I should have thought of it, since within the framework of the film profession all I was able to contribute, not only then but later, was a certain portrayal of reality. A slightly ironic portrayal, at a time when movie telephones were always white, when it never crossed anyone's mind that a star could ever wear the same dress in two successive scenes, when every dialogue was filled with a wit that no one, except a handful of scriptwriters, could have possibly possessed.

But I wasn't wasting my time working in films. I learned on the spot what a situation was; in the dramatic sense of that term, I learned how to tell a story, the internal mechanics of writing a piece . . . The way movie scripts were still being written twenty years ago, that is according to the laws of the theater rather than in a properly cinematic language, they were surely a better school of journalism than writing some thesis for a French university.

I knew I was learning, and learning is always a pleasure. From '37 to '40 I moved steadily up the so-called ladder.

To become an assistant director was a big step forward. I made it squarely. Not like the sons of wealthy fathers who are recommended to some sleeping partner who arranges to have them taken on as a third-assistant-director with the job of Kleenex-carrier, so that the kid can see a bit of what goes on in the movie world, since that's all he dreams about . . .

The director I was working for was a drunkard, but a very distinguished one. He had to direct the movements of thousands of walk-ons, first in a circus, then in a public stadium. And he had to deal with two stars, Fernandel and Raimu, each out to make sure he was not upstaged by the other. Their little game was to see if one could keep the other waiting on the set, were it only for sixty seconds. They really gave me a rough time, there's no other way to describe it.

I stuck to it because the position provided me with my own little dragon to stalk. I had to prove that a girl could do the job just as well as a boy. And since no one else gave a damn about it, I can't say the job was made any easier for me.

— Were you a feminist?

— No, not at all. Girls bored me. I found them dull and tiresome, with their endless stories and the way they had of using their charms to provoke, then crying wolf. Actually, I was the traitor, the one who had gone over to the men's camp. On the social level, I had very vaguely begun to understand the weight of ideology, in the Marxist sense of the term, of infrastructures and superstructures and vice versa — not in those terms, of course. But it was much, much later that I began to see the relation between ideology and the feminine condition.

I was actually in the worst position possible to perceive that relationship, since in a sense I had been spared most aspects of male domination. I hadn't really had to shake myself loose from it, for I had never been economically dependent or imagined that I might be dependent on a man. At that time of my life I found women weak, whining, and underhanded, without having any excuse for being so. On another level, I had been deeply influenced by bourgeois ideology, not so much from my own environment and background as from literature: Julien Sorel and Rastignac. For my mother, my ultimate point of reference, one did not "succeed" socially. One *was,* and one maintained one's position. The façade did not even count. To know "who" someone was, it sufficed to know who his grandfather was.

Events had forced me to realize that you don't pay the butcher with your grandfather. I therefore based my hopes on personal ability, and I did not look down my nose on the possibilities for self-realization that bourgeois society offered — see Balzac — to help restore a certain balance, but exploited these possibilities the way a boy would.

Thinking back, it was mad. All the more so because I really didn't have any gumption. I admire people who do, but I'm not one of them. Fortunately, you never know those things until you're beyond them in life.

Anyway, there I was an assistant director. A bona-fide, certified assistant director. At this particular point, I was working on a film called *Education de Prince* with a very nice director, Alexandre Esway. And there I meet Jouvet. In the film world, that's the last encounter that had a real meaning for me. He helped me become less immature, less green. He made fun of me and it was very healthy. I had endless conversations with him. That is, he talked and I listened. I really knew how to listen. Films didn't interest him in the least. For him, it was a way to earn money. His life was the theater, and in particular the Théâtre de l'Athénée, where he was both the star and the director. To reach him there, you had to climb a steep staircase. His dressing room was a large office filled with books and models of stage sets, with an ad-

joining bedroom . . . the room where he died ten years
later of a heart attack in August 1951 in a deserted Paris
where it was completely impossible to find a doctor . . .

When the Germans occupied Paris, Jouvet had the courage
to leave this theater he loved rather than play for the victors,
or make films for them. He took his troupe and went to
South America. That voluntary renunciation of his public, if
you know what that means for an actor, suffices to describe
him.

There was a brief period in '39 when I found myself out of
work. No film in the offing, nothing. He heard about it. He
called me and asked me to come and see him. He didn't talk
to me about anything specific, only about a scenario someone
had submitted to him that he asked me to read. As I was
leaving, I opened my pocketbook. There was a check inside.
I remember the amount: 3500 francs. I accepted it rather
ungraciously. I mumbled the usual stupidities. He let me say
my piece, then he said to me: "You're taking yourself for
some heroine. And besides, you're making a mountain out of
a molehill. Keep the check. For the moment, it's no problem for me. Someday I may find myself in a bind, in which
case you can help me out."

At the end of '39, during what was referred to as the
"phony war" because nothing was happening while the Parisians went about conscientiously carrying their gas masks
with them, all film activity came to a grinding halt. I took a
job as the secretary to some business executive. A real beast.
As soon as I could, I left him to take the job as secretary to a
lawyer. A lady lawyer, and an overworked one, since she had
taken over the cases of her male colleagues who had been
called up for military service. She was intelligent, brilliant,
and a lovely person to boot. Her husband was away in
service. He had left her a small car, a Simca 5, which she
didn't know how to drive. I had learned to drive, if you could

call it that, during the shooting of a film. One day she asked me to drive her to Fontainebleau. I was more dangerous than an enemy bombing, but she finally arrived safe and sound. It was a tiny car — fortunately, since I never did manage to find reverse gear! To get home, I turned the car around by pushing it till it was headed in the right direction, then I drove off alone. I found that it was very hard to drive as I zigzagged down that darkened road, in and out among the military trucks, which were being driven with their lights out. I brought it back to the garage in Paris and said to the mechanic: "Is this car always that hard to drive? The steering wheel's impossible." He looked at it. He looked at me. Then he asked: "How long have you been driving this car?" I told him four hours. Then he told me the steering mechanism was broken. To grow old, don't you see, is being incapable of doing such things.

I became the proud owner of that piece of machinery because I wore a ring the lady lawyer wanted. We decided to make a trade, without trying to figure out who was getting the worst of the deal. It was in that stout little car that I decided, one fine day in May of '40 — or perhaps it was even later, in June — to go visit, or rather revisit once again, the cathedral of Chartres. I went with the feeling that it might be my last opportunity, that it might be destroyed. By the time I started back the route had already been bombed.

On June 10, 1940, after the blanket of darkness had fallen on Paris, I set out for the south, one among countless thousands of Parisians. The exodus was no worse for me than it was for anyone else. On the contrary, I knew where I was headed, and I knew that I would be joining other members of my family. I took nothing with me, only a suitcase. I didn't wander through the streets of some unknown city in search of a place to lay my weary head. I was young, with a good constitution. And I was fully confident of my ability to cope with difficult or dangerous situations.

— Are you still?

— Slightly less, because I now have to make certain allowances for my physical stamina. I can no longer sleep just anywhere, nor can I run as fast as I used to, or as long; I can't lift heavy things, read without glasses, what else? . . . All of which is simply a way of saying that I'm not as young as I used to be! And I'm also slightly hampered by the lingering aftereffects of some well-placed clubbings.

— But when you were compelled to put your self-assurance to the test, did you find it was justified?

— I'm not self-assured. That's not the right term. I had — and I still have within the limitations I've already mentioned — confidence in my own machinery. It's a good machine that can take a lot of wear and tear. A kind of jeep. It knows how to do all sorts of useful things, quickly and correctly.

— Why did you leave?

— Why? To get away from the Germans! And the bombing of Paris, which everyone was expecting. My reaction was not all that original. Whoever had a vehicle of any kind . . .

— And I would imagine that your faith in the invincibility of the French army was by now a bit shaken.

— Slightly, as you might suspect! But still, even then there was still fighting along the Loire. The Loire of '40 might become what the Marne had been in '14. It was several days before we learned the true extent of the disaster. The unbelievable disaster. A few days of collective disbelief, then dumfounded amazement, then shame when the French asked for an armistice.

— Where were you?

— In Auvergne, at Clermont-Ferrand. In the middle of that extraordinary confusion of Clermont-Ferrand where all the upper crust of Paris — or at least all those who were not hard on the heels of the government in Bordeaux — was to be found. The only reason I was there was because my sister lived not far away. The weather was beautiful, very hot. While the Germans were picking up prisoners wherever they went, the way fishermen catch shrimps in their nets, the displaced Parisians were sitting on the café terraces of Jaude Square in Clermont. Or else they were wandering around completely disoriented, bumping into one another, asking questions. The silent center of the storm: no mail, no telephone or telegraph, no trains, no means of communication whatsoever. Believe me, when people find themselves in that situation away from their normal environment, it has a strange effect on them. It would have been almost comic had it not been for the extent of the tragedy. You have no idea how many people rushed back home as soon as they could because all they could think of was their furniture . . . Others, who had dreamed of freedom, of leaving their wife or husband, of deserting their family, quitting the rat race of boss and office, and who for once in their lives had the chance to make the plunge and disappear, suddenly began searching frantically for those by whom they had always claimed to be enslaved. There's material there for a fascinating study.

— And were you studying it?

— I was too preoccupied and scared! But I did record that impression, as something one ought to remember when one talks about freedom.

— Did you have the feeling that you were going through a historical catastrophe?

— It would have taken far less to give one that feeling. It was an earthquake. I cried, I ranted and raged; I had the impression that what was happening was intolerable, unacceptable . . . I also felt how powerless I was to do anything about it.

— I take it you didn't hear De Gaulle's appeal then?

— Yes, I heard it. In front of one of those big wooden radios on which a loudspeaker was mounted . . . I heard it.

— And what did you think?

— That he was right. In all honesty, I didn't have a minute's hesitation.

— And yet he was nonetheless a "traitor."

— What! Oh, no! The traitor was Pétain!

— In what way was Pétain a traitor? After all, hadn't he simply recognized the weakness that yields to a superior force?

— But who yields or gives in? How can anyone make a pact with the Germans, ask for an armistice while there is still North Africa from which to carry on the fight? I found that inadmissible. On the *Massilia,* that ship which a handful of politicians had borrowed to take them, in fact, to North Africa, was that lawyer-friend of my family's I've mentioned before, Campinchi, who had, I believe, been Minister of the Navy in the Reynaud government. That only added to my conviction, as if it needed any further evidence, of the proper path to follow. Before you are ground down into the earth, liquidated, drained of your last drop of blood, you don't give up by default. No one is ever beaten until he admits defeat. No one, speaking in the name of France, ought to have conceded to Hitler that he had the right to occupy the country. And, as we then believed, to give Hitler a platform from which to launch an invasion of England.

— When you heard that appeal by De Gaulle on June 18, did you have the feeling that it was the basis for a new beginning?

— No, I really didn't. All I thought was: at least there's one man who did what he had to. I didn't go any further than that.

— Do you remember that part of his speech where he talked about the technical superiority of the Germans, who, he said, would in turn be defeated by an even more powerful technical force?

— I have no memory of having heard that precise passage. Since then, of course, I've reread the text, and that part of it in particular, which is extraordinarily intelligent. But at the time I was in such a state of emotion and confusion that my judgment was affected — assuming of course that in those days I might have been able to assess the sense and importance of that portion of the speech, which was not the case.

— I wonder if De Gaulle himself really understood what he was saying?

— Oh, I think he did! I think De Gaulle operated like a computer. Or, if you prefer, like a chess master. He said to himself: "At some point America will get into the war with all its technical power. It's a question of holding out till then."

— Wasn't it rather a verbalized intuition, which he was known to have had, while waiting for events to unfold?

— Obviously that's something I can't say for sure, but I strongly doubt it.

— Did any of your friends go over to join De Gaulle?

— Of course! But I didn't know it at the time. Most of them were officers and men from whom we were cut off . . . But it would be wrong to claim they constituted a vast throng.

— If you had been a man, would you have left?

— Is it right to ask such a theoretical question? . . . My reaction is to say yes. But if I had been a man, I would not have been in Clermont-Ferrand on June 18, 1940, at the age of twenty-three, listening to the radio with my family. What I can say is that I would in all likelihood have been bound and determined to join the combat against the ancient enemy, Germany, as soon as I found a way. And when one became available to me, I did join the struggle. But whether or not I would have tried to join the Free French Forces in London in those early days I can't honestly say. What I can in all good conscience assert thirty years later is this: from 1942 on, any Frenchman who was young and fit who failed to participate in some form in the struggle against the Nazis has to be counted as having, I won't say a character defect but — how shall I put it — a very cautious nature. If ever there was a struggle where the lines were clearly marked, this was it. But who was it who said: "There are things one will never understand if they are not understood immediately?"

The question of collaboration is a whole other matter: it was either a question of the criminal class which exists throughout the world and which Fascism inevitably enlists in its cause, or — and this is far more serious in its spirit if not in its consequences — of the ruling class, with the backing and approval of the high clergy, in fact.

What made that collaboration so serious was the fact that it confirmed in a way the abdication of that ruling class from its posts and responsibilities. If that class had done its job between 1920 and 1940 and industralized France, if it had worked and invested the way the nineteenth-century bourgeoisie before it had done, it would have found the strength to defend its conquests rather than handing them over to the Germans on a silver platter.

It goes without saying that there were some among them who did resist, but they were individual cases . . .

— What you're saying is that in June 1940 there was a kind of enormous silent majority . . .

— Silent and shell-shocked. And with good reason. At

first the French were astounded, dazed, then immediately pre-occupied with personal and material problems. They all thought of nothing else. It's only normal. But I have to admit that today I judge what they did differently than I did for a long time.

— Making more allowances as you grow older?

— No, it's not a matter of making allowances. It's more a question of interpretation. I came to the tentative conclusion that there was in the French character, culture, tradition — call it what you will — an extraordinary aptitude for happiness compared to other peoples at a similar stage of civilization. I have the feeling that in 1940 that aptitude played a role even in the farthest recesses of the collective unhappiness.

— Could you put that into more concrete terms?

— What it means, if I'm not wrong, is that the majority of Frenchmen were — and still are, although perhaps to a lesser degree — sensualists. Capable of being happy and of enjoying themselves, indulging in relatively simple, concrete pleasures. For example, for a long time, and especially during the war, I was extremely exasperated by the importance the French attached to food. I enjoy a good meal, I'm a better-than-average cook, and I fully appreciate fine wine. But to make a cult of that twice a day every day — and during the Occupation, when everything was rationed, a veritable obsession — made me bristle.

There wasn't 1 percent of the population that joined the Resistance, but I swear there were 50 percent who would have risked their necks for a pound or two of butter. And then, about four or five years ago, I began to think that I had been wrong. If the French remain among the least unhappy people, and most enjoyable to be with — everything being relative — it's partly because, twice a day, they know how to make themselves happy by partaking in a pleasure about which they are meticulous.

This same sensualism had also long found satisfaction in the beauties of the country. When you lived in the French countryside, beauty — a gentle beauty — was everywhere. The ugliness of industrialization is relatively new, and surely has a relationship to the increase of ill temper in the country, even among those who fail to see the connection.

And there is also, of course, love. I have no idea whether there is any truth in the saying that people in France make love better and more often than they do elsewhere in the world . . . I distrust these unverifiable generalizations . . . But it's a fact we're not puritans.

To which you might retort: "What a pity!" for there is no strength or power without a degree of austerity, without sublimation. It seems that for a period in their history the French achieved an extraordinary equilibrium, that they managed this impossible mixture. And then the balance was tipped in favor of a predilection for happiness — this zest for life, for pleasure that strikes me as deriving directly from civilized sensualism.

— Are you implying that those in positions of power have no taste for life or pleasure?

— They don't give it top priority in their scheme of things; that's a fact you can verify every day. What they do have, and what they do give top priority to, is a taste for power.

— Does a country like the United States have a taste for the pleasures of life?

— First of all, it's far from sure that the United States wanted the power position they hold in the world. They are, if I may put it this way, imperialists in spite of themselves. But if ever there was a power built on the basis of puritanism, the United States is the prime example. And today a reaction is setting in. That's not an original point of view with me; Max Weber's *Capitalism and Protestantism* is a well-known thesis.

— I'm afraid I don't follow you at all when you maintain
that we're not puritans. When, for example, we refuse to see
Le Chagrin et la Pitié . . .

— But that's not puritanism! In fact, it's quite the opposite. The puritan is forever harking back to his responsibility before God, his unworthiness, his self-denial of the
world's pleasures. The example you give illustrates the contrary of what I'm saying. We don't want to know, since in
the case you're referring to, to learn the truth only makes us
unhappy, forces us to reconstruct a mental image which, however false, is easier to live with than the truth. You may
remember that in the old days they cut off the head of the
messenger who arrived bearing bad news. Why? Because he
obliged the general or prince to whom he brought the news of
a defeat to see himself suddenly in the guise of the van-
quished. And yet that does not change the content of the
message, and its reality. But as far as the Occupation itself is
concerned, the epic of De Gaulle enabled us to erase it. To
bury it beneath the sands of memory.

If everything I have just said makes any sense, the moral
to be derived from it is to understand and appreciate how this
talent — there is no other word for it — this French talent
for life managed to conceal, and still does today, the unpleasant realities, which become even more unpleasant by virtue
of not having been perceived, discussed, and faced up to in
time.

— And what about you: what were you doing between '40
and '45?

— I did whatever I could. Do you know what song was
on everyone's lips in 1940? Anyone who's old enough to
remember will tell you. It was a song by Jean Sablon, the
favorite crooner of the time, whose words went: "I bow and
take my leave, let my steps go where they may, down the

ways and byways of France, of France and Navarre . . ." He
had no idea what he was saying.

During the summer of '40 I bowed and took my leave.
The great advantage of catastrophes is that you tend to forget
yourself in them, lose sight of your own problems. When I
regained contact with myself, as it were, I had emerged from
my youth. The first, the real one. I would have preferred to
have it happen under different circumstances, but no matter
how it occurs it's good to have it over with. My profession
no longer existed, so I started looking around for another one.
It was a period when there were some pretty odd job changes
— people turned to vegetable gardening, lamp-shade manufacture, the canned-goods industry. Anything. As for me,
once again fate played a part, a direct part. But this time I
was unaware of it.

Among the Parisians who had retreated south to Clermont-
Ferrand was the editor of the biggest French newspaper of the
time, *Paris-Soir,* which was owned by Jean Prouvost. He had
his whole team with him — with the exception of Pierre
Lazareff, who had gone to the United States — and they had
taken up temporary quarters in the offices of the Clermont
daily. In the street one day I ran into one of the paper's senior
editors, Charles Gombault, whom I knew from somewhere, I
can't quite remember where, and who was departing the next
day for London. Before leaving he introduced me to the
person who was slated to become the editor-in-chief of the
paper, Hervé Mille.

When *Paris-Soir* left to set up offices in Lyon, I went along.
Newspapers used to print short stories. Every day they carried a new one. There were specialists who wrote them. A
story is not all that different from a film script, and I wrote
some and offered them to the paper. Hervé Mille accepted

them. By a stroke of pure luck, the day when one of my first stories was printed, the sales manager of the paper, who passed Jean Prouvost on the stairway, said to him: "Say, boss, the story in today's paper is one of the best we've had in a long time!" He might as easily have said the contrary — the story he was referring to was hardly tailor-made for sales managers. War sometimes fashions such little miracles! . . .

— Do you remember the story?

— Only vaguely. It was second-rate Mark Twain. With a proper touch of wry humor and mockery. Jean Prouvost looked at the name of the author, which obviously he had never heard before. "Ah, so you're the little brunette . . . Very good, very good indeed. Keep up the good work! . . ." To which I replied: "Yes, Monsieur, thank you, Monsieur." Those who heard me took me aside and whispered that I should address him as *patron*. Call him *patron?* No, I couldn't. I could never bring myself to that.

Fortunately Hervé Mille had taken me under his wing. I still don't know what effect I had on Prouvost, whether I amused him or irritated him. He used to say, with that very special drawl that all his fellow workers could imitate to a tee: "Hervé, she's got a bad temper, that little brunette has . . ."

One night he invited me and five or six other employees to dine with him at one of the bèst restaurants in Lyon. I think it was *La Mère Brazier.* Anyway, we were all sitting at a round table. I don't know what he was eating, but every once in a while he'd say: "Ah, delicious! Here, try it . . ." And he would offer his fork in turn to the people at the table. Power is really disgusting!

He lived surrounded by a court. Like royalty, he never had a penny on him. He stuck his nose into everything at *Paris-Soir* naturally, but also into *Marie-Claire,* a woman's weekly which had its offices in the same building, and into 7 *Days,* a kind of poor man's *Paris-Match* that he had just started, for which I wrote a great many short stories. He was really the boss, the autocratic paternalist; and in fact he was greatly admired and was impressive in his job . . . Where had this wealthy bourgeois from the north of France, who had been born into sugar and textiles, got his nose for what the public wanted? . . . "A crocodile who swallowed a shopgirl," they used to say about him. For it's not enough to want to "sell paper," as the saying goes, you have to know how to. And it's a law of the press, as it is of many other professions, that you only make well those products that you would buy yourself . . . Jean Prouvost was the typical reader of his own newspapers. See if you can make any sense out of that!

He was that rarest breed in the newspaper world, a man who combined, in a single person, the creative sense, money-making and administrative ability. One of the last of the great, autocratic entrepreneurs. Who else is there in that same generation? Marcel Dassault in the field of aviation; Boussac, the owner of Christian Dior, in textiles; Pierre Laguounie, who owns the *Printemps* department store; Gaston Gallimard, the publisher . . . I had lunch one day with Boussac. The atmosphere was so heavy you couldn't breathe; you had the feeling that it would have been unspeakable if anyone had even tried to contradict him. There were all sorts of people there who owed him nothing, but without exception they knelt before him . . . It's strange, the effect that money produces, for we all know that the most you can ever expect from a very wealthy person is that he may be kind enough to bum your cigarettes.

Anyway, that day he had just inaugurated a dressmaking establishment in which he was interested. It was long after Dior. It was called Pierre Clarence, I think. He asked all the women present what they thought of the collection. By offering my candid opinion I had no intention of seeming aggressive, but if I had physically put my feet in his plate, it couldn't have been worse. The hostess turned geranium-red. Pierre Lazareff, who was one of the guests, immediately tried to smooth things over, naturally. I didn't press the point. I didn't give a damn about Pierre Clarence — or about Boussac either! Now Dassault is another matter altogether. There's a man with a real creative imagination, of the kind we were alluding to a short while back. He takes his little pencil, he sketches his little airplanes . . . An extraordinary fellow, I assure you, even in how he throws his weight around. The way he has of buying his way into films when everyone tells him there's no more room there . . . at such a point, the use of money ceases to be obscene and becomes poetic.

Prouvost, for his part, believes he's immortal. I'm convinced he really believes that. He thinks an exception is going to be made for him — that he will at least live long enough to see his great-grandchild, who is his only male heir and, what is more, his namesake, take over. One is eighty-six, the other must be ten or twelve. An interesting succession, isn't it? I don't mean his industrial holdings, nor even his publications. But he is the sole owner of the daily paper *Le Figaro,* and he owns enough shares of R.T.L., the nongovernment-controlled radio network, so that the other shareholders need his agreement to retain control of the station . . . *Le Figaro,* plus R.T.L.: that is what you call having a certain power. Assuming you know how to use it, of course, which today is far from easy.

All these men are from another period. They can't share their power. And besides, can power ever be shared? And if so, how? That is perhaps the most explosive question of our time. Far more explosive than the question of sharing ownership, if that ownership is not accompanied by power.

The unfortunate part is that people who ponder this kind of problem have generally never held positions of responsibility in any business. For that reason alone I'm glad that I have, although I never derived any real pleasure from it. But I would even have liked to work for a while in some kind of industry to see how it operates from the inside. A newspaper is a somewhat special case.

But there are two detonators in the society of highly developed nations: women and popular participation in the decision-making process, both in business and in politics on the regional or local levels.

VI

AT THE TIME I was working for *Paris-Soir,* I would probably never have known anything about Jean Prouvost, or what went on at his level of operation, if all that had happened in Paris. But in Lyon, under those exceptional circumstances, with this heterogeneous collection of fashionable people camping in temporary offices, a kind of soup kitchen set up in a deconsecrated whorehouse, where you would see a Rothschild-in-distress — Philippe — arriving to join the group one day, a French ambassador — Massigli — passing through the next — there we had all the features and habits of refugees, and something of their intimacy . . .

The only Lyon residents with whom I had any kind of sustained relationship during these few months were two prostitutes. They hung out in a bar next to the hotel where I was living and somehow always managed to have cigarettes. They were nice. They never took advantage of us. One day about ten years later I saw a girl walking along the Champs-Élysées, literally upholstered in mink. She flung her arms around me and said: "Don't you remember me? Lucette? From Lyon? How are things going?" I said, "Sure I remember you. I'm all right. How about you?" She gave me an incredible wink, indicating both the mink and the man she was with. I never saw her again. I was with someone who said to me: "Your friend doesn't have exactly the best taste . . ." I didn't even try to explain to him. Those things can't be explained to someone who hasn't experienced them.

So it came to pass in Lyon that I found myself not only in the same office with Hervé Mille but at the same desk, facing him — which again would have been unthinkable under normal conditions.

We had discovered that the readers of the paper had a thirst, which we had to slake, for "Parisian life"; they wanted to read about the shows and plays, about the stars, and so forth. It was an area I knew, so I wrote a few articles, fillers, little pieces. I no longer remember the subjects. I had to write fast, and Hervé Mille took the sheets off my desk as fast as I finished them and passed them on to the compositor . . . I didn't enjoy it: the rush, the writing tossed off because there was no time to think . . . That's why I never liked daily papers. But I must have learned some things in spite of myself, from the very fact that I was seated across from the director of the paper, that everything came across his desk, that I listened and watched.

— That was really your debut as a journalist, wasn't it?

— It would be fairer to say it was my debut on a newspaper. Because at *Paris-Soir* I didn't do any reporting or any research. I was living off the material I had already accumulated.

As far as the stories and features were concerned, I used gimmicks, tried and true techniques. It was purely a way of earning a living, but under tolerable conditions due largely to Hervé Mille's tact and decency. In fact, he played a decisive role in my professional life since it was thanks to him, five years later, that I took up journalism seriously. He was one of the benevolent figures in my life, and not only in mine. A veritable Pygmalion of the press. His worldly, Parisian exterior conceals the strength of his character and the inflexibility of his positions on everything that really matters.

There were other interesting people working in those days on *Paris-Soir*. Jean Prévost, for one, who was later killed — horribly mutilated — in the Vercors underground. And there was a good journalist named Robert François with whom I lunched practically every day for six months — sharp, effeminate, on drugs, and fascinated by the personage of Pierre Laval. François passed into posterity under the name of Roger Vailland.* We got along very well. And although we didn't see each other very often in later years, it was an affection which lasted until his death.

That sophisticated community aspect, the hotel life, those friendships more easily fostered and maintained than would have been possible under normal conditions, that inscrutable city between its two rivers — I like cities that have rivers running through them — all that had, by its very precariousness, a certain charm. It was tucked in a time where the whole tone was dramatic, like some plaintive music, full of inexplicable sobs.

It was in Lyon that I saw Saint-Exupéry for the last time. He took from his pocket the pack of cards he was forever carrying — he was the best card trickster I've ever seen — and he said to me: "I'll do whatever trick you like . . . And then after I've done it I'll show you how to do it yourself . . ." He had never before wanted to reveal any of the secrets of his magic.

And then after a while the film industry started up again, in both zones — the unoccupied, so-called free zone of the Vichy government and Pétain, and the occupied zone, which

* Pen name of a well-known French novelist of the postwar period. — *Translator.*

was Paris. Between the two zones was a line of demarcation that you had to have a permit to cross in either direction, like a frontier. In order to work in films in both zones, you needed a work permit from a corporate committee called the C.O.I.C. Not long ago I happened to be talking about this period with Simone Signoret, who in those days had only walk-on parts in the theater — or, as she puts it, she was a sham-actress. She was as fresh and pretty as could be. Anyway, the C.O.I.C. refused her a work permit because she was half-Jewish, but she managed to get a part in a film anyway. When she went to the producer to claim what he owed her, he threatened to denounce her. That was the least of what was going on in those days.

I worked on films in both zones. One, made in the unoccupied zone, was called *Promesse à l'Inconnue,* and wasn't half bad. And then I pulled up stakes and went back to Paris for good. A lot of films were being made. The movie houses were packed — they turned on the lights during the newsreels to prevent people from demonstrating — so there was no shortage of work. I also wrote some songs. Paris was less sad than the unoccupied zone, where people really felt like refugees and cried when they heard Charles Trenet sing: "If you go to Paris, say hello to all our friends . . ." I went back and forth fairly often between the two zones. There was nothing suspicious about it. I had left my mother and son in Clermont-Ferrand. In 1941, my sister had created there the nucleus of one of the first Resistance networks. There were a great many pro-German Alsatians in Clermont, and in '43, *La Milice* blew up her house — my son, who was inside, miraculously escaped — and then she was arrested by the Gestapo. After that I brought the rest of my family back north. In Clermont there was a big wave of arrests. Jean Chappat, my sister's husband, who was the head of the Resistance movement in the whole region, was also arrested. And later I was arrested in Paris. My sister was deported to Ravensbrück, then to Flossenbürg. Chappat was sent to Neuengamme. As for me, they imprisoned me in Fresnes.

The day I was arrested the room on the ground floor of the Rue des Saussaies where people were first brought was jampacked. In the prison van used to transfer us to jail there was no room on the benches so they let me stand in between. As we drove over the Pont Alexandre-III I could see through the grill the blue sky fresh after a rain, and outlined against the sky the streetlamps with their spherical globes, those very special streetlamps that flank the bridge. And I said to myself: "It's all over. You're never going to see this again." When we arrived, it was too late for any formalities. They locked me in a cell with two other women, a mother and daughter. It was a windowless storage room, without any light, no benches or beds, with puddles of foul water on the floor. I hesitated for a moment, then lay down on the floor. The two women were standing, clutching each other. One of them said to me: "You're going to get your coat dirty." I said, "I know." And I went to sleep. When I woke up I saw them still standing there, right where they had been when I lay down. They had spent the night standing up. They looked at me with a kind of horror on their faces. The mother said to me: "I don't understand how you could have . . ." I answered: "We don't know what's in store for us. It's better for the nerves to have had some sleep. It helps you to act less stupidly . . ." And that woman, who the day before had been arrested by the Gestapo, said to me: "You're right! But meanwhile you've ruined your coat."

That's a characteristic I noted not only at that time but also at others — only then it was a question of life or death: an almost complete lack of any sense of priority. It often occurs when one is "in shock" in the true sense of the term. Your mind keeps clinging to the idea that you forgot to turn off the gas. I don't know whether it's a way of avoiding reality, responsibility, of fending off fear . . .

— Weren't you afraid?

— Of course I was. Often. Especially later. I was afraid when I heard the screaming of the prisoners being brought back after they had been interrogated. But that night I wasn't. I was simply exhausted, at the end of my rope.

A short while after the Allied landing in June 1944, a message slipped into a package informed me that I was going to be deported. I waited, believing, in my ignorance — we were all ignorant of the deeper truths of deportation — that I was simply going to rejoin my sister. It was a thought I found rather pleasant.

One day I heard my name called, among some fifty or a hundred others, and the number of my cell. They came for me. There was a great deal of commotion and activity in the prison that day. They took me and several other women to the prison clerk. "All right, you can leave. You're free."

My immediate reaction was to think that there was some mistake. I was weak; they had not made it any easier for me to walk off, as I was perched precariously on thick wooden-soled shoes. And prisoners' feet become fragile from lack of use. Anyway, I walked as fast as I could, first within the confines of the prison itself, which was vast, on my way to the street. Then down the street to the Métro, which was a good distance away.

I was almost at the Métro when I heard footsteps running behind me and someone calling my name. Two Germans came up to me, and I thought that I was done for. One of them put his hand in his pocket and handed me something. "Here," he said. "They forgot to give you your watch back." And they turned around and left.

I know that story sounds made up. But it's not; it's the

gospel truth! What I like about it is its absurdity. A completely German absurdity.

I arrived home, took a bath, tried to make contact with someone who could furnish me with false identity papers, and went into hiding. A month later, Paris was liberated.

— Were you arrested under your real name?

— Yes. Someone denounced me.

— How would you describe what Paris was like under the Occupation to people who never experienced it? To young people, for example?

— The Occupation? Which one? Everyone riding bicycles; Paris completely silent; the curfew; the lack of anything to buy; the black market; bare legs painted because there were no stockings; the films of Cocteau, and those of Carné and Prévert; Sartre's play, *Les Mouches;* ration tickets for everything; crazy hats; zoot suits? Or the yellow Star of David worn by the children on their coats and smocks, the police raids, the red posters, your heart pounding every time the doorbell rang? Or the rich manufacturer from the north celebrating his first million at Maxim's?

I'm afraid it's an experience impossible to relate. When you try to tell about it you condense, and through the very fact of condensing you tend to make it false . . . And besides, everyone experienced his own Occupation.

— If you could summarize it in one word, though, what would it be?

— In one word? Devastating — despite the moments of intense exhilaration that come from living with danger. It was long, very long. And sometimes unspeakable. Any situation which offers a great number of people the opportunity of behaving badly is one to be avoided at all costs. When cowardice, venality, and betrayal become not only useful, but are also esteemed and rewarded, they come into their own, it's only to be expected. The same people who under normal or unpressured circumstances would never reveal this side of themselves are triggered into action. It's like pressing a button. There were others, of course, who when the chips were down revealed qualities of courage and unselfishness that were impressive. But any situation where good and decent people are getting killed is obviously bad.

— Did you know any people who broke down and gave in to their baser instincts?

— I'd rather not discuss that. No one who lived through the Occupation — unless perhaps it was in some tiny, remote village, and even then I have my doubts — can think back on it without some degree of skepticism and leniency. Not for those French who killed, tortured, and informed on their fellow men, but for the others . . .

— Did you feel that way at the time, or only later?

— Oh, not at the time! Nor even right afterward . . . Anyway, "leniency" isn't the right word. It's more complex than that. I realized that many people — a great many — are capable of anything. Which includes doing good. Ultimately, they're the same people.

— Did you think the Germans would win?

— No. Oh, maybe for half an hour or so when the news from the front was discouraging. But otherwise never.

— Why?

— I don't know. Maybe because I stupidly believe in the triumph of good over evil. I never for a minute doubted the moral superiority of England, and for me that explained how she was able to hold out, with nothing more than that. You remember Churchill's famous phrase: "I have nothing to offer but blood, toil, tears and sweat . . ." When he said it he put his hand over the microphone and half whispered: "And for ammunition, beer bottles . . ." The point is, England did hold out. I never doubted the power of America either, or that it would come into the war on our side . . .

— But what about Pearl Harbor? Didn't that jar you?

— On the contrary, Pearl Harbor was a pure stroke of luck. Democracies, for obvious reasons, are always slower to get underway than totalitarian countries. As for the Russians' ability to resist I had no idea, but we did have the precedent of Napoleon. We knew that military strategists had always said that deep penetration into Russia was death. Since then I have gone to Russia — in winter — and when you see those endless, snow-covered plains stretching as far as the eye can see, until they meet the gray horizon at a point in infinity, you begin to understand why no invading army has ever returned victorious. You can feel it in your bones.

No, I was never pessimistic as to the outcome of the war. In any case, not for very long. What I was pessimistic about was my ability, and the ability of my family and all the people I loved, to endure long enough to be there when the end finally came. Especially in the beginning of '43. I had an impacted wisdom tooth, which developed into incipient blood poisoning. And at the same time there was an epidemic of scabies going around Paris. I caught it. I was really miserable, at my wit's end. I think what kept me from slipping over the edge was a feeling of the absurdity of the whole thing. You don't die of an impacted wisdom tooth during the war!

— How about in prison?

— No, in prison I was fine. Prison is a strange experience. You become all flabby on the outside, soft and greenish-white. And all hard within. Hollow and hard.

— Didn't you ever hope?

— No, never, not while I was in prison. Not out of courage — unfortunately, it was much less positive than that. It was just that I don't believe in hanging onto life for the sake of living. I require certain conditions, as it were. I only felt that for my mother to lose both daughters would be just too much . . . But it's better to lose your children in a war than in an accident. At least people tend to believe so.

— Do you remember the Liberation?

— I won't say that it was the most beautiful day of my life, because the shadow of those no longer with us was terribly present. And then, as they say, reality never quite lives up to the expectation. But still . . . De Gaulle marching down the Champs-Élysées, in that kind of crazy confusion, that clamor. It was like a steel corset being unlaced, when you begin to breathe again . . .

— What about De Gaulle? Did you think of him as a great man?

— During the war? He was more. He was the symbol. With that extraordinary name . . .

— Later, though, you were worried about him being Fascist . . .

— De Gaulle, Fascist? Never! I defy you to find a single word I ever wrote even alluding to such an idea. In fact, such a notion never even crossed my mind. Fascist? Certainly not!

— And yet, it would seem that in May of '58 you at least feared that he might become Fascist, insofar as he had been brought to power by a Fascistic coup d'état.

— In May of '58 this is the gist of what I wrote — and it's easy enough to check: "If the French want a king, are looking for a father, they can never find a better one. He will be the State. We will be the people. And without doubt he will rule his people well." I remember it very well — although I usually have little interest in what I write once it's printed — because the article was written right after the famous Quai d'Orsay press conference which nipped my potential Gaullism in the bud while it seemed to give strength and purpose to François Mauriac's. We were at the press conference together. I could literally see him melting, while I could feel myself turning into ice.

And yet it was moving to see De Gaulle again. After the war I had only seen him twice, once in '46 or '47, at an immense open-air meeting one Sunday in Vincennes. He had just announced the creation of his political party, the R.P.F.: *Rassemblement du Peuple Français.* I had gone to the meeting with Pierre Lazareff, who kept murmuring: "It's Nuremberg! It's Nuremberg!" as he watched the flags whipping in the wind and the crowd going mad. And I saw him another time at once of his increasingly rare press conferences that I had been sent to cover. It was no longer Nuremberg, but a man alone, solitude draped around him like a mantle of stone. André Dewavrin — Colonel Passy, head of the French secret service in London during the war — who is a friend of mine and who had never stopped seeing De Gaulle had said to me: "You have no idea how alone he is. Write to him. Go and see him." I had written to him, on the Liberation anniversary of June 18, simply because he was De Gaulle and for no other reason! He had of course replied. He always replied — who doesn't have a letter from him? It was early '58, when it was clear that the time of his return to power was fast approaching.

I had had a long discussion with Malraux, who as Mauriac used to say had retired to his study with his album of memoirs, and he had described to me his plan for Algeria. An original plan, and a pretty wild one, I must admit! Anyway, we arranged for a completely private and confidential interview between Malraux and Mendès-France. What a pity no record of that was ever made.

When the Tunisian ambassador to France, Mohammed Masmoudi, was recalled by his government in the wake of the bombing of Sakiet, Jean-Jacques Servan-Schreiber went to say goodby to him. In the course of the conversation, Jean-Jacques suggested: "Before you leave, why don't you drive out to Colombey and say goodby to De Gaulle . . ." Masmoudi followed his advice. It was on that occasion that De Gaulle uttered his well-known phrase: "One should not insult the future."

In any event, in May of '58, as successive governments of the Fourth Republic fell like so many dominoes as soon as they had to try and cope with the question of decolonization, as we watched that dizzying lack of character and political vision, that talent for running scared the minute three tomatoes were thrown or two colonels refused to follow orders, the way Ho Chi Minh, Bourguiba, and the Sultan of Morocco were treated like so many despicable dogs, I was really ready and willing to applaud De Gaulle's return. But not on the shoulders of seditious soldiers whom he refused to disown. Do you remember his declarations, such as: "A man whom I hold in high esteem, Guy Mollet . . ."* or: "A man whom in fact I think of as my friend, Robert Lacoste . . ."† Who wasn't De Gaulle friends with in '58? To whom did he refuse his esteem, he who had always been so sparing of it in times past!

And then there was that deliberate lie, about the balcony scene at the town hall of Arras, where De Gaulle related that he had stood next to Guy Mollet at the Liberation, a sob story aimed at softening up the Socialists, who are always ready to shed a tear or two. Whereas De Gaulle knew perfectly well — he had a memory of steel — that it was a complete fabrication.

It's only a detail, I know, and one does not assume power

* Guy Mollet was head of the French Socialist Party for twenty-five years. In 1956 he was Premier. — *Translator.*

† Robert Lacoste was a Socialist Party minister and special government representative to the Algerian government during the war. Several times he announced that the Algerian War was winding down to its conclusion, that it was in its "final quarter hour." — *Translator.*

through openness and candor but by resorting to wile and ruse; De Gaulle himself said as much quite clearly in his writings. Only the end counts, providing the end is noble . . . Great men would quote the devil if it suited their purpose, wouldn't they?

The week before the press conference when De Gaulle announced his willingness to assume power, François Mauriac had ended his article for *L'Express* with these words: "We all place our hopes in De Gaulle, but not in a De Gaulle who would respond to a call from General Massu.* May he not say a word or make a gesture that would link him to the generals involved in the coup d'état." But after hearing him, Mauriac realized — and wrote — that these coup-d'état generals had not in the least been disowned by De Gaulle. Nonetheless the seduction had still worked, and Mauriac couldn't help letting it show.

For me it was the opposite, and I do not believe that these reactions can by explained by any logical analyses but by what basically determines political attitudes in the broadest sense of the term, that is by what is commonly called one's make-up, one's temperament. In essence, what De Gaulle was really demanding was that we ought to have faith in him because, no matter what happened, he considered himself the best judge of what needed to be done and more able than anyone else to carry it out. All this without in fact knowing — this appeared clearly only later — what had to be, or what could be done with Algeria.

The blind faith that binds one person to another is something to which some — as in my case — are allergic, as they would be to the most serious sort of abdication of one's

* Jacques Massu was a French general in Algeria who in the government crisis of 1958 formed, with General Raoul Salan, a committee of public safety, which seized control in Algeria and faced France with the threat of civil war. — *Translator.*

responsibilities. Alienation results. Besides, even if I wanted to, I am incapable of such sworn devotion. Mauriac's very nature, on the other hand, tended to push him in the opposite direction.

I'm not making any value judgments here. I'm not saying: this or that is what should have been done; I was right and he was wrong. You can change your mind on an issue, but you cannot retract on a basic stand.

— And what about Mendès-France's attitude at that time: how do you explain it? The same way? A matter of character?

— It's up to Mendès to explain it himself. Assuming of course he understands what makes him tick, which I don't believe he does. What did become clearly apparent in the course of a luncheon at Mendès-France's when an emissary from De Gaulle arrived — it was Lucien Rachet, a friend of ours and a real hero — was that his entire reason, his whole concept of the primacy of civil over military power, his rigidity with respect to compromise, all prevented him from going over to De Gaulle unless he clearly and unequivocally disowned the Algerian dissidents. I don't think I'm telling you anything you don't already know by saying that not only is Mendès not conciliatory by nature, but that he's delighted any time he has the possibility *not* to be. Nothing, it would seem, pleases him more than a break in relations where he can say to himself: "I'm suffering; I'm alone. But no matter, *I'm* the one who's right."

In that particular situation, however, he wasn't alone: he wasn't the only one to remain untractable. Mitterrand was beside himself.* I must say that that is the only time — those

* François Mitterrand, present head of the French Socialist Party, who has twice run for President of France. The first time, running against De Gaulle in 1965, he polled a surprising 45 percent. In May 1974 Mitterrand's Socialist-Communist coalition lost by a tiny margin to

days of May 1958 — when I saw him in that upset state. And yet their relationships with De Gaulle were not at all the same. Mendès had been his minister and unquestionably admired him even though De Gaulle had refused to listen to him in 1945 and Mendès had resigned because his financial policies had not been accepted. Later Mendès saw De Gaulle again, and it was he who advised him to adopt the electoral system we have today, which is supposed to prevent any electoral landslide. Can you imagine what might have happened under a system that favored landslides! Mitterrand, on the other hand, had once had a meeting with De Gaulle in wartime London where he reproached him for not having flown to England in a French plane! Relations between them had always been very poor, and they did not improve when at the Liberation De Gaulle ran into Mitterrand again at the Hotel de Ville. And again in 1958, when Mitterrand was a minister, and together with all the other ministers of the government was called to a meeting at the Hotel La Perouse. When De Gaulle saw him he exclaimed: *"You* again!"

— And what about Servan-Schreiber? Did he influence the Gaullist opposition, or was he in turn influenced by them?

— Neither one, I think. They simply saw eye to eye.

— Looking back, couldn't one say that they were mistaken? That De Gaulle could not immediately disown the military rebels since they were the ones who had brought him to power, and political realism required that he deal with them? After all, he subsequently did get rid of them.

— Yes. The same way he got rid of any ministers who tried to warn or advise him against his will . . . But the

France's new President Valéry Giscard d'Estaing. Mitterrand was minister in a number of governments during the Fourth Republic but after De Gaulle's return to power in 1958 had been a steadfast member of the opposition.

question you raise is a very important one. In politics should you be a "realist," that is, in the final analysis should you resort to guile in order to force men and destiny? That's one question. The other is to find out if this guile — which is perhaps inseparable from the art of ruling and perhaps has to be used by the man who manipulates the marionette strings — has to be blindly subscribed to. Not because you conceive of where the ruse will take you, the way a good chess player can see and plan the moves even when he's merely observing another player but because you blindly trust the player. Which brings us right back to the problem of faith in a great man, that absolute faith that De Gaulle demanded.

There's no point in mulling over what might have been, what might have happened in Algeria, and in France, without De Gaulle. No one can even guess. And maybe he was the only person who could make mainland France swallow the bitter pill of Algerian independence without too much inner turmoil — even making the retreat look like a victory. That was really his genius: to transform everything into a victory for France.

And yet this regression, this return to a kind of "gift" from the country to an all-powerful military man — and I'm willing to concede today that he was an uncommon soldier — was very serious indeed. In any case, the least one can say is that those who "gave" themselves in this way had no idea where he was leading them.

The optimistic hypothesis is that the French are very cunning and very rational. They took De Gaulle when they needed him to accomplish a certain task, and once the job was over they ousted him. And, after all, why not be optimistic? . . . On the subject of the French and their collective political sense, I am perfectly willing to be so.

As for Servan-Schreiber, since you asked the question, he was remarkably steadfast in his basic political options.

Mendès-France and Mitterrand were both equally steadfast in their opposition, but they had a political career behind them, a political physiognomy and they had made a choice: to incarnate the opposition to the regime.

If Servan-Schreiber had been a pure political climber, without any real convictions, he would have gone over to De Gaulle, he would have been a *député,* a minister, God knows what, like all the other ex-ministers of the Mendès-France government. I don't find it shocking that people evolve politically or that, as one grows older and has the taste for power, one is tempted to try to operate within the pale of government. I simply note that Jean-Jacques has never done it, nor has he ever been tempted to do it. That said, what was termed in our quarters rabid anti-Gaullism — which was basically a rightist trend — was never rampant in our ranks. And, to come back to your question, none of us ever said, thought, or wrote that De Gaulle was hatching any kind of Fascism whatsoever.

— And yet, when he died, you didn't write about him. Why?

— You're right, I didn't. I went to Notre Dame the day of the funeral. And afterward someone said to me: "I saw you . . . I couldn't believe my eyes. You were crying." And why not? At funerals, we all know that we're crying for ourselves. First of all, De Gaulle's departure was admirable. Worthy of the highest respect. And besides, he was the man of the Liberation. And certainly the Gaullist politicians and their gang could not deprive me of four years of my life during which De Gaulle was my guiding light — the head of free France.

But to write a piece on this subject in *L'Express,* which at that time was suffering from a kind of conformism, of deferential respect, of what I used to call, in an effort to shake the magazine up, an appalling "Timization," no: I couldn't.

For me his death was a private matter, if I may use the term. The public matter, with all those people changing coats and speaking with quavering voices as they saw how the public was reacting to them, was more than I could take: I would frankly have been too ashamed to be part of it.

— A little while ago we talked about the Occupation. Could you tell us anything about the Resistance?

— It was inefficient and sublime. But what can I tell you about it? The Resistance is something you do, not describe. Right afterward, it's only normal that those who were part of it wanted to relate their adventures, were they big or small. And then came the balloon effect. All the heroes. And after that, the historians. And then there was also the effort on the part of others for whom it was the "great period," as it were, to freeze it the way one tries to stop time. And then, and then . . . Not that I was exempt myself: between the Liberation of Paris and the end of the war I tried to put my experiences into writing too. I wrote two hundred pages.

— Were they ever published?

— No. I tore them up. May '45 arrived, and with it the ever-growing list of those whom we would never see again, plus those who came back in the condition you're aware of. Those who had seen the Evil. Evil with a capital E, whose eyes were filmed over with it. That tended to put my own prisons, my own resistance, into a whole other perspective, where suffering and courage had to be measured on some common scale. I shouldn't even say that. There is no such scale. In short, I rid myself of these memories when my sister came back from the concentration camps. She made an astonishing entrance. She was wearing her striped prison garb and weighed only seventy-seven pounds, although she is tall . . . She handed me something. It turned out to be a very heavy Bohemian crystal ashtray. And she said to me:

"Here, I brought this back to you from Czechoslovakia . . ." After two years of concentration camps. There's nothing I can say that would be any more illustrative.

Two weeks later we talked, alone, the way sisters and brothers do. That relationship, as you know, is a strong and hardy one, indestructible actually, one that's like no other. She talked about the whole experience. All night long. And she knew how to tell a story. That was the first and only time she ever talked about it. I never heard her husband talk about it at all.

Later I learned what a veteran was. A veteran is someone who killed the dragon and believes that in order to keep it from rising again from the dead, he must "remember," pay tribute to the dead, tend to the fires of sacrifice, keep reminding young people of what happened so that the world will never forget, etc. I don't believe a word of it. While they are busy parading past the remains of the dragon, it has already assumed another guise, tiny but growing in another skin.

The Nazi survivors do not interest me in the least. That is, they don't interest me anymore, since none of them is able to explain how, in the midst of the twentieth century, in the heart of a presumably enlightened Europe, a Christian country with a high degree of civilization toppled headlong into barbarism. One German Nazi, plus another German Nazi, plus another German Nazi does not make for a completely consenting Nationalist-Socialist Germany, intoxicated by that super-Fascism which was called Hitlerism, with the working class leading the way — that German working class that was supposed to be one of the most articulate and enlightened.

After that, all you can ask yourself are questions for which there is no answer. And, too, you become alert, on your guard, hypersensitive to any resurgence of Fascism in its newest, underhanded forms.

That is one of the things that really frightens me. I'm

afraid of the time when there will no longer be enough people in France who will know, from having experienced it, what Fascism really is. I'm afraid of the temptation Fascism holds for a portion of the Left, the little Robespierres of the Left, those who look in the mirror and take themselves deadly serious; I'm afraid of what might happen when we run into some really serious financial difficulties. Fascism's favorite breeding ground is in the soil of economic crises. Fascism is a phenomenon of the masses and the lower middle class, when people find themselves up against the wall because of unemployment, payrolls not met, inflation getting out of hand, while they can see a handful obviously reveling in the lap of luxury, which raises the hackles of those struggling to keep their heads above water. When political leaders seem incapable of coping with the situation, or are simply corrupt: Those are the times when one of those authoritarian socialisms is ripe to take over; only once it does, there is more and more authority and less and less socialism.

Why, in times like these, does a Germany give itself to Hitler, an Italy to Mussolini, but the United States gives itself to Roosevelt rather than to Huey Long? . . . Why has Great Britain been able to suffer an excessively high rate of unemployment without being in any danger of Fascism? . . .

Why didn't the graft take in France? The Italian writer Elio Vittorini hypothesized that the freedom, relative but undeniable, of the French in the realm of sexuality kept them immune from the Fascist virus. And that relates to what I was saying a while back when I was discussing the French impulse to happiness. But the point is, one would like to be certain of the immunity, the way one would like to be sure that there is never any pre-Fascist tendency among those often very bright or even brilliant minds whose hatred of capitalism, while real, may blind them to other dangers.

— Do you think there is a real possibility that we could

have another economic crisis of the kind or proportions of 1929?

— Not the same kind, no, insofar as, theoretically anyway, we today have sufficient knowledge and enough built-in early-warning systems, not only internally but among nations, which ought to prevent any such cataclysmic crisis. Theoretically. But this presupposes that politics is becoming rational, which it is not, at least with respect to the notion we have of reason. It also presupposes that our Western civilization stops hating itself, has the strength to renew rather than destroy itself . . . There are also fruitful crises. But that's a subject that might lead us far afield. What I'm trying to say is simply that the massive manufacture of a great many bitter graduates who despite their diplomas cannot find jobs, together with a serious economic crisis, contains the seeds of dangers far greater to public freedom than all the police at the disposal of the Minister of the Interior.

— But didn't Fascism seem crushed once and for all after the war?

— Yes, of course. There was a moment of euphoria. The French even managed to convince themselves that they had won the war. It was a necessity . . . I can't say that I honestly shared the euphoria. I remember the period right after the war as a time of great inner turmoil, a time when I had a great deal of difficulty adjusting my values. First of all, Hiroshima. Then, for days on end I went to the Hotel Lutétia, which was the reception point for the convoys of returning deportees, those who were on stretchers. I kept searching among these living dead for a few faces that I never found; I kept waiting, and I thought: "God's only excuse is that He doesn't exist. I will never believe anymore in anything, neither in God nor the devil, nor in any man, any faith, any law." I thought that everything I had ever been taught was false, that the world, France included, was a jungle in which one had either to be the predator or the prey.

I kept wavering between the temptation of succumbing to cynicism and that of going off and working in a leper colony. I was confused and unclear. So was France, where the good and decent souls had thought that as soon as the war was over everything would be "as before." And as it turned out nothing was the way it was before, in any case the food wasn't. The actors, those weathervanes who always tell you which way the wind is blowing, fell over one another to sign the anti-A-bomb Stockholm Appeal, with Maurice Chevalier leading the pack. That was the sign that the Communists, who already head a number of ministerial posts, would soon be in power.

It was a time when a great many ambitious young men, most of whom had been in the Resistance, flung themselves into public affairs. I did the opposite. I got married, to someone straight out of a Dostoevski novel. Impossible to be more Russian than he. Handsome. With a sharp sense of the absurd, which fit right into my own frame of mind at the time, and stimulated it. We've been separated for a long time, but I'm still very fond of him. He taught me a great many things.

— You say that about most of the men you refer to . . .

— I do? It's natural enough. Women are formed by men. And the converse too. This is learning at the level of higher education, don't you think?

There's a story, by Chekhov I believe, in which he tells about a charming lady friend whom he sees only occasionally but whose lovers are an open book to him because of her conversation. Once when he sees her she knows all there is to know about irrigation; another time, all she talks about is the army; and still another time, she goes on and on about legal and judicial questions . . . And then one day the protagonist goes to see her — by this time she is already well along in years — and she begins to talk impassionedly about elementary mathematics. And he says to himself, "Really, at her age, with a student . . ." At which point an adolescent boy comes into the room, and his lady friend says to him: "I want you to meet my grandson . . ."

That's not exactly what I wanted to say about "learning." I don't have that marvelous plasticity of certain women who really can become somebody else. No, I've always felt that I'd been formed from some kind of potter's clay.

 VII

— WHAT DID YOU DO professionally after the war? What were your hopes and ambitions at this juncture?

— As far as slaying the dragons went, I had about had my fill. I worked on some films, which I didn't like very much but which were quite successful commercially . . . And I wrote some songs. I've always had a talent for that kind of thing. I needed money. My expenses had sky-rocketed to a dizzying height. The problem was, I was beginning to hate my profession, and myself for being in it.

There's something very frustrating about being a script-writer. Except under exceptional circumstances, where you are working hand-in-glove with a director, what you conceived, imagined, wrote never comes out quite as you felt it. And besides, the film world had become boring. All its spangles, its marvelous madmen, its inventors, its creators were gone.

Anyway, I felt like writing about something else, in another way. I felt clearly that a certain kind of film was outdated and outmoded, but I couldn't figure out what to do to change it. I've already mentioned that I'm not really an innovator. I know how to seize the brass ring, how to recognize

it and put it to good use, but it has to come by. I don't know
how to provoke it into coming. That bothers me, but it's
better to recognize it. Perhaps I simply have a greater faculty
of implementation than of creation, a doer rather than an
originator . . .

— And an opportunity did arise?

— Yes. One day in January 1946 when I was invited to
lunch at Madame Lazareff's. At that time I had never met
her. I remember the date because I had no sooner arrived at
the Lazareff's on the rue Kleber when a very short, very ugly
man came in and said: "De Gaulle's resigned." It was the
day when De Gaulle quit, and the man announcing the news
was Pierre Lazareff. I thought he was in a state of extreme
anxiety. What I didn't realize at the time was that that was
his normal state.

I was there — something I learned only later — because
Hervé Mille, my old wartime colleague at *Paris-Soir* of whom
I've already spoken, had said to the Lazareffs when they returned from America, "I'm going to give you a gift. I'm going to give you a piece of paper with the names of three
people on it whom you don't know." One was Raymond
Cartier, another was me, and I don't know who the third
was . . .

Hervé Mille was also the moving force behind the newly
published women's magazine *Elle.* If I'm not mistaken, the
magazine had been financed by three people: a munitions
manufacturer from Marseille, a Parisian antique dealer, and
Paul Valéry's son, Claude. And it was Hervé Mille who put
them onto Hélène Lazareff. Today, *Elle* is the most important
woman's weekly in France and the biggest moneymaker for
the Hachette publishing empire, which purchased it from
that curious threesome, the original backers.

I don't think the story has ever been written about the press
at the time of the Liberation and later. Someone ought to.

For it's all there: the glorious incompetence, the dark machinations about who should get how much paper — which was rationed, the lyrical illusions, the farce of nationalizing the distribution processes, the political wheeling and dealing that went on about setting the date for sabotaging the papers that had appeared during the war . . . The date had to be set late enough to save this or that paper, but early enough to make sure not to save some other . . .

Try to picture this situation: no television; newspapers and radio stations disappearing from one day to the next, and with them the writers, commentators, administrators, etc., who ran them; a virgin terrain, with the public hungry for news; paper strictly allocated; the buildings, the equipment, the machinery of collaborating newspapers confiscated and transferred to this person or that . . . On one side, you had people who had immediately understood the capital that could be made from such a situation, and I'm speaking monetarily. On the other side, you had those who saw in the situation an opportunity to gain control of a political instrument. And then there were the innocents, the purists, the intellectuals who published newspapers the way the young Marx had a hundred years earlier when he published the *Gazette Rhénane,* trying to change the fate of the proletariat by reaching two thousand readers.

There's a great story to be written there, and one which would doubtless bring on dozens of lawsuits. But let us let the dead bury the dead.

Elle was a respectable little business which arrived on ground already occupied by two other women's weeklies, *Marie-France* and *Claudine.* I can only describe what happened between Hélène Lazareff and me as love at first sight. On both sides. She was irresistible. A little bird of steel. I guess you can say that I'm vulnerable to such strokes of lightning, since I was hit twice in my life. The first one was at that luncheon with Hélène, and the second was much later, the day I met Jean-Jacques Servan-Schreiber at the French book publisher, René Julliard.

What I mean by "love at first sight" — which does not properly convey the French *coup de foudre* — is that immediate shock from which emanates an intense flash of lightning, in which you are able to see the other person completely, in all his or her facets and ramifications. You see what other people do not, for love, far from being blind as the saying goes, is extra-lucid. It's desire that blinds and endows its object with all sorts of beauty and imaginary virtues until that desire passes and the object of desire is returned to its truth, which is stripped of its imaginary trappings.

But not love.

And what existed between Hélène Lazareff and me was a kind of love, there is no other word to properly describe it. The proof is that there was never any friendship between us; quite the contrary. And I think I can honestly say that I know what friendship is and means; it's something I practice with men, carefully and meticulously. No passion can enter into such a relationship, for it would change and destroy it. It's a-passion. With Hélène, all there was was passion, be it negative or positive.

The strength of that tiny, frail woman, her ability to see things the way she wanted them to be — which in principle is a derangement of the mind but which above all is a way of making these things inflexible, making them conform to what you want — her way of "tidying up" reality without turning it into a lie, since she was the first one to believe in her version . . . All that and a great deal more: her complete submission to her emotions; the way she had of ignoring anything that stood in her way; and whenever those obstacles were human, her ability to make them invisible. In the eyes of those who really knew her, Hélène Lazareff was a heroine straight out of some Russian novel: captivating, really; someone you couldn't judge or measure by any normal standards.

And besides, she had come from another world. For those of us who for five years had been hemmed in by blood and death, she was like a traveler who arrives from the ends of the earth with a hundred many-colored suitcases full of exotic treasures. She was life, gaiety, optimism . . . She brought America with her.

She asked me to write an article for her, then another and another . . . I dropped in on the magazine more and more often. Three rather grubby rooms on the rue Réaumur, packed with the strangest bedfellows. Do you know that it was Pierre Gaxotte, the historian, who for several years wrote the first pages of *Elle?* We were old friends. Every day, at the stroke of noon, he put on his hat and off he went. Noon was the hour of Hélène's arrival. Although they at least liked and admired each other, there was something basically incompatible about this sharp, witty native of Lorraine who was incredibly well organized and that completely unpredictable Slavic-American.

There is nothing any more exciting than the pioneer period of a newspaper or magazine when there is a real creative spirit — or spirits — behind it. Hélène was one of this rarest of species. But I didn't yet feel ready to commit myself to a career of journalism. This was the time when Jacques Becker and I were writing a film called *Antoine et Antoinette,* which had that new tone I was looking for.

And there was another factor: the postwar "baby boom" was in full swing, and either the virus struck me or, simply, it was rediscovering sanity and health: I wanted to have a baby. And this time I wanted to do it right. So in September of '46 I made up my mind to take it a bit easier. It was the first time in my life that I had allowed myself to slip into that almost animallike torpor, that delightful self-involvement which, when circumstances are right, so often accompanies the first weeks of pregnancy. I reveled in it — I knitted, I spent hours trying out names — I had decided it was going to be a girl — I imagined all sorts of pretty maternity dresses.

But in my life something always happens.

No sooner had I chosen bliss as my way of life when Hélène fell seriously ill. She had to have an immediate operation, and it very soon became obvious that she would not be able to return to the magazine for three or four months. It was a young and fragile magazine, whose very existence was in question; till then it had been improvised rather than published, and it was totally lacking in any editorial structure.

I went to two or three meetings where the magazine's fate was being discussed. I heard things from journalists far more experienced than I — men who were on the editorial board of *France-Soir* — that made my hair stand on end. I realized that with all their experience they had no understanding of the tone and style that Hélène had been trying to impart to *Elle,* and had begun to find. So I said to Pierre Lazareff: "If you like, I'll take over the editorial responsibility of the magazine until Hélène comes back . . ."

Pierre was having his own problems with *France-Soir.* "Thanks, *mon chéri,*" he said. *Mon chéri* was a generic term he used when addressing all women; with men, it was *mon coco.* "Just be sure not to strain yourself."

It was a pure formality, that admonition. But I was in the peak of health, and the Lord had endowed me with a capacity for work which, I later learned, was far from common. It's a real gift from heaven. I've heard tell that it's all a question of your thoracic cage, the width of your thorax. I have no idea whether it's true or not — in any case, it's something you don't acquire.

In short, I began to spend my days putting out *Elle,* and I kept on doing so for seven years, with forays into the film world and to other publications. I got into the habit of working twelve hours a day seven days a week, which is not what could be called especially intelligent.

I wrote a weekly column for *Carrefour,* the best weekly newspaper at that time. Jacques Chardonne, the editor of the paper, recruited me via the intermediary of his daughter France, stating that he thought I wrote French less ineptly than most journalists. Maybe he didn't believe a word of what he said, but in any case he said it, and I found it agreeable to believe him.

I also wrote a weekly column for *L'Intransigeant,* a very Parisian evening daily. After it merged with *Paris-Presse,* the editor — that is, Eve Curie — one day cut ten lines, which she found impertinent, out of one of my pieces. I slammed the door behind me as I left.

I also wrote . . . Oh, I don't really remember anymore! I wrote a great deal faster than I do today — fortunately. Journalists are very poorly paid in France.

— But why *Elle?* What did *Elle* represent for you?

— Several things. One, which nobody ever talks about, is what happens when you wake up in the morning. Do you or don't you look forward to going to work, to meeting your colleagues? To me that seems of prime importance. Life isn't short, it's long, and so are the days. Today, the place where you work has assumed the importance in our daily lives that the village had in earlier times. Everything is concentrated there. And the more you enjoy your work, the more you find it interesting and absorbing, the more involved you become.

I enjoyed seeing Hélène every day. During that entire period we were very close, we understood each other. As for Pierre Lazareff . . . he never had a court around him, which is remarkable considering how important he was. Later, after '58, and especially after '62, he became an unofficial VIP in the Fifth Republic, with close ties that went back a long way to Georges Pompidou — he had ties with all the politicians in fact. Among other things he told me that in 1969 he was asked to undertake the delicate task of telling Pompidou that he was no longer Premier — and I saw no reason to doubt the story.

It was Couve de Murville who reportedly made the request, in these words: "The General has informed me that he has named me Premier. Now Georges has to be told. It would really seem out of place for me to do it . . . Could you tell him? He's one of your friends . . ."

Maybe Pierre was simply bragging. But the secret role that he played on various occasions was known to enough people to make the story credible. Those political connections, plus the strength of his position within the Hachette publishing empire and his influence in television could have made him unbearable. But the fact was he never really took himself very seriously. To take himself seriously was the thing he feared the most. Maybe too much. As a public figure, there is a minimum importance that has to be associated with anything you do.

Pierre was the most winning man who ever lived. And all this charm and modesty and creativity that went with him wherever he went resulted in a trailing wake of the strangest, most disparate collection of hangers-on you ever saw, whose ranks were forever being swelled by some minister or other.

And, last but not least, there was the magazine itself. I don't want to relate retrospectively that in editing *Elle* I had any illusions about changing the world. Nonetheless, it was an instrument, a liberating instrument. But when I first started working on the magazine I thought of it basically as a professional experience.

I think I mentioned earlier how the events of my childhood had instilled in me a deep-rooted hatred of amateurism.

And, conversely, the greatest respect for professionalism. The racing car driver, François Cevert, says that Jackie Stewart is the greatest racer we have today, not because he drives any faster than the others, but because he makes fewer mistakes. That's professionalism: to make fewer mistakes than the others, the fewest mistakes possible. Not many people know that to put out a magazine or newspaper is above all a matter of professionalism, and when you really are a professional you can publish *Elle,* you can put out the magazine of the merchant marine, edit *Le Monde* or *Animal Life.* And you can do it well, providing you enjoy it. The best newspaper publishers and editors are not necessarily the people who write the best. That's a whole other matter. When you write, you tend to attach more importance to your own article than to your colleagues'. To edit and publish is to strike a proper balance in a mosaic whose overall design you have clearly in mind.

Hélène Lazareff was a remarkable professional. And she was light-years ahead of her French contemporaries, because she had just spent five years in the United States working on the best paper in the world, the *New York Times,* and then on a woman's magazine.

On the technical plane, for instance, she mastered the use of color photos, which was still completely unknown in France, and in any case impractical because of the lack of proper film. In the prewar *Marie-Claire,* the photos had been colored, an entirely different process.

On the question of color photography, the energy with which she imposed her will on everyone around her, starting with her husband, was nothing short of amazing. All the raw material was imported from the States. Each time a shipment arrived, we had to go down in person to the Ministry of Finance to get it through customs. I've never seen a Minister of Finance so often!

Hélène knew all there was to know about the presentation of a magazine. In the beginning, the editorial content was off target, because she was terribly Americanized . . .

— What did that mean: to be very Americanized?

— Hervé Mille reminded me only the other day that at the time I had said to him: "It's strange that Hélène wants to publish a woman's magazine in France; she loathes women, and she hates France." It was an outburst of ill temper on my part, out of all proportion to the truth, but there was an element of truth to it nonetheless.

In her heart of hearts, Hélène never really believed that women had any other function in life except to seduce men. To catch a man, as the American women used to say in those days. To hold a man, or several men, was for her the epitome of female gamesmanship, the only thing that made life meaningful. What war is to men.

As for France: she had just come back from a country where everything that wasn't new was considered ruined, to be discarded, which suited her personality to a tee. It amazed her that anyone would take the time or trouble to check the quality of a piece of cloth by fingering it. Nor could she even begin to understand how anyone could prefer an object that was worn and repaired to an object that, while it might be of a lesser quality, was new; how anyone could make jam when you could buy it.

My husband used to tease her by saying: "Why do you think that I married Françoise? Well, you're wrong. It's because she knows how to make raspberry jam with the whole berry intact." That made her double over with laughter. Since then I've forgotten the secret of making raspberry jam, and today I too buy it ready-made.

One of the reasons, I'm convinced, that Hélène Lazareff succeeded so brilliantly with her magazine was that her arrival on the scene coincided with the beginning of vast social changes in France, of a break that came out of the war and the lack of consumer goods, which she sensed before anyone else, and she went with the tide rather than trying to swim against it. In the same way, she sensed the appetite for frivolity, for changes of taste in clothing and dress that the war had wrought.

— Did that desire for clothes affect you? Were you interested in fashion?

— I've always been interested in fashion. The day when dresses, or whatever takes their place, are no longer of any interest to me, I'll have one foot in the grave. What fascinates me above all, though, is the language of fashion, what people express, individually and collectively, through clothing, adornment, the signs they reveal. The way a woman — or, today, a man, though to a lesser degree nonetheless — presents herself, dresses, does her hair, says as much about her psychic state as a medical examination would reveal about her physical condition.

There is the fashion of a society, which reflects a time or moment in history, and there is individual choice, which is the reflection of each woman's relationship with her body, her image, with what she would like to be, and the way she assumes her responsibilities, disguises herself, or refuses to be herself. I've often been struck by the fact that women who appear the least frivolous are the very ones who always remember what they were wearing in important moments of their lives. When they are novelists, they describe their outfits and usually produce poor works of fiction. What ought to be described is the character projected by the dress one is wearing and why that dress was thus able to dictate certain conduct. No one is quite the same when they are wearing white as when they are wearing black, when they wear pants as opposed to crinolines. That's a question I'd like to ponder some day, because I have a feeling there is a direct relationship between women's condition in society and the clothes they wear.

And besides, I like what's beautiful, or at least what strikes me as beautiful. A fabric, a cut, harmonious colors . . . A pretty woman who is well-dressed is very pretty indeed.

But I would not have been able to make fashion my profession, or my main interest. In that regard, in fact, Hélène Lazareff and I were worlds apart. I wore black, she wore red. You had to be healthy to dress in red twenty-five years ago, that American kind of healthiness made up of equal portions of optimism and dynamism . . . In those days, an American woman was someone whose hair was always freshly washed and combed, who wore a hat and a suit and looked as though she was newly minted. The antihippie.

You have no idea the degree of optimism, the exhilaration, the generosity emanating from the United States in those days! Anyone who hasn't seen that with his own eyes doesn't know the meaning of a happy country.

And anyone who wasn't in France in those days cannot understand what it means to be hungry for consumer goods, from nylon stockings to refrigerators, from records to automobiles — to buy a car back then you had to get a purchase permit and then wait for a year . . . Something similar is going on today in the Eastern European countries.

It's very simple: in 1946 in France there was literally nothing. If I remember correctly, we even had to have ration tickets for bread.

Yes, Hélène Lazareff and I were worlds apart. But we formed a good team, and that included work. I tend to be a good long-distance runner; she's a sprinter. For a time we shared not only an office but also a chair, a big leather easy chair, because there was no room in the office for two. Then, for a long time, we shared the same desk, sitting across from each other.

The battle of *Elle* was a tough one. *Marie-France* had a substantial lead. And *Claudine* was a serious competitor. There's something exciting about a professional battle, when it means something more than pure commercial success.

— And in this case, was there something else?

— Indeed there was. In those days, *Elle*'s candor, its openness, was really revolutionary. Just think, before the war *Marie-Claire* refused to allow the word "lover" to appear in its pages. Women had husbands or fiancés. That new candor didn't help the magazine to grow and prosper, for whole regions refused to handle it. But at the same time that openness, that freedom of tone and expression, made its reputation. It was highly regarded for its originality. It was the subject of a running battle between Pierre and Hélène. He was constantly disapproving, saying that she was completely unaware of the effect some of her daring innovations could have in Brittany or Alsace. She refused to listen to him, and she was right. *Elle* was Hélène. It was a very costly magazine to manufacture, because, for one thing, she employed the most expensive photographers in the world, and with them the top models. *Elle* never managed to reach the large-circulation figures some women's magazines — whose names you probably don't even remember — attained for a time. Yet today those magazines are in total decline.

But *Elle* was a real honest-to-God magazine which, during its first few years, was brought out by a mere handful of people working under what can only be described as absolutely insane conditions.

I remember one English novel we were negotiating for with the intention of serializing it in several issues. We announced it as forthcoming in one of our issues, under the French title we had picked for it. Then at the last minute the rights somehow slipped away from us. The illustration for the excerpt had already been engraved. In a matter of hours,

I wrote a chapter to fit the illustration. The problem was
how to carry it on for another six or seven weeks. Each
week's publication ended on a note of suspense that was all
the more exciting in that I had no more idea than the reader
what next week's installment would bring. The real principle of a serialized novel, perhaps! And to think that a
great many nineteenth-century novelists used to write that
way year in and year out.

As for *Elle*'s famous "Magic Coupon," which today is a
mail-order selling arm for the magazine's readers, it was one
of Pierre Lazareff's brainstorms. One day *Marie-France* had
announced the creation of a "Marie-France House." We had
to counterattack. But with what? Here it became a question
of the magazine's commercial policy, which was Pierre's
domain. He had a kind of stamp glued to the cover of the
magazine which said: "Thanks to this magic coupon, this
issue will pay you back 100–1." It was obviously a good
idea. But how was this reimbursement going to take place?
And where? By cutting out the coupon and presenting it with
your purchase of this or that product, on which you would
get a substantial reduction. But what was the product
going to be, and where would the readers go with their
coupons? I don't know through what miracle we were able
to find a stock of Pyrex dishes and saucepans — which in
those days were literally scarce as hen's teeth — at some
manufacturer's. And it was we, the staff members of *Elle*,
who lugged them back to the offices and there turned ourselves into temporary salesladies. The readers were delighted.

All that was hardly what you could term serious, a far cry
from the basic rules of management, marketing, and elementary organization. Anything that had to do with the
Lazareffs was always chaotic, the only difference being that
Pierre denied it while Hélène openly admitted it. But it was
out of all this chaos that they both evolved magazines and

newspapers which were very successful commercially. For others, of course. They were never very successful in managing their own finances.

I have no liking for disorder. But if I were a financier, I would exchange all the orderly gentlemen of the press for one Lazareff, for the creative spark of a Lazareff of twenty years ago. You don't publish magazines or newspapers with functionaries. And I say that with all the more conviction because, starting in 1952–1953, I found myself in basic disagreement with Hélène, both politically and from the viewpoint of professional ethics.

But when Pierre Lazareff saw a double-page headline in *Combat* — "Should We Burn Kafka?" — he said, "I don't know about Kafka. But with a headline like that, we sure as hell ought to burn *Combat* . . ." And he was undoubtedly right, from a purely commercial point of view, for only a handful of readers could have heard of Kafka in those days.

— A little while ago you said that *Elle* had been an instrument of liberation. In what way?

— It brought women a new vision of their place in the world, by saying, and saying to them personally, certain truths.

I really put my heart and soul into that effort. And I had complete freedom to do so. It was a question of vocabulary. The more subversive ideas are, the more moderate the language ought to be in expressing them. And if you look closely at most of the ideas expressed with violence, you begin to see that, once you've scraped away the terminology, you're usually left with the worst platitudes. I was subversive on a number of levels. In particular, I think I was the first woman to talk about frigidity in a general publication.

The only scandal I caused unwittingly was with a public-opinion poll entitled, if I remember rightly, "Is the French Woman Clean?"

—Why? Wasn't she?

—As recently as 1972, a poll showed that only one French person out of four used a toothbrush. In 1972, mind. So you can imagine what the percentages were in 1947! I'll admit that investigation was really meant to provoke.

—Didn't it also have a moralizing quality to it?

—Moralizing? No, I don't think so. I'm not much inclined to moralizing, and if I've ever done it, I regret it. Sometimes you moralize without meaning to. In any case, when dealing with something like cleanliness, it was interesting to tell women the truth. "You buy a dress because you want to look good, to please, but under your dress what are you wearing? A garter belt that hasn't been washed in two years. That's the national average. So don't go around scolding your child because he doesn't wash his hands before sitting down to meals. You're the one who's dirty."

This type of truth is, I think, useful; irritating, but also useful, in an area where moralizing would get you nowhere. It's journalistic truth, the truth I'll stick to till I draw my last breath, even if the misfortunes of politics outlaw it. I'm referring to information gleaned via carefully conducted research.

—Wasn't that kind of research done back then?

—Not in women's magazines.

—And did you play any part in the homemaking boom?

—Not personally. And so far as I remember, I had already left *Elle* when that boom hit France. In the years right after the war, we didn't devote much attention to producing goods and appliances for the house.

 VIII

— YOU LEFT *Elle* in 1952?

— Yes. It's strange that most people have such a dim memory of that period, of the material conditions of the country in those days.

I left *Elle* because I had come to the end of a personal cycle in my life which coincided with the end of a certain postwar period.

These things don't happen from one day to the next, of course. After the initial charm of adventure wore thin, *Elle* began to pall for me. It was because it had become successful; we had moved from the artisan stage to the factory level, and our tiny office had given way to sumptuous quarters. With it came commercial considerations, whether real or imagined. A weekly horoscope, to name but one. I found myself circumscribed by a number of specifically feminine interests which I didn't scorn — not all of them anyway — but which began to bore me.

One evening in 1951 François Mitterrand came to dinner at my house. He was in a somber mood, looking for all the world just like the political cartoonists of the time used to picture him. He was minister of something or other. As always. I first met him when he was thirty, and he was already a minister then. After dinner he began to talk about Indochina. I think it was the evening when the great French military defeat at Cao Bang had been announced. There were about a dozen people present, and as soon as he began to talk politics, a kind of spontaneous division took place. The men formed a circle around Mitterrand. The women moved away. One of my male friends makes the reassuring remark that at least in those days women kept quiet when serious matters were being discussed.

In December of '51, Jean-Jacques Servan-Schreiber, whom I had just met, took me with him to the Chambre de Députés to hear Mendès-France, who that day was supposed to speak both on the budget and on the question of Indochina. The whole thing was terribly impressive. The place itself fills you with anxiety the first time you visit it — a kind of sinister vat into which no ray of daylight ever seeps. The attentive silence which suddenly fell when Mendès began to speak, whereas most of the speakers talked to an audience busily reading its newspaper, writing letters, chatting. And then the speech itself. The courage required to make it . . . There are many kinds of orators who take the dais: aside from the poor speakers, there are the clever ones, the brilliant, the memory-magicians who can flash facts and figures at you, the flowery, the quotation-stringers, the pungent wits, the lyrical. There are speakers who say important things but in such a boring way you'd never know it. And there are others who spout banalities but do it so cleverly and amusingly that you're amazed, when you read the texts of their speeches, to find that they contain nothing.

That day Mendès put it all together, as he so often did: the great speaking voice, the eloquence, the clarity, and the strength of conviction. I felt sure that his speech would cause a sensation, as it had with his audience as they heard it, and afterward when they dashed up to the podium to surround him with congratulations. He took us with him to dinner, where he elaborated further on what he had said. At the time, the way he dealt with problems was totally new to me. He articulated his entire political speech around economics. The next day, with the exception of *Le Monde,* no newspaper devoted as much as ten lines to what he had said in the Chambre.

I had a weekly column in *France-Dimanche,* and the following week I devoted it to Mendès-France. The *France-Dimanche* of those days had nothing to do with what the scandal sheet it has since become. Nonetheless, the editor-in-chief was surprised. Mendès-France? Not very well known. Indochina? Ugh . . . It made you wonder whether the French even knew they were fighting a war over there.

It should be added that no one was making any effort to remind them. The rule was: don't talk about it. Don't talk about anything. That good old French rule . . . I was beginning to discover it.

For me this speech marked the end of the postwar era, that period I had lived egocentrically, concentrating on my private life, my children, my house, my work, carefully avoiding any real commitment, scrupulously playing — not without pleasure — the game of integration into that elegant, Parisian, and, in fact, brilliant French society of the time. It was a society which still retained a degree of polish and subtlety, which had not yet been devasted by attacks of bad conscience.

I'm not trying to disown the person I then was. I think one has to have lived in that world for a time, if only to know whereof you speak when you declare that nothing is more deadly than formal dinners, those parties where everything hinges on who your dinner partners are.

Materially, between journalism and the film world, I was doing better than I ever had before or have since. I won't pretend I didn't work my head off for it, but after all I did enjoy it. The only thing was, something had gone wrong. The irony, the humor, the mockery, a certain form of dandyism: all that had been a refuge. And what do you do in refuges? You watch things go by, rather than becoming involved in them. You say: do whatever you want, but count me out.

The intellectual terrorism that the Left wielded at the time, and continued to wield until the Twentieth Party Congress, its Stalinism, its ex-communications, that religious and frankly paranoid way it had of viewing political issues and of accepting unquestioningly, even adoringly, Mother Russia in the person of Father Stalin, the morality lessons that the inhabitants of the Latin Quarter were forever dishing out over any matter at all to the people who lived in the wealthier sections of Paris: all that hardly gave one any great desire to enlist under its banner. And since the other banner was ill-suited to my beliefs and opinions . . .

I was still doing a film or two a year. One of them was chosen for some festival, which resulted in my being part of a French delegation at the beginning of 1952, in South America. In Peron's Argentina, in Uruguay and Brazil . . . When I came back to France I wrote an article in which I said, among other things, that Punta del Este, in Uruguay, was a concentration camp for millionaires, a contention that had the French Foreign office on my neck almost immediately. It was an undeniable fact, but France needed Uruguay's support in the UN for something or other.

Pierre Lazareff gave me a fatherly slap on the wrist. I was genuinely upset. What was the press then? Was it simply an adjunct of the Foreign Ministry or the Presidential Palace? What was the line of demarcation between responsibility and passivity? Up till then, I had never had to ask myself such questions.

I have a feeling that if 1952 wasn't felt by the French as a whole to be a major turning point in postwar history, it was nonetheless an important date. It was in that year that people began to be aware of the burning issues which involved the French: the war in Indochina with all its attendant consequences; Tunisia, which was a veritable tinderbox; the degree to which France was dependent on the United States. All these things were actually felt by only a handful of people. Who in France in those days knew who Ho Chi Minh was? Or Bourguiba?

Perhaps I was especially sensitive to change in 1952, because for me it was a year of rupture, therefore a year of death, therefore of rebirth. A break with a man, a magazine, a life-style, a break with a degree of notoriety that I enjoyed and that I was about to give up. A comfortable crutch that I was throwing away. But no such break can ever be made without leaving some parts of yourself behind: the best, the worst, the best and worst all mixed up together, I have no idea.

Jean-Jacques Servan-Schreiber had asked me if I were ready and willing to start a magazine with him. I had said that I was. He was political editor of *Paris-Presse,* where he had moved after having left *Le Monde* because of the neutralist policy that paper had adopted. At that time, you'll remember, we were in the middle of the Cold War.

All we needed to start the new magazine was a backer. Jean-Jacques was working on it. In August 1952, the banker who was supposed to finance us let us down, and that was the end of the project, which was to have been called *Bref.*

Then, in October, I asked Pierre Lazareff to send me to the States. "Go right ahead, *mon chéri,*" he said to me, "if you'd like to. But don't go with any illusions of 'discovering America' the way so many people have already. There's no room for another article on that subject."

Anyone's first trip to America is always a shock, and twenty years ago the shock was enormous. We belonged to another planet, not only on the material level of our daily lives, but also insofar as human relations were concerned.

In order to get a closer look, I took a job as saleslady at Lord and Taylor. The woman in charge of the store opened all sorts of doors for me. The first thing that shocked me was to see the salesladies sitting down waiting for customers. I knew how different the same situation was in France. The first remark I remember hearing was a saleslady saying to a customer who couldn't make up her mind about a dress, "You'll be happy with that one," and to convince her, adding: "I bought one just like it for myself."

I realized that I had only scratched the surface of this country and that my eyes were about to be opened to a whole host of new ideas.

— And did your views on America finally coincide with those the Lazareffs had brought back?

— They didn't share mine, and I didn't wholly agree with either Pierre or Hélène about the United States. Pierre had spent a frightful five years in the States during the war, and for him it was a terrible memory. He was never able to learn a word of English. Had he been capable of hating anything, he would have hated America, which has no pity for the weak. Pierre's real country was Paris, the people of Paris. It was only later, much later, that he stuck his nose outside and looked further afield. His wife, on the other hand, was bilingual.

Personally, I like America, or rather the Americans. I found the country bracing, exciting . . . Even today, when everything has changed so radically, you still find that same sense of intellectual stimulation peculiar to New York. And when you come back to Paris you have rather the same impression Parisians do when they visit the provinces. The provinces are pleasant, full of charm, you live better there, more peacefully . . . But they also lack something: a tension, a pace . . . You grow dull and sluggish.

Twenty years ago this contrast was less noticeable, but there were other things that were startling.

I'll always remember my arrival at Idlewild Airport, as it was then known. I had brought a small, portable typewriter with me. The customs inspector seemed to be looking at it suspiciously, trying to figure out how to open it. I quickly blurted: "I can show you the receipt for it . . . I'm a journalist. I need it for my work, you see . . ." At that he started to laugh and said to me: "I don't doubt it, but that's not what interests me . . . I just want to get a closer look at it. It's really very light, isn't it? Well-made. Are you happy with it?"

That was a remark unimaginable in France.

I thought that I had simply chanced on an especially eccentric customs official. And then that same evening I bought a newspaper at a newsstand in the street. You know how difficult it is in the beginning to figure out the value of foreign coins, so I held out a handful of change to the newsdealer so that he could take whatever it was I owed him. As he did, he touched my hand and said to me: "Hey, your hand's very warm. Are you sure you haven't got a touch of fever? Better be careful, there's a lot of flu going around town."

Things were getting stranger and stranger. Now when I go to the States I know that the waiter who will bring me breakfast in my hotel room will say, when he sees the magazine on my bed: "You shouldn't be reading that [on my last visit the periodical in question was *Ms.*]. The women are crazy. I'm all for equal salaries for the same job, but as for all the rest of it . . ."

I've gotten used to that casual kind of relationship, which so far as I know doesn't exist anywhere else in the world:

casual, but nonetheless not familiar, a relationship unencumbered by any sense of indiscretion. It's something else very basic, an interrelationship expressing the lack of any difference among people insofar as their social position is concerned. The very essence of democracy, actually.

This behavior, so interwoven into the fabric of American life, can only exist in a country which has never had any blood aristocracy founded on the fields of battle, that is, a class which deems itself to be superior *a priori,* not because of what it may have done to ascend to the top of the social scale — something someone else could in theory emulate — but because of its birthright.

Americans will nonetheless tell you that there is in their country a high degree of snobbery. In America there are those who trace their lineage back to the *Mayflower,* the way we trace ours in France back to the battle of Agincourt. One either has the good manners of Boston or Philadelphia and has gone to a top university — which costs a small fortune — or you have the bad manners of Brooklyn, or a Southern accent. Instead of an inherited title, you can be named Henry Ford III. It's what we would call bourgeois snobbery, based on money. Actually, the very term "snobbery" eliminates the notion of aristocracy, since aristocracy cannot be acquired. For Europeans who take the trouble to understand it, American snobbery, although it may be arrogant at times, is like a veneer on its society, without the traditions that you still find so deeply imbedded in the subconscious of French and English society.

And I am also touched by the way most Americans have of being truly democratic, by which I mean that they don't play any role, they make no distinctions between the job and the person. For example, it's common practice for someone to whom you're paying an office visit to introduce you to his or her secretary, if the secretary happens to be present. She's a secretary, but she is also Miss or Mrs. or Ms. So-and-So. She's a human being who exists. If you are introduced to her, you acknowledge her existence, you exchange a few words. In France, a secretary doesn't exist for the visitor. She is a functional object, like a telephone. You don't introduce the telephone.

That, too, is a carryover of aristocratic manners whereby all the people who "served," all those who worked, were lumped into one overall category.

The inferiors. My own grandmother still used that incredible term. I wonder to what extent it may still exist in the minds of white Americans when they think about the blacks. . . .

In order not to discover America through the big hotels, the French restaurants, and some friends who lived on Park Avenue, I took a room in a hotel reserved exclusively for women: the Barbizon. Can you conceive of such a hotel in France, a hotel where men don't even have the right to cross the threshold?

I should add that at the time the United States was still puritan. In one major New York hotel, I saw the reception desk refuse a room to an unmarried couple. Each had to have his or her own room. It's true that the same situation existed in those days at the Hassler in Rome, or the Ukraine in Moscow. But in New York! They've come a long way, the Americans, in the past two decades.

And since Americans never do anything by halves, I would not be overly surprised to see the bell captain of the Pierre or St. Regis provide you with whatever you might need to round out a threesome or foursome. He will, if you want, provide you with the local abortion guide.

New York is a fascinating city no matter how you look at it, whether it be from its luxurious center or its violent, dirty extremities. I buried myself in it. In spite of what Pierre

Lazareff had said, I was determined to write about it, and to find some new angle I wrote a whole series of profiles about women at different economic levels. One was a co-worker of mine, a saleslady at Lord and Taylor; another was a suburban housewife with three children; there was also one of those terrifying career women who never removed her hat. A woman of café society. And some others.

The way American children were brought up — permissive theories were already in vogue — struck me as immoderate. My own children never opened their mouths to speak at table unless they were spoken to. Was I right? Or had the Americans found the key to happiness by literally allowing themselves to be tyrannized by little savages to whom nothing was forbidden? Thinking about it over twenty years later, I'm not at all sure that the method produced such brilliant results . . . But then ours didn't either. Maybe there just isn't any good method.

I stayed in New York for three weeks, intoxicated with it, welcomed with that casual good grace, that warmth of hospitality, unknown in France.

Everyone goes out of his way to make you feel at home, gives parties for you, introduces his friends to you. In return, when Americans come to Paris, nobody opens his door for them. A lunch, or dinner in a restaurant; that seems the most anyone can offer visitors, though not always for reasons as mean as they may appear.

I've sometimes tried to explain to my American friends why it's so difficult to get invited into French homes. There are our bourgeois background and traditions, whereby everything has to be perfect when you receive guests . . . Everyone, depending on his social level, does more than he's able to. Small plates are put on top of larger plates; embroidered tablecloths are taken from the linen closet; a manservant or maidservant is engaged for the evening, perhaps a cook as well; the host may even go so far as to stint himself and his family in order to put on a good appearance when guests come to dinner. The torn lampshade is replaced; the floors are waxed. At least that's the way it was only a few years ago — and still is in the provinces.

To entertain is therefore a real effort, and a costly one. The Americans are much simpler about it and welcome you into their everyday life. They don't die of shame if one of their guests happens to push open the wrong door and discovers an unmade bed. And most aren't in the habit of being waited on at table. The French bourgeois, as a matter of fact, are also losing that habit, but I'm not sure it makes them any more hospitable.

Finally, it was in the United States that I discovered television in action. I was there during the '52 presidential campaign, Eisenhower against Stevenson. These two gentlemen paid me daily visits in my hotel room, looking me straight in the eye as they made their speeches. On election night I was introduced to Eisenhower. And for a fraction of a second I was surprised he didn't recognize me, since I already knew him so well!

Servan-Schreiber, who was covering the elections for *Paris-Presse,* arrived in New York. I went to pick him up at the airport, and in the taxi going back to New York, he asked me politely who I thought was going to win. I say "politely" because he knew the ins and outs of the States extremely well, already had his own opinion about the outcome, and knew that I had only been there for three weeks.

I said to him: "On one side, you have Maurice Chevalier; on the other, Jean Vilar.* In a country where everyone has a right to vote, who's going to win? Maurice Chevalier, of

* A famous actor and director, who was the moving force behind the Avignon Festival, and was long the director of the TNP — the *Théâtre National Populaire. — Translator.*

course. Therefore Eisenhower. This said, I admit to knowing nothing about American politics."

"No, I can see you don't," he said. But Servan-Schreiber has the peculiar characteristic of always weighing the judgments of people whose opinions differ from his before rejecting them. Or agreeing with them, which he sometimes does. My method of determining the outcome had puzzled him. He himself had used more rational methods to reach the same conclusion. And he was the only French journalist who, against all the forecasts made in the States, and against his personal preferences, correctly predicted the election of Eisenhower over Stevenson.

At this point I'd like to stop and say: "After that there was *L'Express,* and that's the end of the story." First of all, it bothers me to be constantly talking about well-known people, and I don't quite know how to avoid it. How can I bring people into this story whom I would have to describe, physically reconstitute as a novelist does, with their many-leveled complexity, so that the reader can picture them and establish some kind of contact? I'm afraid that the kind of conversations we've opted for makes that virtually impossible.

If I ever have time, I'll one day write a book about the "unknown" people in my life. A girl I was in prison with, who today tends a wine shop. The headmistress of a boarding school. A bicycle delivery man who worked for *France-Soir.* My great-uncle Adolphe who always used to say: "As long as I'm alive, no woman in my family is ever going to work for a living!" I'd also like to write my "true stories" — stories I've either experienced myself or know about, whose characters are no one you have ever heard of. Here: I'm going to tell you my Guerlain story. That's one way of delaying the time when we'll have to move on.

It was a twenty-third of December when I was twenty,

with not a franc to my name, and I mean really not a single franc. In those days, nobody went away for Christmas. Quite the opposite. People put up huge Christmas trees decorated with real candles, and children didn't receive their presents on the fifteenth "because on the twenty-fifth they'll be in the mountains skiing." It was an important, elaborate holiday.

I was invited out for Christmas eve. I had a pretty dress, really lovely. But no shoes, nothing even remotely resembling dancing shoes. And no one who could lend me a pair. There was no way one could buy shoes on credit. And the only money I had was put aside for a bill falling due the thirty-first. It was out of the question to spend it on any frivolity. I was in a blue funk, trying to figure out what to do, when a delivery boy brought me a little package. It was a bottle of Guerlain perfume, a present.

It just so happened that the day before someone had given me the same present. I rushed over to Guerlain's on the Champs-Élysées, armed with both my bottles, and I explained to a lady — who was very courteous, I must say — that I was overwhelmed by both these two gifts but that one of the bottles was as much as I could use. And besides, it was a perfume I had never tried, I said, lying through my teeth, and if perchance it didn't suit me . . . Would Guerlain be good enough to take back one of the bottles?

"But of course, Mademoiselle," I was told. "I understand perfectly well. Nothing is easier."

There, in the space of a second, I foresaw everything. Perfume, as you well know, is expensive, and the bottle I was returning was decently large. I pictured not only my dancing shoes, but all kinds of other delightful pleasures which were going to decorate the holiday, presents I was going to give others and offer myself. For several minutes, I really believed in Father Christmas.

I went over to the cash register and waited, without daring

to ask how much I was going to get back. "Your name, please," the lady cashier asked me. I gave it to her. She wrote something. Then, with a charming smile she handed me a piece of paper and said: "Here you are. This is a credit. You can use it whenever you like. We're happy we were able to be of service to you. Goodby, Mademoiselle, and a very Merry Christmas!"

I also know other stories with happier endings. And others even sadder. But I can see that you're not really interested in my stories . . . You're right. But I needed to pause and get up my courage. It's relatively easy to talk about the real past, the past you've dissected so often that you can talk about it almost as though you were talking about someone else.

L'Express and everything around it is not the past; it's yesterday, today, and tomorrow; it's living history, that pulses, that implicates people in the middle of their professional lives about whom I cannot speak with complete detachment. What is more, it has importance.

 IX

THREE STORIES are intermingled. The story of a man and a woman, the story of a magazine, and the story of a group of people who wanted with all their might to move France out of its rut.

It goes without saying that I won't tell you anything about the first story: someone once said that you should never tell the story of your life because it is made up of the lives of others, and you have no right to talk about other people's lives. Quite simply, the discretion necessary here would create mystification, a mystification I want to avoid because it might lead people to believe that there is no special obstacle in the way of a woman having a career, even when women's ambitions are such as to put them into direct competition with men.

Until *L'Express* came into being, my relationships with this man or that never helped or hindered my professional life. I would just as honestly tell you the contrary if it were true. The men who helped me, and they are legion, were my friends, not my lovers.

Besides, I have grave doubts that I would ever have allowed the two types to intermingle. On that score, I was a bit of a fanatic. The only way I ever even conceived of the possibility that a man might be my superior was for him to compete with the image I carried in my mind of my father. And nothing is more difficult than competing with a myth.

On the other hand, would I ever had had the courage to enter into the crazy adventure which *L'Express* had to be unless I had complete confidence in the indestructible ties that bound me to Jean-Jacques Servan-Schreiber? . . . Actually, it was he who had that confidence. And not without reason, since so many years have gone by, and so many storms have come and gone, bearing with them — quite naturally — a great many autumn leaves, without that bond ever breaking. Only the future will reveal whether it is, in fact, indestructible. But to all appearances it must be of a very tough metal.

And on this point I would like to be especially precise. In the combination of circumstances I found myself in in 1952, I don't claim that it was easy to change my life. It wasn't.

When I told Pierre Lazareff that I was leaving *Elle,* he understood immediately that there was no point trying to keep me. And I believe that he hoped from the bottom of his heart that the change would be for my good. Hélène, who was more stubborn, went to see my mother and said to her: "Françoise is about to do something completely mad. She's leaving a solid fortress for a castle built on sand. You've got to talk her out of it." Needless to say, she had knocked on the wrong door if she was counting on my mother to help her.

Nothing was easy. But whatever two people do together is never of heroic proportions. I think that I felt obliged to tell you that, and not be dishonest enough to imply, by blurring the focus, that I could have founded a political magazine by myself, that people would have had the same confidence in me alone, that I would have had the drive necessary to bring it off single-handed.

As soon as a woman crosses the border into male territory, the nature of professional combat changes. I often wonder how many men would be capable of demonstrating the virtues that are, under these circumstances, demanded of a woman.

As I said a short time ago, the present evolution of women, and the way it will turn out — and it may veer more sharply than anyone suspects — is to my mind the most profound revolution that highly developed societies will have to contend with — that and the highly charged question of sharing the power of decision. A fire has been lighted which affects the basics, beginning with the family. It all started with the pill, of course. Not because it enabled women to avoid having children. That's the secondary aspect, no matter how convenient it may be. It was because, for the first time in the history of humanity, that decision belonged to women. And not only is the decision theirs, but in a sense they cannot avoid it, for not to make it is another way of making it. This major assumption of responsibility is clearly at the basis of this deep-rooted movement that is taking place now, and it is leading to the demand for equivalent social responsibilities.

But all that is very complicated. Women are not afraid of losing what they don't already have, right? . . . Authority, control, in a word "power," the decision exercised by someone who does not feel his virility threatened or who does not constantly need others to reassure him, will be both different in nature and have different effects. Therefore, any widespread accession to power on the part of women ought to have widespread, incalculable repercussions in the conduct of human affairs.

But when will it take place? And will it take place? When that antidote to anxiety is not necessary, will people search for responsibility? I am not talking about individual cases based on personal neuroses which may, in fact, happen

more frequently. I'm talking about the whole female population, that part of the human race referred to as "women."
Aren't they going to be paralyzed with fear — which you can
be sure will be played upon — that they may lose their
femininity? As though femininity is something you can lose
the way you lose your pocketbook: hmm, where in the world
did I put my femininity? And just what is femininity exactly,
I mean that really irreducible part of woman — aside from
the anatomical differences — which is in no way related to
culture or civilization, that which actually constitutes the
female of the species? We have not managed as yet even to
define it; in fact we're not even close. But we have not heard
the last of that, believe me.

Ever since Freud's famous remark about the "dark con-
tinent," as he referred to female sexuality, which he admitted
was all Greek to him, ever since his question: "But what is it
women want?" and his inability to answer it, progress in the
area generally lumped under "the feminine mystery" has not
been exactly staggering. It is obvious that women themselves,
and only women, have any hope of finding the answer.

It remains to be said that theories about women are one
thing, while practice is quite another, especially when one is
a woman. At birth, our place in the world is determined, and
whether we accept or reject it we have constantly to cope
with it in our daily lives.

I loathe those who send others to their deaths. I'll never
send another woman to her death by urging her to live psy-
chologically above her capacity, whether it be alone or di-
vorced or having a child without being married, whether it
means her feeling unhappy or guilty. That's some progress,
at least.

In the past I was irritated by the positions that Simone de
Beauvoir took, not because of what she said, but because the
woman who was urging others to assume their freedom was

herself assured — on the material plane — of a professor's salary and — morally — of the unfailing support of a man. "I knew that if Sartre agreed to meet me in two years on the Acropolis, he would be there . . . I knew that he could never do anything to hurt me . . ." Who wouldn't opt for that kind of freedom? But it's what I would term "snug freedom": material security . . . Simone de Beauvoir's personal life is beautiful, because there is nothing rarer than a successful human relationship, but nonetheless, as it relates to women in general, it's a kind of involuntary imposture, since she can't say: "Do as I do . . ." She is the example incarnate of a woman living for and through a man, a woman who, if I read her rightly, never really had to give up anything in her relationship with that man because it intruded on her work.

It is probably an enviable success, and one devoutly to be wished. But strictly speaking it is inimitable, a success which does not add constructively to the life of "Everywoman." And these Everywomen have a life which is too difficult for them to be lied to. You don't become Simone de Beauvoir-hyphen-Sartre because you make up your mind to have an abortion and to live together without being married, any more than you become Brigitte Bardot because you use the same beauty cream she does.

All you can do, if you want to badly enough — and if you are properly prepared — is to make yourself economically independent, without which I don't even know what the word freedom means. You can work it so that you never give up that economic independence which is the basis for all the others. On the other hand, you can revel in being the woman who regularly says, "Don't forget to leave me some money . . ." to the man who is depressed at the very thought of having to pay the gas bill, and who replies: "I don't know what you do with it, but we sure spend far too much money . . ." For me, that's sheer hell.

But even if you have that independence, if your professional credentials are impeccable, it's still difficult to have enough confidence in yourself to go hunting in pre-eminently masculine territory, especially if it's at the level of actually running a magazine.

It was a preferential entrance, in that Jean-Jacques never let me doubt for long about my abilities. On the contrary, he made me use them, try things I never would have attempted without his urging. At the outset he unequivocally established the principle of equality, and applied it assiduously; without it, who knows, I might have been tempted for a time to willingly submit to the role of the devoted collaborator. I don't think I would, but who knows?

The point is he never tried to create such a situation, and therefore I never had to fight, were it only against myself, to keep it from arising. The frustrations of such a situation were spared me. As were the conveniences.

Servan-Schreiber also has that special faculty of ignoring other peoples' "dark side" — to always play on their bright side, their good side rather than their bad. He has the ability always to see the best in people, and to uncover in them talents and abilities they themselves didn't even know they had. That's why people react so strongly, and get so angry, when for one reason or another they lose contact with him. It's as though a spotlight that had been directed on them had been turned off, or directed at something else. Their first reaction is be grateful: that exclusive attention he pays to whatever it is he's working on makes people feel guilty for anything they may happen to do which doesn't directly relate to the enterprise.

He turns even the most innocent pleasures into duties, and if he isn't doing something he's planning his next move: for example, he exercises not for the fun of it but simply in order to keep in good shape. Anyone who likes the theater, con-

certs, or any kind of spectator sports, who goes fishing, tourist-
ing, or who spends time painting, at the races, lingering over
gourmet meals, or in frivolous conversation is as strange to
him as a man from Mars would be. He can admire, if necessary, but with a kind of wonderment. All those things have
nothing to do with him, and any pleasures which might sap
his energy have to be kept on a leash. People involved with
him are all more or less caught up in this system, and they
struggle as best they can to preserve some vestige of personal
life from this pace, in this assault on Mount Everest under a
glaring sun. When they do untie the climber's rope they at
first feel relieved to be free of him. But later they generally
can't forgive him both for having known him and for having
lost him, and all that submerged darkness resurfaces.

François Mauriac, who without the help of Freud knew a
thing or two about human ambivalence, saw that very clearly.
And he didn't hesitate to say it, at least in private, with that
supreme simplicity that was his. "Beware," he said to me one
day, "of all those who can't get over having known Jean-
Jacques . . ." Dear Mauriac . . . There was no one quite
like him. They say that cemeteries are filled with irreplace-
able people. It's probably true. But there are times when
they aren't replaced.

It was really an extraordinary moment, the spectacle of this
elderly gentleman, weighed down with all the honors with
which the Establishment endows its own, leaving the ancient
and honorable paper *Le Figaro* to join forces with two rebels
who were putting together a new and virtually unknown
magazine. We couldn't even pay him what he had every right
to expect by virtue of his position.

We were running the magazine on a shoestring — ten
people in three rooms. And he understood that, and approved
of it. Actually, magazines ought to be slim when they're
children, to remain healthy as they grow up. When young

magazines absorb money as though there was no tomorrow, it means they're ill.

We got Mauriac because of a handful of outraged colonials, among whom was one who signed her letters "The Countess of X . . . Catholic-one-hundred per-cent." They finally prevailed on Pierre Brisson, the director of *Le Figaro,* to act. Did he let himself be intimidated, purely and simply, or did personal feelings play a part in what he did? Be that as it may, he asked Mauriac to tone down his articles, which appeared every Thursday in the paper, and in which he was coming down hard on the Moroccan situation. The upshot was that for one, two, three weeks in a row there was no front-page Mauriac column. That alerted me to the fact that something was up.

And when Jean-Jacques said to him: "Would you like to have a page in our magazine?" he accepted. His first column appeared in November 1953 and was entitled: "The Pretenders." In it he literally tore to shreds the various candidates vying for the French presidency at the end of President Auriol's term. "One must give Monsieur Joseph Laniel his due," he wrote. "Here's one pretender who doesn't pretend. You can see at first glance what this massive president incarnates: there's a gold ingot in that man." He was off and running.

But one shouldn't forget it, because this period was really a glorious one for Mauriac: contrary to so many other polemicists, who most of the time turn out to be anarchists of the Right, Mauriac never tried to foist off on the public the notion that politics is an area limited to mediocre careerists and men who are corrupt. In that same article, in fact, he said to these candidates: "We have no quarrel with you for being ambitious. If any one of you harbored the high-minded desire of restoring the state to its power, we would get behind you enthusiastically. For every Frenchmen sees that there is

Françoise Giroud and her older sister
with their mother, 1917.

André Gide in 1930. Françoise Giroud first met
him a year later, when she was fifteen.

Left: In 1933 at seventeen, when she had begun working for film director Marc Allégret.

Bottom: On a movie set as a script girl, 1934.

During the filming of Antoine de Saint-Exupéry's
Courrier-Sud in 1935. From left to right:
Saint-Exupéry, director Pierre Billon (with bow tie),
actress Jany Holt, Françoise Giroud,
and actor Charles Vanel.

Top: In 1937, while working as assistant to Jean Renoir and Erich von Stroheim on the filming of *La Grande Illusion.*

Left: 1943 — in Paris during the Occupation, shortly before her arrest by the Gestapo.

As editor of *Elle* magazine in 1950:
Françoise Giroud (left) and publisher
Hélène Lazareff (center)
with members of the staff.

Françoise Giroud's mother, in 1951,
with Françoise's daughter, Caroline.

Left: Maurice Thorez (1953), the long-time leader of the French Communist Party.

Bottom: At *L'Express* in 1954: publisher Jean-Jacques Servan-Schreiber and editor-in-chief Françoise Giroud with François Mauriac (center), who was then writing a weekly column for the magazine.

Top: Albert Camus (left), also a regular contributor to *L'Express,* at the magazine's press in 1955.

Left: January 1956: Former premier Pierre Mendès-France (left) with Socialist Party leader Guy Mollet, who was shortly to become premier of the new cabinet.

François Mauriac and Jean-Paul Sartre, June 1957.

On a reporting trip to the
Soviet Union, 1960.

Jacques Boetsch, *L'Express*'s
Washington correspondent,
in 1970 — a year before his
tragic death.

At home in her Paris apartment with daughter, Caroline, 1973.

Opposite, top: Françoise Giroud just after introducing Jean Monnet (left), principal founder of the Common Market, to Bertrand de Jouvenel (right), political philosopher and writer (1973).

Bottom: During a recent editorial staff meeting at *L'Express.*

With François Mitterrand, present head
of the French Socialist Party (1973).

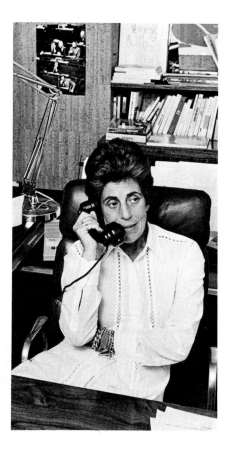

Left: In her office at *L'Express,* 1973.

Bottom: With France's new president, shortly before his 1974 election.

FRANCOISE GIROUD

V. GISCARD d'ESTAING

With Jérémie, her second grandson, 1973.

no longer any state, and that his country is in its death throes."

Starting in January of '54, as I recall, his column began to appear regularly. He still wrote for the *Figaro Littéraire,* some brilliant and beautiful articles where he dealt only with literary questions — Chateaubriand and Barrès — which could be counted on not to upset any countesses. Thus his friendship with Pierre Brisson was preserved, and for Mauriac that was important. But he never wrote any more political articles for *Le Figaro,* at least not under his own name.

All *L'Express* had done was take advantage of a fortuitous coincidence: a new magazine, a conflict of a writer with his old publication . . . But in fact, it was one symptom in a whole syndrome. Mauriac had a radar. Not only did his sensitivity send him warning signals in areas that his intelligence may have neglected, but also he had acquired a position in life where nothing could escape his gaze. I have no idea what manner of man he may have been in the days when he still had his full voice, when he may have dreamed of becoming a member of the French Academy, or of winning the Nobel Prize. Courageous, without any question, at the time of the Spanish Civil War, especially when you consider the Rightist world out of which he evolved. It was a world which had taught him as a child to call his chamber pot Zola, in the wake of the Dreyfus affair. But he was also no doubt a man like any other caught up in the network of his ambitions, his interests, his desires.

By 1953 he had played all his cards. And won. Even his health, which used to worry him and which he complained was fragile, had become as strong as iron, and his hoarse voice only added to his charm. He was free the way no one is ever free, or only very rarely. Free from others, and from himself. He had done what he had to do, he was sure of being loved by Someone up above, Who forgave him his unworthiness, in

word and deed. To write was a pleasure for him, not an effort.
So he was in a position to pick up every wavelength, without
any static. First and foremost, those emitted by people, of
course, which provoked those opinions full of fire and brim-
stone. And by following his instincts. "I'm like a cat, my
dear friend," he said to me one day. "I pick my own basket."
Everything about him, not only the scratches he was capable
of giving, reminded you of a cat. The distance; the independence; the haughty discrimination in deciding who could get
near him and who couldn't; and he would sit there purring
with his eyes half closed, his claws in, when all of a sudden,
zip . . . up he'd climb, back into his tree. The infallible
instinct.

The "basket" we offered him was, he knew, one where he
could stretch out to his heart's content, and feed on whatever
seafood delicacies he desired: that was one aspect of the
matter. There were also other reasons for the harmonious
relations that existed between us.

There comes a time in life when you have the feeling that
you're a walking graveyard. Your memory is filled with so
many dead about whom you soon won't be able to talk with
the living, for the simple reason that no one but you will have
known them: so many feelings and emotions, so many hopes,
memories, fears, so many vanished, and therefore incommuni-
cable, joys . . . And then that impression that each of these
people, when they died, took your childhood with them, your
youth; that as long as they were alive, that childhood, that
youth, was also alive somewhere, because someone was carrying around in his mind the picture of what you then were.
Because the fact is, we die a little every day, don't you agree?
There is simply one time which is the last. And we look at
ourselves, and in vain we search in the mirror, scanning our
present features for the reflection of the person that was, and
often we appear dejected, like some faded flower, because we

can only see ourselves in relation to what was, or what we hoped to be. The transition from one stage of life to another is always difficult, that renunciation of a person you once were that others don't see. Who knows, really, what stages anyone reaches before complete self-realization? This is as true at fifteen as it is at forty-five or even much later, no doubt. And it applies equally to both men and women. I have a feeling that men are more prone to mimic an age-category they no longer belong to.

If, instead of being rejected by those who come after them, by the rising generation or generations, people are treated with friendship and respect, deference and appreciation, it's obviously easier to accept the process of aging. When an older person is spontaneously offered the company of younger people, it acts as a mirror in which he sees himself not as young, but loved and needed.

I sincerely believe that we gave that to Mauriac. That feeling he had of belonging, of being part of our little group, someone who was contributing to the cause, he was part of the struggle. All of us are made up of both masculine and feminine components, in varying proportions, and Mauriac possessed a larger than normal share of the latter. He liked being pulled by someone else's motor. And yet he would never allow himself to be led anywhere he didn't want to go. He immediately recognized in Jean-Jacques one of those motors, those mobilizers of energy. And he also undoubtedly saw something more in him since, with that foresight and freedom he alone possessed, he wrote in one of his last columns, in 1969 — in November of '69 to be exact:

> Let me go on record as stating, from my own personal experience and association, that if Jean-Jacques Servan-Schreiber ever came to power he would display considerable political ability. I remember once, when Jean-Jacques was still quite young, having dinner with Bourguiba. Throughout the evening Jean-

Jacques, who was defending French policy with respect to Tunisia, held his own with the wily Tunisian. I admired him for being both so clear and so convincing. Ever since that evening I have always thought that politics was Servan-Schreiber's real vocation — politics in the best and noblest sense of the term — and that only in that area would he be able to demonstrate his real worth. But what I cannot see is how the yoke he's saddled himself with can help him advance in that direction. He would doubtless answer me that it is not he personally who is in question, that he never needed anyone to help him steer his own ship, that what is needed is to inject new life into the Left, to deliver it from the Communist nightmare and anchor it firmly in the center through some kind of rejuvenated radicalism.

He ended with a "We shall see what we shall see" which still obtains today.

If I quote that text, it is because it seems to me to illuminate everything we're talking about. Mauriac acted as a witness, which is a journalist's natural vocation. A witness who can never be muzzled but who reserves for himself the right to withdraw from the game at any moment. Jean-Jacques is not a witness. The journalism in which he excels is the kind that gives expression to an overall plan which affects both events and the acts of men. It was this participation in action that *L'Express* gave Mauriac, and in return he gave it all the things of which you are fully aware.

The M.R.P. — the Christian-Democratic Movement on which Mauriac based such high hopes — let him down, and let him down badly. He used to paraphrase Corneille: "I see, I know, I believe, I am disillusioned."

Mauriac was going to be an actor on the stage of politics, but in the noblest sense and in the way that suited him best, since it was not a question of helping to satisfy any base political ambitions, but of trying to bring Mendès-France and his ideas to power, to translate Mendès-France's ideas into action, for the good of France. In that kind of orchestra that we all played in, he was for seven years the soloist. And I think he was happy in the role, although he provoked some deadly hatreds, which were accompanied by threats, even including threats on his life. Not to mention the disgraceful insults.

It wasn't the first time — nor the last — that a group of people have banded together within a periodical in order to crystallize certain ideas and give voice to them. But, on the one hand, these efforts only succeed when the time is ripe. A newspaper or magazine can only act as a catalyst; it cannot give rise to something which does not exist potentially. On the other hand, it was a rather original adventure in that it brought together a handful of real journalists, including Pierre Viansson, that is, people capable of translating ideas into writing in such a way that they became clear and striking, of simplifying them, of disseminating them; and it also brought together a handful of important government officials, university professors, business leaders, and politicians, all of whom had the experience and ability to furnish us not with bits and pieces of information but with the whole picture, the basic elements of judgment and analysis which formed our policy positions.

I don't think I'm saying anything out of turn — since it's common knowledge — when I note that Mendès-France, who is a truly magnificent speaker, writes poorly. Nor that Simon Nora and his friends, the people he brought with him — he could have been a character straight out of Balzac's *Histoire des Treize* — that Simon Nora, whose mind and thought are very rich indeed, has a talent for complicating, through an overaccumulation of data and ideas — rather than simplifying. And that Louis Armand, a brilliant man, was as gifted a speaker as he was inept in writing. And many others . . .

Generally speaking — and with the notable exception of Alfred Sauvy — everyone in France who is the proud possessor of any kind of knowledge or information used to think — and often still does today — that he is dishonoring himself as soon as he is understood beyond the circle of his peers. Everyone speaks, or writes, for the people that he expects to meet at dinner. It's an illness that affects some journalists, in fact.

The cooperation of these different elements bore its fruits. And as for me personally, it was a veritable education in economics and political economy, private lessons that were more effective than if I had been at a graduate school of political science!

The necessity to translate what people told me into a language accessible to all — and in its early days all the articles, interviews, muckraking reports, and economic cartoons were written in a style meant to be readily accessible — was an exercise which utilized all the muscles of the mind. As in learning a foreign language, the first stage is to understand it; the second, and more difficult, is to speak or write it.

You may remember that at the time economics, in the broadest sense of the term, was virtually unknown to the press, aside from a few periodicals that specialized in it — and even today . . . Those that did deal with the matter dealt with it generally from a financial point of view. L'Express was founded in 1953. And it was only in 1968, as I recall, that a paper such as Le Monde* began to include in its pages a separate section devoted to economics. In its political ramifications — and the overlap is constant — economics was the very *raison d'être* of L'Express. If you doubt it, look at the first issue. At that time, who was Mendès-

* The most serious newspaper in France, roughly equivalent in importance, if not in scope of coverage, to the *New York Times.* — *Translator.*

France, after all? He was a gentleman who kept on repeating: we must invest, we must reduce our nonproductive expenses — the foremost of which of course was the war in Indochina — we must provide the country with adequate housing, invest our capital in machinery, factories, and schools; we have to create jobs for those who today are six, seven, and eight, and who a decade from now will be coming onto the job market. We have to put an end to the endless stream of governments who go to Washington for their seal of approval because we are living at the expense of the United States.

He was an advocate of government planning but also a staunch supporter of the market economy; authoritarian but democratic; he was a liberal and steadfastly wedded to the parliamentary system — in fact, he would have liked ours to model itself after the English system; he was vigorously opposed to Communism both rationally — he saw nothing in Communism that he deemed desirable for France — and personally, that is out of an innate horror of coercion of any sort.

He used to relate the following story that had taken place in London during the war, which he had heard about firsthand. A Communist *député* had fallen in love with the wife of a fellow Party member, a love that was requited. The order came down from on high to break off the relationship. Both lovers persisted, refusing to follow the order. For Mendès-France, that story was a kind of prelude to the nightmare. I heard him tell it a dozen times. And there was good reason to, I might add.

As for the rest of his political thinking, Mendès-France believed that the war in Indochina was ruining France and compromising the future of North Africa where, according to him, progressive decolonization should be put into effect: the first stage would be to grant internal autonomy to Tunisia and Morocco.

You may remember what happened: during the short time he was in power, Mendès-France did not grant Tunisia full independence but internal autonomy, which was what Bourguiba was demanding.

The Empire Peddler, they called him! No one was less disposed than Mendès-France to give anything away, much less peddle it at bargain prices. No one was a tougher negotiator than he, when he was given free reign to negotiate, if only because he has very set ideas, is very slow to accept change and the advent of new concepts. He accepts change only through reasoned thought, through intelligence rather than spontaneous understanding. Accepting change is all the more difficult for him because he has such a basically analytical mind. I know no one whose analysis is clearer, more rigorous, or more convincing. Except that, his analyses often fail to take into account some little factor that has been lingering on the sidelines, whose incorporation into the concept alters everything.

His distrust of anything with which he is unfamiliar, and a great deal with which he is, is boundless. For instance, he firmly refused to believe that a break would ever occur between China and the Soviet Union. I must still have the letter he wrote us castigating *L'Express* for having published reports of the rumored cracks in the Sino-Soviet wall which were the forerunners of the ensuing break. The greatest politicians have made mistakes at one time or another about the future; history is full of their false predictions. What is interesting is not that they were made but why they were, what there was about this or that political leader that caused him to make such errors. Actually, it would make a good subject for some Ph.D. thesis. Fortunately, though, people do make these mistakes: it's the proof they're human and not simply computers.

X

THE ORIGINAL GOAL that *L'Express* set for itself had nothing to do with what it became up until the end of the Algerian War because of the horrors of decolonization. Its original mission was to support and nurture a policy of rebuilding France, a policy backed up by solid information. And it is to that initial mission which the magazine has reverted today.

Without doubt we were — and I fear still are, relatively — the people the most ill-informed about themselves. I don't think I'm wrong in stating that, today, our statistical apparatus is far less sophisticated than that of the United States or Japan, where in the space of fifteen minutes you can obtain literally any piece of information you're looking for. It's all there, and it's all available. And yet we had the agency, which Mendès created in fact, called the *Commission des comptes à la nation,* whose purpose was to provide statistical information about France. But the tendency to — I'm tempted to say the mania for — secrecy that still informs so many French companies whose directors would be offended if you asked them for the basic figures about their businesses — and would be even more upset if you dared to make them public — renders the problem of gathering and disseminating information in France a difficult one. The same tendency applies to the affairs of state. There's another problem: the so-called sophisticated Frenchman, who thinks of himself or his ideas as advanced, is contemptuous of any notion that might cause him to readjust his ideological convictions. It may all boil down to the truth that the French don't like information because it pitilessly reduces their margin of illusions or hopes, because it impinges on their intellectual comfort. It's true that reality is always less pleasant than the notion of reality one has made for oneself. Flaubert maintains that autointoxication is a national illness. "The mania not to see the truth," he said. But I strongly suspect that this is merely a facile excuse for a great deal of cowardice and a multitude of sins of omission.

In any case, if that illness indeed exists, it has to be treated. But on the Left it's: "Put us in power and we'll topple the economy from top to bottom, gratis." The Right retorts: "If we gave in to your demands, the economy would fall apart."

And you begin to wonder what kind of civilized government would coldly publish and promulgate, during the Algerian War, a document purporting to show that if we lost the war one out of every five workers would be unemployed and the port of Marseille would be in jeopardy. That's the sort of thing they tell the Egyptian fellaheen.

It makes you think of the famous address to Charles X by the bourgeois members of Parliament in 1830: "An unfair distrust of the feelings and reason of France is today the basic thinking of the Administration."

Doubtless the press has to share a large part of the blame for that "distrust of reason" which is still rife today. But you have to go back and try to see the roots of the French press, the climate and soil out of which it evolved; you have to see why, contrary to the English and American press, it has no tradition of information behind it.

The French press is less than two centuries old. During these two hundred years there have been some thirteen or fourteen regimes in France, each of which, in coming to power, took it out on the preceding regime by closing down the newspapers and throwing the journalists in jail. You may recall the definition of censorship that the philosopher Louis de Bonald gave in the middle of the nineteenth century: "A sanitary institution set up in order to protect society from the contagion of false doctrines, similar in all respects to the measures taken to eliminate the plague."

Journalism over this long period did not consist of passing on information but in doing battle with the enemy, accusing, inflaming . . . The powers-that-were never for a moment thought that their difficulties with the opposition might be the result of their own policies; they knew the press was to blame.

It's an infernal dialectic, at the end of which, quite naturally, you find perfectly respectable people saying in the 1970s that the war in Indochina or the Algerian War was lost by the journalists, as you found a government minister, Monsieur René Pleven, seizing *L'Express* in 1953 because it contained the report by Generals Ely and Salan on the state of military operations in Indochina. In other words, it contained the intolerable, the "truth."

To seize a periodical is an incredible reflex! And an act of pure illegality to boot. That was the first of a long series of seizures.

And today, when we see in *Paris-Match* the photographs of the bloody repression in Sétif which occurred prior to the insurrection in Algeria,* and we are coolly informed, "Needless to say, we were unable to publish these photographs when

* A repression in Algeria that took place the same day as the signing of the armistice between the Allies and the Germans, May 8, 1945.— *Translator.*

they first came into our possession . . ." what are we supposed to think? What do *you* think? As for me, it makes me want to change professions. Why *not* have published them? Who knows whether their publication might not have changed the course of events . . .

And what about the incident with Raymond Aron, a man who can hardly be classified as a subversive? Do you know that he was the first person who had the courage, in a brief memorandum he wrote, to set forth what might have been the conditions for Algeria's independence? He sent the memorandum to Jacques Chevallier, the liberal mayor of Algiers, asking him what he judged were the chances of having the French in Algeria accept such a plan. That must have been in '56, since Chevallier had asked Jean-Jacques to come and have dinner with him at the town hall of Algiers before answering Aron. You never saw the slightest mention of this memorandum in any newspaper, did you, including the paper that has the honor of counting Aron among its regular contributors?

I doubt that there is any such thing as the press being capable of a crime of indiscretion. But there is such a thing as a crime of silence. Mauriac wrote that. Between the periodicals that are afraid to offend their readers, and the television, which is afraid of offending the U.D.R.,* you have to conclude that any Frenchman who wants to be informed really has to work at it! In '53, in any event, we had our work cut out for us on that score.

— You mean you had a very clear idea of what you wanted to do when you started *L'Express?*

— Exactly. Despite the fact that it was badly undercapitalized in the beginning, that's why it was started. And that's why it was so innovative. I'm not saying that *L'Express*

* Union pour la Defense de la République — the early name for the Gaullist Party when De Gaulle returned to power in 1958. — *Translator.*

invented the current-day press. But it is only natural that its purpose coincided with the times to which it belonged.

What I would term, for the sake of simplicity, the Prouvost press and the Lazareff press — since they are both newspapers that characterized their era — were simply mass-market periodicals which, in the case of Prouvost, brought to the middle class, and in the case of Lazareff to the working class, the varied and distant murmur of the world and of life in all its facets. It was a press that opened windows onto the five continents, onto the customs and mores, the vast panoramas of the world; a press that took on the best writers and reporters and sent them wandering across the face of the earth, not in search of food for thought or reflection, but to see and to write about what they had seen. To see what was happening in Hollywood and in the lower depths; to see what was going on at your next-door neighbors, by reporting on the scandals near and far. Both Prouvost and Lazareff posed as a basic principle that ideas are of interest to no one — or at least to only a few — unless they become incarnate. It was an entertainment press, in which quantity was the order of the day. Those who produced those papers were in no way cynics or simple paper-peddlers, but people pleased with themselves the way someone is who performs a good deed, like taking an armful of flowers to some solitary old lady. They were, obviously, conservative politically, but then, that was their perfect right!

The only thing was, the printed press ceased having the monopoly on these flowers, with the advent first of the transistor radio, and later of television. As for their tried-and-true journalistic style, such as: "It was 2:35 P.M. when Mr. Jones, dressed in a blue suit and wearing a red tie, climbed into his gray Chevrolet" — all those details of the "who-what-when-where-how school" you have to give but which have no relationship whatsoever with meaningful information — it very quickly struck the rising generation, which was much more informed than its parents had been, as insignificant. Compare how many students there were in 1939 with the number in 1950. It was the latter who became our initial readers, and the readers of *Le Monde*. And compare how many students there were in 1950 with the number in 1970. It was logical that this new public wanted a new press; and, what was more, the public as a whole became increasingly demanding. That, simply, was what we felt. And we figured that if we, as readers, had nothing to read that suited our wants and needs, that answered the basic demands we thought a periodical ought to offer, there must be others out there like us. The problem was how to bring off this journalistic "renewal" and do it successfully — I don't think I need reiterate my feelings about professionalism in this area. From the format to the contents, not to mention the writing style, the selections, the use of captions, the typography: we invented it all. Later on, I doubt if any periodical has ever been more copied, more plundered. And I take it as a compliment. In fact, discoveries are made to be lost and picked up by passersby who are incapable of making their own, while the more creative minds move on to other things.

I'm more interested in what *L'Express* will become tomorrow than what it was yesterday. A writer can rest on the laurels of what he has written. Not a magazine.

— And you never doubted that *L'Express* would be a success?

— We never doubted that we had to publish it so that it could play the role it has played. The question of success is another matter altogether. *L'Express* began with a circulation of 35,000 copies, and a capital I can only call ludicrous: $20,000. But it began with the help of one very simple idea. Like all simple ideas, it was one you had to come up with: Jean-Jacques' father and uncle owned a weekly newspaper concentrating on economic matters called *Les Echos,* which as I recall they had founded in 1908. It appeared five days a week and had a circulation of . . . 35,000. The subscribers were informed that they would begin receiving a weekly supplement — a Saturday *Echos* as it were — which would be called *L'Express.* In return, the price of their subscription would be increased so much, if they agreed to receive it. Virtually everyone did. At that point we thought: wouldn't it be incredible if we could raise our circulation to 75,000?

— What's your circulation today?

— Ten times greater: 750,000. But at what point can one say that *L'Express* was a "success"? And what constitutes a magazine's success anyway? I would say, its influence on influential people, its circulation, and its good management. For the most part, newspapermen hadn't the vaguest notion how a paper ought to be properly run . . . thanks to which, Claude Bourdet and Albert Camus lost *Combat,* Emmanuel d'Astier lost *Liberation,* etc. There always comes a moment when you have to choose between the infusion of outside capital needed to keep the paper going, or growing, but which usurps your freedom — no one ever invests that money without exacting something in return — or throwing in the sponge. Camus and d'Astier threw in the sponge. But wouldn't it have been better if there had been some way for them to hang onto their papers?

That is what Jean-Jacques has always been able to avoid: getting himself into a situation where he had only one alternative: seek outside help, or give up.

— You mean he was obsessed by the idea of raising his circulation . . .

— No. There you're making a classic error. To have good management does not necessarily mean selling more copies. It means balancing expenses and income, growing according to a carefully conceived plan, and deriving a suf-

ficient profit from the business to have some kind of reserve
if and when you have to pass through difficult times.

— Still, you have to sell!

— Of course you do. But *France-Soir,* which lost something like a $1,500,000 in 1970, sold a lot of copies, that I
can assure you. Many more than *Le Monde.* Then why does
Le Monde make rather than lose money?

I have a feeling I'm annoying you by suggesting that the
newspaper world does not consist of paper peddlers on the
one hand and heroes-with-pen-in-hand on the other. The
landscape of the press is a bit more complex than that. It's
not an old-time Western we're playing.

What continues to amaze me is the number of people who,
in their own professions, are money-oriented, think only in
terms of commerce, who are bootlickers and cowards when
dealing with public officials — because everyone in France
depends more or less on the State — but who, when it comes
to their newspapers, demand a courage and unselfishness of
which they themselves are completely incapable. Sometimes
you feel like saying to them: "Why are we the sole reposi-
tories of virtue?" I don't know enough about the European
press to make irrefutable statements or comparisons. But we
do have a very clear idea about how the press operates in the
Eastern countries on the one hand, and in England and
America on the other.

In the East, the press is strictly controlled by the government. The people, too. Therefore, since there is no ambiguity on that score, no one expects or hopes to have any influence on the government leaders, nor does anyone worry
about expressing public opinion.

In Great Britain, not only is it inconceivable that the
government interfere with the workings of the press, but in
general the weight of the government is considerably less
than it is in France. The head of this or that business is not

kneeling in supplication before this or that minister, who in turn is not on bended knee before the powerful financiers. The English citizen therefore would have every right to censure the press if it was guilty of ignoring or glossing over some important issue, or if it was overly circumspect about those in power. But, so far as I know, that never happens. And there are very strict libel laws if the press defames someone without proof to back it up.

In the United States, the instances of the press's freedom with respect to the country's government officials are legion. Watergate is but the most recent example. Perhaps it is hard for Americans to conceive of the French journalists' frustration at seeing how Watergate, involving the highest political personages in the land, was dealt with in the States, but the fact is they know that in France they would doubtless not have been given a chance to ferret out such skeletons from the political closet.

It's true that the American press — and especially the magazines — have been jeopardized by the massive increases in postal rates over the past few years, which has made the acquisition of new subscribers more and more difficult. Subscriptions, which have never been an important part of the life of the press in France, are the lifeblood of the magazine press in the States. But the United States government did not raise the postal rates in an effort to make the press toe the line, nor is it even conceivable that it would resort to such blackmail.

As for the mass of American citizens, they find it perfectly normal that newspapers make money; in France, the notion of profit is somehow still connected with the notion of sin, in keeping with the good Catholic tradition. But Americans live under a free-enterprise system. Even if at one point the present administration, because of inflation, had to initiate price controls in some sectors, there is simply no comparison between the Frenchman's dependence on his government officials, and the American's. As for price controls, a 1945 ordinance in France stipulates that the government can set prices on any item whatsoever. For virtually anything we want to do, be it build a building or seek a subsidy, we are dependent on the government officials. The press is not an industry like the others. Not to offer an opinion is to offer an opinion. To publish *France-Dimanche, Ici Paris,* or *Jours de France* is to have a conception of man and woman and their place in society, therefore to have a political attitude in the broadest sense of the term.

Some newspapers also serve another function, one I would term therapeutic. They soothe and alleviate hatreds, which are better being exorcised through reading the paper than by resorting to physical violence. Other papers offer comfort to the ugly, the lonely, the forgotten, the failures by informing you that Queen Elizabeth, believe it or not, has her own problems of infidelity, my dear; and as for Jackie and Ari, well let me tell you . . . We care for, we poison, or we offer strength, in any case we nourish with print and paper just as much as with meat and potatoes. Therefore, we can never escape or deny that responsibility, no matter how we set out to fulfill it.

Even when that crass commercial consideration we refer to deprecatingly as "profit" is the only apparent goal of any paper, there is of necessity a parallel or secondary aspect involved, which is the policy of the paper. I will go even further: any paper which is given the chance to live and prosper and grow and does not have some stance, some clear policy, is suffering more from irresponsibility than from disinterestedness.

The only problem is, management of any periodical is difficult, because it requires that the person responsible for the commercial decisions remain fully aware of the very special nature of his or her product. Ideally, such a person ought to incarnate both the qualities of a journalist and those of a good manager. Beuve-Méry, who founded *Le Monde,* is one good example of someone who could handle both functions himself. It infuriates him to be told that he's a good businessman. But it's true. *L'Observateur* only began to find its real stride after many years of effort when Claude Perdriel, a graduate of the polytechnical institute, took over the reins as business manager, leaving editorial matters to Jean Daniel. Jean-Jacques Servan-Schreiber, like Beuve-Méry, is capable of handling both roles.

— Was it he who managed the business end of *L'Express?*

— Yes. I don't think he particularly enjoys it, but he knows how to do it. And since he was doing it, he wanted to do it well, and he also wanted to give himself, as quickly as possible, the financial independence that being the majority stockholder of a thriving enterprise inevitably brings. All that did not take place overnight, I assure you. It was a very long, troubled, and difficult struggle, which took place in the midst of all sorts of political and professional adventures and misadventures, some of which are still going on today. When you are carrying on a struggle, you have to accept the notion that you will have enemies. Ours resorted to methods which were at times . . . curious, to say the least. For example, recalling Servan-Schreiber into the French army in 1956. It was, obviously, a way of stilling his pen, and it was also doubtless thought to be the most expedient method of bringing *L'Express* to its knees.

It was something the Minister of Defense, Maurice Bourgès-Maunoury, dreamed up. He was the gentleman who accused us, along with a few others in whose company, in fact, we were honored to be included — of being "exhibitionists of the heart and mind." As for himself, he didn't risk making any such claim. We had just finished turning *L'Ex-*

press from a weekly into a daily, and the situation was as delicate as our assets were dangerously low. And then suddenly, in July of '56, no more Jean-Jacques. Swallowed up by Algeria, and in serious danger.

For a devotee of black humor, it was a delectable comedown after the success of the preceding three years. In a nutshell: 1953 — *L'Express* is founded to give voice to the ideas and policies of Mendès-France and to help bring him to power. 1954 — Mendès is Premier for seven months, a period of such brilliance that his term is still looked back on as an important moment in history. It was Mendès-France who negotiated the end of the war in Indochina with Molotov and Chou En-lai, who worked out the Geneva accord, which was unanimously approved by the French Parliament.

I might add parenthetically that if these agreements — dividing Vietnam in two along the seventeenth parallel and providing for elections in 1956 — had been respected, if the Eisenhower administration had not encouraged Diem to refuse these elections, John F. Kennedy would not have inherited the American involvement in Vietnam with its attendant and all too painfully familiar consequences. Arthur Schlesinger, Jr., gave an admirable account of that in his *A Thousand Days.*

But that is another story altogether. In 1954, ours took us to Algeria, the French colony where, on November 1, an insurrection broke out. When Mendès-France was voted out of power the following February, it was because he ruffled a great many feathers, but especially because his own party turned against him, with René Mayer, the representative from Oran who was worried about Mendès' Algerian policy, leading the way.

1955: the insurrection is spreading. Every effort must be made to enable the Left to win the elections scheduled to be held in '56, to stop the spread of the Algerian gangrene.

Mendès-France must be returned to power. At great cost and risk, Jean-Jacques decides to turn *L'Express* from a weekly into a daily paper in order to have a more efficient arm at the service of what he called the "Republican Front" — socialists, radical-Mendèsists, Mitterrand's U.D.S.R., and the U.R.A.S. headed by Chaban-Delmas, the former leader of the Radical Socialist Party. Albert Camus, haunted by the deteriorating situation in Algeria, joins *L'Express* to add his weight and voice to the battle.

But Edgar Faure dissolves the French Assembly. The elections are scheduled six months earlier than originally planned. The newspaper is caught short, its transformation into a daily takes place much too quickly, which is explained to our readers as being "due to the exceptional circumstances." They help us, they participate, send contributions, but nothing can compensate for the lack of time necessary to prepare properly for such a drastic change in a paper's life, especially since few of us had ever had any experience working on a daily paper. We're forced into a situation where improvisation is the order of the day, and that is not Jean-Jacques' style. The paper takes the plunge, designates the candidates for whom its readers *must* vote, in other words puts its very existence on the line . . .

After the elections, in order not to lose control of the paper, *L'Express* hastily turns itself back into a weekly, while there is still enough money in the till to give departing employees severance pay. It is an agonizing decision, but ultimately a wise one; in a sense it is a defeat, but one has to know how to face and clearly recognize defeats.

But the success, for which we risked everything, is also there. The Republican Front is in a good position. And it's obvious that the President of the Republic will call on Mendès-France to form the new government. It is he to whom the French, who for the most part are upset at seeing their sons shipped off to Algeria to wage a war — which is then called "the Algerian pacification" — have turned to restore peace. During the electoral campaign, Mendès-France declared, echoing Eisenhower's "I shall go to Korea," "I shall go to Algeria . . ."

1956: a series of really extraordinary scenes occur.

First there is a luncheon, immediately after the elections, at the home of Gaston Defferre, who is both the mayor of Marseille and *député* from that region. Defferre is a leading member of the Socialist Party, whose head is Guy Mollet. In the course of this lunch, Mendès-France exchanges niceties with Guy Mollet as though it were a question of which of the two would have the opening move in some chess match. Not only does Mendès not come out openly and say, in no uncertain terms, that he will be the next head of government, he also fails to state, or even suggest, that if the President should happen to call on Mollet to form a government, he should defer to Mendès.

It is an historical scene in the true sense of the term, where a man who rightfully is willing and eager to be an agent of history, and who is given the opportunity to do so, mysteriously passes it up.

Why? We'll come back to that later. It's fascinating. And exasperating too. For the moment, let's stick to the immediate consequences: Guy Mollet, not Mendès, heads up the new government. And quite simply, he is not up to the task, especially in such a situation of crisis. He would have made an extraordinary union chief, fighting with passion, cleverness, devotion, and disinterest for the rights of the workers. But he is not a statesman.

Scene two: Mendès has said that he would "go to Algeria." So it's Guy Mollet who is to go in his place. The original idea was to arrive in Algeria unannounced, strike a blow, provoke a shock, show the extremists that you mean business, that you are head of a strong government fully resolved to take whatever steps are necessary.

Jean-Jacques has a premonition that Guy Mollet is somehow going to let himself be sidetracked from this plan. Late one evening, Jean-Jacques rings Guy Mollet's doorbell and offers him this advice: "Don't let them know when you're arriving. And don't arrive during the day; you'll be booed and attacked. Leave right away, without warning anyone in advance. Let them find you already set up in Algeria." Guy Mollet receives Servan-Schreiber in pajamas and tells him in substance: "I appreciate your advice, but I had a long conversation today with Monsieur de Sérigny and his friends [the extremists]. I can assure you I'll be warmly received in Algeria. Good night."

The official scene which ensued is a matter of history: on February 6, in Algiers, the Premier is pelted with tomatoes in the streets; his hasty retreat . . . and everything that followed, that long, agonizing train of events set in motion by that moment . . . On February 7, Camus, who up to then had harbored the utopian dream of effecting a truce between the French and Algerians, gave up all hope.

Here, too, let's not try to remake history. I don't know what would have happened if Mendès-France had been head of the Republican Front instead of Guy Mollet any more than I can predict what would have resulted if it had been he who had confronted the extremists in Algiers . . . Algiers where he himself had appointed Jacques Soustelle a year earlier, the Soustelle of those days, who was fiercely anticolonial. In any case, it is safe to say that the history of the years following February 6, 1956, would not have been the same. And since what did happen could hardly have been any worse . . . How heavily those years weighed on us, not only on individual destinies — which does not strike me as being quite so unimportant as historians tend to make out — but also on our collective destiny . . .

In May, Mendès-France resigns from the Mollet government. He's how old today? Seventy-one? He held power a grand total of nine months. Nine months out of seventy-one years. It's true there is no age limit in politics. And in July 1956, Jean-Jacques Servan-Schreiber, a lieutenant in the reserves, is recalled into the army and sent to Algeria.

It all makes quite a sequence of events, no? Grim humor? But a sense of humor — be it black or rose-colored — is not what characterizes the period. And at the time I can't say that I found it very funny.

Mendès-France lost his temper. "I don't want you to go back into the army," he said to Jean-Jacques. "Once they get you in Algeria they'll kill you." And he demanded that Bourgès-Maunoury demobilize him. Then Jean-Jacques lost his temper and demanded to be remobilized. We were playing Corneille scenes from morning till night.

The whole thing was gruesome and ludicrous at the same time. I must say the ludicrous aspect was less clear to me then than now. And then I was suddenly saddled with the full responsibility for the magazine, even those areas where I had not previously had to carry any load. While on the one hand it was challenging and exciting, on the other it was painful and nerve-racking. Jean-Jacques never had any doubt, I suspect, that I would somehow manage it. And within the magazine itself, all my co-workers were more than cooperative, great. No one added to any of the existing difficulties.

As far as the outside world was concerned, there was a challenge that had to be met, a challenge of which I was actually unaware, because I knew very clearly how important my role was on the magazine. But since I was a woman, in both political and professional circles, the full credit for the success of *L'Express* had always been attributed to Jean-Jacques.

I don't know what was in people's minds at the time. That the magazine would fold, or that I would resign. Not that it matters what they thought. Or rather, it wasn't important to me at the time because I was blissfully ignorant of the problem. It was only later that Beuve-Méry of *Le Monde* told me — he was the first to say it — with what misgivings he had observed the experiment. He doesn't mince words. He has a reputation for being a misogynist, which made what he said all the more meaningful to me. I respect him and I like him.

In October, the financial situation of the magazine was shaky, to say the least. What was I to do? Try and borrow money? I don't think I'll ever really know. What I did was like a sequel to my childhood experience. I chose what was most natural to me — that way you have the best chance of succeeding — that is, I chose to gamble. In fact, double or nothing was the name of the game: I doubled the cover price of the magazine and added a weekly four-page supplement. The readers could resist the price rise, in which case the game would be over. But if they accepted it, the game would be won.

I don't know whether it was, as people said, a wise business decision, but it worked. I was also helped out by the incredible events of 1956: the kidnapping of Ben Bella; the nationalization of the Suez Canal after the Americans refused to finance the Aswan Dam; Budapest; the Suez expedition . . .

Politically, it was difficult to steer a reasonable course considering the many complex and often contradictory pressures exercised by everyone who had decided to give me the benefit of his or her opinions. What made things even more difficult and complicated were the events themselves, which, as always, provoked a variety of emotions. Politics, which claims to be an exact science and involves the strategy of a chess player, also brings out everything irrational in people. It's comical, except that political mistakes so often lead to tragedy.

What is more, people also act in relation to the past: the execution of Louis XVI because Charles I of England was put to death, the Paris Commune imbued with the memory of 1792, etc. Valéry put it better than anyne: We walk backward into the future.

At the time the Suez Canal was nationalized, I went to visit Mendès-France at a spa where he was taking treatments for his throat, which tended to be delicate. He told me he thought the Egyptian pilots would turn out to be incapable of replacing the European pilots and wouldn't be able to take the ships through the canal. In nationalizing the canal, seizing it from the hands of the capitalists and imperialists, Nasser calculated he could block a vital part of the world's maritime traffic, and at the same time, when he reopened it, the canal would provide an important source of income for Egypt. What upset these carefully laid plans was not the inefficiency of the Egyptian pilots, but the fact that with huge tankers you don't need the canal. It's been closed now for what? Six years, seven? . . .

At the time of the Franco-English expedition against Suez, one of our closest friends, about whom I've already spoken, Lucien Rachet, who was very close both to the magazine and to Mendès-France, was fanatically pro-Israel and all for the expedition. Mendès-France, however, was adamantly against it. I can still hear him when he learned the news, picking up the phone and in that terrible, icy voice, telling Guy Mollet what he thought. Jean-Jacques called from Algeria, where for once he had been able to get to a phone, and reported what those fellow officers who had become his friends were saying. They wanted the army to break off all relations, once and for all, with the Arabs. As for Jean-Jacques himself, cut off as he was from everything, he refused to offer any opinion.

I was ridden with fears and doubts, I remember, when I wrote the lead article for the magazine — unsigned, by the way; I signed them simply *L'Express* — after long discussion and argument with our executive editor, Philippe Grumbach, who was very lucid. It was his idea to publish in full Nasser's own *Mein Kempf.* The following week, as I recall it, it was Sartre who, overwhelmed by the crushing of the Hungarian rebellion, gave us a very long and beautiful piece on the subject . . . I have a very fond memory of that issue, for all the reasons you can imagine. For other, more personal reasons, too . . .

In short, it was a tense and troubled time — I am tempted to say: "Yet another." But major responsibilities always carry with them that dual virtue of stimulating even as they stretch your nerves to the breaking point. The truth of the matter is I enjoy them. For some strange reason I tend not to aim any higher than I have to. I assume responsibilities when they come my way, I don't try and avoid them, but on the other hand I don't go running after them. Maybe because I no longer have anyone to whom I can offer the dragon's head. Or because I don't think I'm worthy of them. Passive, shy, and modest: would you say that's an accurate self-portrait? I know you find it hard to believe, don't you? It doesn't matter. Anyway, I may be fantasizing by telling you all this in order to avoid going to the heart of the matter, to avoid analyzing the reasons why I like power and at the same time fail to go after it. But let's not get sidetracked into idle speculation.

What matters is, we survived the difficult period from 1956 through 1957 and came out with flying colors. What it means, I suppose, is that we're not people who thrive on routine and stability. Each troubled period through which we've gone has been marked by a new thrust forward, a renewed vitality, on the part of the magazine. That has been the case without exception, including once fifteen years later when I really had myself a time!

 XI

IN 1971, *L'Express* (which by then no longer had 50 employees but 500) once again became my sole responsibility. It was like taking a cure at the fountain of youth. This time, the enemy did not attack from without but from within. In fact, it was Jean-Jacques himself who had brought into the magazine the elements that almost did us in. He is generally a very good judge of people, but this time his insight failed him badly. He would have had to be a psychologist to foresee what was coming, and that he has always refused, claiming it tends to soften and weaken. And to some extent it's true; if you spend too much time trying to fathom why people act the way they do, you can drive yourself mad. I've been guilty of it myself.

Nonetheless, it's sometimes useful to understand why, in a given situation, a friend is going to turn into an enemy, to know that the only thing someone holds against you is the fact that you've helped him in life . . . It's as pointless to try to find the will to power concealed beneath this or that humiliation the person may have suffered as it is trying to figure out why self-sacrifice can lead to implacable hatred . . . It is useful to realize that you can go on for years not knowing who the people around you are, because you weigh on them. And if that weight remains, nothing will happen. But when it's removed, suddenly the coiled spring extends. The jumping jacks spring out of their boxes.

It is useful to know who will ineluctably betray you.

I know all these things. I've often felt I was at fault for not having tried to make Jean-Jacques see more clearly the serpents he was creating out of those seemingly innocent little lizards.

But logic, reason, and good sense were all on his side. When he decided to throw his hat into the ring and run for political office by accepting the chairmanship of the Radical Party, he thought he ought to resign from the management of his magazine and even from the board of directors of the holding company he had built up, which by now controlled several businesses.

Morally, his position was impeccable. As the major stockholder, he would continue to participate in the companies' profits. But what he was doing in a sense was giving his own magazine its independence. That too was beyond reproach, but here he was guilty of that candor which he at times displays by naming, as the head of the company which published *L'Express,* one of his so-called "friends" who didn't know the first thing about newspaper or magazine publishing.

I voiced some objections about the very principle of this decision. But my objections seemed motivated by a kind of pique at finding myself suddenly provided with a "president" who, at least legally, was my superior.

I was, as a matter of fact, in a state of ill humor, not very clear in my own mind as to my position or why I was objecting so strongly. I suspected that some of my reasons were ill-founded — and indeed some were — and I was afraid they were blinding me to reality. In short, I failed to carry the day. And besides, perhaps I didn't want to badly enough. I still wonder sometimes whether or not I wanted Jean-Jacques to learn a lesson.

His own responsibility is considerable, in that he was blind, and after he was elected he disappeared into Lorraine, as though he were invulnerable.

I have a share in the responsibility too. First, I saw that the goals of the magazine were going to be corrupted.

The board now consisted of five members, including me; Jean-Jacques' brother was chairman, and with the consent and agreement of Jean-Jacques, he had decided to have the company go public. *L'Express* formed part of this company, and the idea appalled me, thinking of it only in terms of the magazine. I expressed my opinion, but of course to no avail. At which point I should have resigned.

I almost did. *Vogue* in the United States offered me a post as its monthly columnist. I also wrote occasionally for the *New York Times* Sunday magazine. Combined, it would have been enough to live on. But I was afraid that my resignation would be misinterpreted. And there was something else: it's hard to resign from a magazine . . . it's a living organism — especially when you gave it birth . . . But the things I see clearly today were less obvious then.

In December 1970, though, I would have resigned if Jean-Jacques had lost financial control of the magazine and sold part of his shares, as everyone was urging him to, with tempting sums to back it up. Did he hesitate? Whether he did or not, the point is he finally refused. After which his brother decided to resign. The plan to make a public offering was adjourned *sine die*.

But one full year had elapsed since Jean-Jacques had cut his ties with the magazine. After he had won election as a *député* from Lorraine by a landslide, he decided to challenge Chaban-Delmas, the then Prime Minister, in his own bailiwick of Bordeaux, where a partial election was being held.

That tactical error ruined his political image. The person he had put in as president of the magazine, who was both a friend and a shareholder, and another to whom he had given an important position in the company, both turned against him. They exerted as much pressure as they could bring to bear on the brain trust of *L'Express* to force it to become daily more hostile to Jean-Jacques. A kind of court clique formed, whose avowed goal was to rid the company of Jean-Jacques and force him to sell his shares. Some members of the clique even went so far as to declare that they wanted to ban him from the pages of *L'Express* when, after several months, he wanted to start appearing in the magazine again.

It was this that brought on the crisis of June 1971. It was high time, because aside from any other considerations, the magazine was being badly run and was sinking into an attitude of respectable conformism with regard to the government. It was also becoming boring, therefore bad.

The confrontation between the clique and Jean-Jacques was rough. Thus it was that, from one day to the next, eight people — the president, the managing editor, and six senior editors — left, convinced that by arranging this sudden, collective departure they would sink *L'Express*. And once again I found myself with complete responsibility, with an editorial and administrative staff traumatized by the experience, the union nervous and upset — in short, a situation that was, frankly, hard to control. I was named president; I also took over the position of managing editor for a three-month period, and I somehow managed to pull it off. And that was that. At least materially. The other aspect is psychological, revealing both in what it says about Jean-Jacques' character — I'm sure he won't make the same mistake twice — and about French society.

— Can you describe this second aspect?

— I'm not sure Jean-Jacques will like it. But I'm going to

anyway, because, if my analysis is correct, it may have a general application.

Up until 1969, Jean-Jacques was always the *wunderkind* — the boy prodigy with a circle of adults applauding his every move. He had an entourage — he worked with men considerably older than he or who, in any case, were in a "paternal" position with respect to him. Protective. Either because they were well along in their own lives and careers or because they were able to experience certain things vicariously through him, they were pleased by his successes and saddened by his defeats.

Then, little by little, things began to change. First, there nonetheless did come a time when he was no longer thirty. He found himself exclusively surrounded by men of his own age whom he had deliberately chosen because of their brilliance, without being overly concerned whether or not they were also the most ambitious or greedy. Then he wrote *Défi américain,* which became a worldwide best seller, and that irritated a lot of people, starting with those who write political works whose sales only reach 5000. Or even 25,000. It irked those who say to themselves: "I could have written that. After all, I knew everything he said in the book." It galled those who would have loved to see their own names in headlines in the papers, or blowups of their faces in bookstore windows. Why not! It's childish, but that kind of envy is understandable. It's only stupid to think that someone else's success is what is keeping you from getting ahead. The success of *Défi américain* was nonetheless enormous, and in that sense unforgivable to the kind of people I've mentioned — and Jean-Jacques is not someone they easily forgive.

I'm convinced that he neither suspected nor wanted to suspect the existence of that envy, that sad passion he aroused in people . . . In any case, he opted to try and give a number of men of his own generation a chance, as though they too would, if and when it happened, take pleasure in contributing to his success . . . as faithful lieutenants.

What occurred was the direct opposite, of course. He was generous; they were humiliated by his generosity. It was no longer a circle of warm, attentive "fathers" but one consisting of potential rivals. They were men who were not happy to see him win the Lorraine election. What bothered them most was the aspect of personal exploit; if he had simply been swept into office on the coattails of some general-election landslide, it would have been different. And they of course were not willing to close ranks behind him after he made the mistake of challenging Chaban-Delmas in Bordeaux.

I'm not saying that mistake can't and shouldn't be judged harshly. That was how I judged it. It upset and hurt me. But it's one thing to judge, it's another to turn your back on someone to whom you have up till then claimed to be loyal. And it's still another thing suddenly to no longer see, in a person you know well, anything but negative traits, whereas a week or two before you couldn't stop singing his praises.

It's a defense mechanism, of course. People flee from the defeated the same way they tend to keep away from someone in mourning — that's the reason for mourning clothes, in fact: it shows that you have been touched by death, therefore that you're contagious, therefore to be avoided for a certain length of time. People want to keep away from the defeated person for fear that he may be contaminated, and since they know that their attitude is reprehensible, they immediately begin looking for reasons to justify it. What better reason is there than to convince oneself, and then convince others, that the defeated person was a pompous ass who has at last been deflated?

All politicians have experienced that reaction in times of

setbacks. After the events of May 1968, how many of the late Georges Pompidou's friends — and I'm referring to so-called close friends — suddenly did a disappearing act, repeating far and wide, "Poor Georges, he really didn't live up to our expectations, did he!" And later, after De Gaulle dismissed him as Premier, you can imagine what the exchanges were!

Or ask François Mitterrand what icy wastes he had to travel through during his postdefeat periods.

There is, in a literal sense, something "inhuman" about keeping the faith with a defeated person, at least as a reflex. It reveals all the more surely a strength of character.

Anyway, there were, orbiting around Jean-Jacques, a series of gentlemen-satellites whose reflexes can only be described as terribly banal: pleasure at seeing a rival receive his comeuppance; excuses proferred for taking such pleasure in his defeat; a self-righteous attitude by those who stomped on his prostrate figure rather than trying to help him up — if that help took no more than the form of giving him hell, yelling at him! — telling themselves it was for his own good, or that his defeat would serve some higher purpose. Have you ever noticed that the foulest deeds are inevitably committed with a good conscience, a holier-than-thou attitude? Men are strange creatures, incapable of open cynicism. When Hitler had his good friend Roehm assassinated, it was in order to save Germany.

To trample on someone who has stumbled, when that person is supposed to be a friend, is a daily occurrence, whether the people involved are little boys in the schoolyard or big boys who are ministers, high officials, or Nobel Prize winners. It's every man for himself, right? The whole thing is to realize it. It takes far too long to learn, especially since one is tempted for a long time to think that the motto really is "Every man for me." "Every man for himself" might have been Jean-Jacques' motto, with this one reservation: never did he fail to back up and help a friend who came to him in a difficult situation.

When the stakes involved in the "every man for himself" game happen to be a magazine that is both powerful and prosperous, a magazine that a certain number of important and well-heeled people would love to control, and who in gaining control would be wresting it away from a vocal and unruly opponent, well . . . how shall I describe the situation? . . . It's a thorny one, I can assure you.

What happens when two rival financial groups, both of which are powerful, fight for control of a bank or business is like a fencing match with the foils covered compared to the unholy desires aroused in the battle to gain control of a major magazine or newspaper — the sums involved, the low blows struck by one faction or the other. And compared to the vigilance with which the government places its own men wherever they effectively can, whose role it is to seduce, or at least to neutralize, journalists who are in a position to serve them. What is more, in France this kind of battle takes place within the confines of a very narrow caste and its periphery, that consisting of graduates of the National School of Business Administration,* a certain number of whom are either themselves ministers or work in high ministerial posts, while others hold key positions in banking and industry.

I'm not saying that there is any overall plot by the enarques to retain power — and I mean the real power — in France. It can even happen that these gentlemen do not always see eye-to-eye with one another, or that some among them are idle dreamers. But, as was the case in *The Jungle Book,* they say to one another: "We're blood brothers," and they always

---

* The French name of the school is *L'Ecole nationale d'administration* and its graduates are sometimes referred to as "enarques" after the first initials of the school: ENA. — *Translator.*

bail one another out. It's the freemasonery of our time, where a favor is never forgotten. A little while ago I mentioned Balzac's *Histoire des Treize*. There are more than thirteen of these men. There must be thirty, maybe as many as fifty . . . divided into rival clans, which are constantly shifting and changing, however. Everything in France passes through the hands of at least one of them. What makes them so powerful is that incredible concentration of power. A great many men, especially those at the head of big businesses, have come to realize that they have to use them, and they pay whatever the going rate is to their enarque personnel, after which things run smoothly. When you've seen how the system operates, you obviously prefer to have it for you rather than against you.

What *L'Express* was faced with between October of 1970 and June of 1971, was a collusion of money and political forces, fired by a number of personal ambitions. All of this took place, naturally, without the knowledge of the magazine's employees, and especially the journalists, who were only used, when the time was ripe, and were adroitly maneuvered. And at times it worked.

I'm hardly a saint, and I've seen a great many things in my life. In general I prefer to understand than to judge. I am in no way paranoid. I don't have any persecution complex; quite the contrary. Nor do I feel that I have been vested with some grandiose mission — such as having the independent press, for example — or with any other mission which my many opponents, whose numbers are constantly growing, are trying to thwart.

I can honestly say that I have never been caught up in this kind of closed system. And besides, when it happened, I wasn't the target. On the contrary, people thought they could use me against Jean-Jacques. In order to undermine eighteen years of confidence through eighteen months of intrigues, I would have had to be given more convincing proof than the ill humor of a difficult partner. He *was* difficult, and as I've said, I'm no saint. I'm tempted to fall back on Mauriac's words: I do know how to choose my nest. And I find certain odors offensive. I will say, weighing my words very carefully, that what transpired around *L'Express* between January and June 1971 was nauseating, both in its maneuvers and its goals. And very enlightening too. For me, surely, and I am sure for Jean-Jacques. For me it was an eye-opening experience: suddenly I understood what happens when you suddenly learn power has changed hands in the Kremlin. Or in China. When you learn that Mao had disappeared from the scene, and then is back. Or that his dearly beloved comrade-in-arms and friend, Lin Piao, had purely and simply been plotting to get rid of him and toss him over the Great Wall of China, but it was he who ended up dead in the wilds of Mongolia . . . In short, all things being equal, it's the old, classic, eternal struggle for power, wherever power happens to be. Can I pursue the comparison? Yes, because it's a way of making myself understood. Mao returned, Lin and his clique were ousted, and Chou En-lai sends you his best. Translate that any way you want to.

After a period I can only describe as turbulent, the magazine took a valiant leap forward. And the key positions on the magazine are now once again held by the people who made it, with all their qualities and shortcomings.

Since no newspaper or magazine can ever stop, no matter what happens, I spent several rough weeks following the ouster of Lin Piao and his terrified clique. Since then, they've obviously all been welcomed back into the bosoms of their own families.

But these weeks were also in a way a kind of liberation. I would actually have counted them among the happiest of my life had they not coincided with the agony and death of someone I loved, a man who, with all the remaining strength at his command, helped in that struggle for liberation, and helped me.

His name was Jacques Boetsch. He was forty-two. He was dying of cancer and he knew it. He had been the deputy editor-in-chief for the preceding three years, and it was he who single-handedly had put together the foreign-affairs section of the magazine. Then, in May of 1970 he had urgently requested that I send him to the United States as our permanent correspondent there. Although our relations were close, he didn't tell me why he wanted to be transferred. His explanations were vague, but I didn't question his motives. Much later, I learned that he saw or sensed what was coming at *L'Express* and didn't want to be mixed up in it in any way.

Three months after he arrived in Washington, he learned, in keeping with the American method of medical candor, that the slight pain he had had in his jaw was cancer. Inoperable cancer at age forty-one. Madly in love with his young wife. Three children, the youngest of which was a little girl, an infant. A man ambitious in the best sense of the term. And then death took him by the hand. And suddenly he was aware of it.

From the depth of the pain I felt when I learned the news, which still remains with me to this day when I think about it, I realize how close we had become through working together . . . Work is a curious relationship, one in which nothing or almost nothing personal may ever enter, and yet paradoxically deep feelings can sometimes evolve out of it. Sometimes, when we had been working late into the night, I would look at his bullish head and his lack of color, and I would think a little selfishly that I too was tired and then some, that I was even more in need of fresh air and sunlight than he, but I would also say to myself that there must be something wrong with a man who's only forty-one and looks like that just because he's a few hours underslept. I thought he must be living a very unhealthy life. But those are things you think about but rarely mention.

The only sign of affection he gave me was that when he came into my office he always left something behind: his pipe, or a piece of paper, or his pen. Therefore, he wanted to come back. He was one of those who could always walk into my office without my feeling a trace of irritation or boredom.

Our mutual affection for each other was doubtless great, but we may never have discovered it had it not been for that cancer . . . That life now was ebbing, that dark life in which he dwelled, knowing that a sword was hanging over him held by the thinnest of threads . . . That fear he dominated day after day, the big, black voids out of which he constantly climbed . . . It's beautiful, a man battling to maintain his dignity, and completely tragic. He wanted everything within him and around him to be esthetic, including his death.

From the States, where he was still working as our correspondent, he wrote me a great deal. And I answered him. That's a whole other kind of relation, one carried on by correspondence . . . Most people do a better job at epistolary relationships. I do, anyway.

And then, in May of '71, he came home for good, to die in France. He didn't know how much time the "little animal," as he used to call it, was giving him. There were times, of course, when he hoped for a long remission through some operation, as there were others when he knew how pitifully numbered his days were. He had no sooner returned to Paris — undergoing various treatments, filled with cortisone, pale, breathing with great difficulty — than the crisis he had been anticipating and whose nature he immediately grasped, broke out at *L'Express*.

He lived in the suburb of Villejuif, and as soon as trouble

started he came to the magazine. And there, very simply, day after day, he worked, superbly as only he knew how. Coughing more and more, his breathing increasingly labored, covered with cold sweat . . . He had got into the habit of embracing me when he arrived at work each morning. No one could have wanted to embrace that stricken man, and I knew that he was doing it because he was on the lookout for the day, the moment in time when the least hesitation . . .

That was the only thing I was able to give him — an affectionate response to that embrace — in exchange for what he gave me in return, which was priceless. On the eve of his departure forever into darkness, and fully aware of it, in that living limbo beyond hope and expectation, Jacques Boetsch, whom ultimately I knew only slightly and whom everyone judged to be a man of complete honesty, made up his mind that morally I was right.

Having come to that conclusion, he threw himself into my corner with all the waning strength at his command. And then one evening he came into my office and said to me: "I'm sorry, but I can't come in tomorrow . . . In fact, I don't think I can come to work anymore . . ." And I answered him: "I wish you would. With all my heart I wish you would . . ." And he said: "I'll try. I promise you I'll try." But he couldn't. He no longer had the strength.

Those last days in a man's life are heavier, more compacted, more difficult to bear than I can describe, those last days of a young, perfectly lucid man in full possession of all his intellectual faculties, that moment when you know that you'll no longer see that face, no longer hear that voice, when a bond between two human beings, made up of warmth and friendship and need, is about to be cut forever. Everything becomes precious, unique . . . No more commonplace or perfunctory words, because they may be the last to be heard. He was so painfully aware of that that he solved it by simply omitting the verbal niceties, the idle chatter that is part and parcel of everyday conversation. He limited his words to those things he had a right to say, things that were serious, and sometimes frightening . . .

In the welter of my existence at the time, and the overriding necessity to get the magazine out, it was difficult to go and see him every day. But perhaps even more important in the priority of things was the need to help Jacques Boetsch to die, since the brief moments I managed to spend with him gave him real comfort, his wife used to tell me, and eased his pain.

One day in August it was all over. And there was a gaping hole in my heart.

Later this hole became very disconcerting. I began to think that I was the person described by some Chinese philosopher, I forget which, who one morning goes to his doctor and says: "I'm sick. I'm no longer interested in my personal or business affairs, I no longer look at my garden, it even happens that my children don't interest me anymore. Doctor, I'm ill . . ." The doctor takes him over to the window and places him against the light, then says: "No you're not. I can see very clearly the seven holes in your heart. Six of them are pierced; the seventh is half-pierced. All you have to do is give up the idea that you're ill."

Holes: I have several in my heart. Like all the men and women my age, no doubt. Maybe a few more, I don't know. But I'd be hard-pressed to know whether there's much room left for any more. Or whether, by now, the last hole is half pierced. But what in the world am I telling you?

I was starting to tell you . . . what in fact was it we were talking about? Tell me, please, where you want me to pick up.

 XII

— I'D LIKE TO CLARIFY a few points. I think it's safe to say that the emergence of *L'Express* as an important periodical made a considerable impact on French society. Looking back, how do you account for it? And what are your feelings about that period?

— I think I've explained that to you in another way. I think that *L'Express* was the first magazine to bring together what you might term a doctrine — if that word didn't have such rigid overtones — and a journalistic technique capable of making it lively and sensitive to the needs and mood of the times, together with a politician who personified that doctrine. It was the combination of the three, the multiplication of each of the factors by the other two, that constituted the real originality of the magazine. Plus the climate of independence and irreverence in which it all took place, the irreverence being inseparable from the independence, since that is what constitutes freedom of thought and expression. That is the rarest thing of all, and the most difficult to retain, believe me, because it frightens people so. How many people are there who only feel comfortable behind bars, and who from their self-made cells shout, "Freedom! Freedom!"

There was another factor too: *L'Express* came into being at a time when a new generation was coming of age and clamoring for its place in society at the same time as it was manifesting its desire to change it.

— In that respect, can we make a comparison with what is going on today?

— Yes and no. One can compare the advent of youth, searching for its place in the sun, which is the eternal movement of each rising generation. But today's youth is different from those who came of age in the '50s, first because the war had affected the birth rate so that there were many fewer young people coming of age in the '50s than there are today, and they were less demanding, less . . . imperialist. And also because those who were between eighteen and thirty in 1953 had gone through the war and the Occupation. To be specific, unhappiness was not fashionable in the '50s. When you are just emerging from . . . France was like some enormous, frozen body in which the blood was beginning to circulate again.

"France and its Future" was the theme of a forum that we organized to celebrate the first anniversary of *L'Express* in May of '54. Through announcements in the magazine, we invited the students of all the major universities to join us for dinner — each student had to pay for his own, of course — and postdinner debate. More than three hundred showed up.

The tables were very well arranged, the dinner was decent enough. The microphones were working. It was a memorable evening, taking into account the fervor of those posing questions and the quality of the people fielding them: François Mauriac, Robert Schuman, Louis Armand, and Mendès-France . . .

Debates such as these can be disastrous when men put on the same old show they've done a hundred times — a show in which they themselves no longer believe, when their speeches are threadbare and weary. That night there was fervor, conviction, and a sense of the new. It was an electrifying occasion. Including the laughter that accompanied Mauriac's rejoinders — Mauriac who was literally shaking in his boots before dinner, because he had never taken part in a question-and-answer period before and also because he felt himself to be at a terrible disadvantage because of the problem he had with his voice. He was shaking, but he came, as a stouthearted soldier ready to join the fray, and he was brilliant. His initial interlocutor began to take him roundly to task because of his Christianity. Mauriac's opening words, in replying, were: "My dear, dear brother . . ." The day was his.

Mendès-France was at his best. Louis Armand, the future president of Euratom,* displayed qualities of warmth, dynamism, and optimism rare for France. Robert Schuman, finally, who was then Foreign Minister, the man referred to as the Father of Europe, made up for any lack of personal charisma by a generous dose of candor. He was the very spectacle of faith, of the man wholly devoted to the notion of European unity. I remember the ringing conclusion of his speech: "I couldn't care less whether it comes to pass with us, the elders, or even in spite of us. But it has to come to pass, and it will."

To hear him talk, there could be no doubt that it would. Robert Schuman was very close to us at *L'Express*. He was one of those who agreed to contribute regularly to the section of the magazine we called "Open Forum" in which he answered questions posed by readers.

— You liked stars, didn't you?

— I could respond by telling you that we enjoyed making stars, and that we did fairly well in that department. But why do you think people become "stars," as you put it, at

* European Atomic Community. — *Translator.*

least in the area we're talking about? Did it ever occur to you that it might be because they have something to say and the talent with which to say it? So when you're publishing a magazine, which has to make an immediate impact, which can be one step ahead of people's thinking but not five—it is indeed better to open your columns to people whose authority is impressive. It was better to open the pages to the most famous of the young French philosophers, Maurice Merleau-Ponty, and the High Commissioner of Atomic Energy, Francis Perrin, than . . . But I don't feel like picking a quarrel.

At the dinner we were talking about, someone suddenly stood up in the room and with a steady voice said: "I'm an agitator." He was also underground. It was Mohammad Masmoudi. In a way that was harsh and unsettling, he talked about his struggle for the independence of Tunisia.

As I talk to you, I'm trying to reflect honestly and sort out what twenty years after that dinner makes me, us, different today from what we were then, and what makes us similar, plowing the same furrow. There is the magazine itself, the men involved with it, and me.

The magazine: that evening we didn't have enough money to pay a decent commercial photographer. The photographer who did come, a top-notch American named Kammerman, worked for us because he liked us and what we stood for. To-day, *L'Express* is a powerful magazine, known throughout the world — we distribute 100,000 copies outside of France. And it's prosperous. Neither one of those factors ought to blind us to the vulnerability of all periodicals, especially when they loosen their grip. But in any event, it's a magazine in good shape. So much for the material aspect.

The role, the function, the vocation: we're right on course. If you had asked me in the beginning of 1971 I would have told you, at least confidentially, that *L'Express* was founder-ing. Today, that's no longer true. It's back on course.

Over a period of two decades, it has changed, obviously. But then so has French society. Considerably. And the place France occupies in the world. Think for a moment that during these twenty years we've seen de-Stalinization, decolonization, the creation of the Common Market, the Sino-Soviet split, the end of the bipolar world, with the United States on one side and the Soviet Union on the other. Think that within that short space of time the first Sputnik was launched, no bigger than an oversized balloon, and the first man has walked on the moon. The meteoric rise of John F. Kennedy, cut off so prematurely. The victorious revolution in Cuba and the coming of Castro. The return and departure of De Gaulle, with its most obvious legacy: a stronger president than under the Fourth Republic. The tragic involvement of the United States in Vietnam, and the incredible — and hopefully fruitful — upheaval it produced in American society, which virtually overnight had to readjust its thinking and realize it no longer represented all the wealth and power in the world. It was an evolution that would have occurred in any case, but perhaps, without Vietnam, much less quickly. Think of the youth rebellion that occurred in the industrialized countries, a youth that has never known either poverty or war and yet is in search of its own combat. Think that the French standard of living has more than doubled in the past two decades, and imagine the acceleration this has brought to the middle classes. Remember how we have seen, and are still witnessing, their desire to accede to the amenities generally associated with a "proper bourgeois life-style" but how, as they achieve it, they run into the problem of numbers. Because as soon as you have numbers you no longer have luxury, that is privileges, and even if you're driving a Rolls Royce a lot of good it does you if you find yourself at the tail end of a ten-mile traffic jam; and, with everyone off on vacation the major cities shut down for the entire month of August; and someone with a Bachelor's or Master's degree in sociology or literature earns less, since there are tens of thousands of them, than a plumber, since there are too few plumbers . . .

I remember a passage from Nietzsche, perhaps prophetic, in which he said: "There will come a time when workers will live the way the bourgeois are living today. Above will live the superior caste, which will be notable for its lack of needs. Since it will possess power, it will be simpler and poorer." Perhaps we're not all that far away from the fulfillment of that prophecy.

And there is another thing, as the same gentleman also put it: God is dead. Killed. But am I mistaken? Today we're only beginning to realize that by killing God we're killing the devil. And to the need for transcendence there corresponds the need to localize Evil, which results in little girls going off to rob some fancy shop or department store, an Evil which gives youth the illusion that they are practicing fraternity. And they do practice it, often in a touching way. But what enables them to? The fact that they band together against a common enemy: adults, society, capitalism; almost anything will do.

It's a fact that people are uncomfortable in the world we live in. They are worried and ridden with anxiety, and the most fragile, as is true in any troubled times, are capable of grasping at any branch extended to them, to shift with any change in the wind. It's also a fact that the church, after having been the whore of the Right, might be turning into the whore of the Left, and that it no longer is an element of internal solidity but on the contrary tends to add to the confusion.

All that happened in the space of a mere twenty years, and I'm sure there's much I've forgotten.

The people generally referred to as "intellectuals" are also in a state of disarray — not that there's any reason they should be the exceptions to the rule of confusion prevailing in the world. Actually, they are often among the first to flounder. During the '50s, one could find enough things in common among Mauriac, Camus, Merleau-Ponty, Sartre, and even Malraux so that they could all contribute to *L'Express.* If Camus and Merleau-Ponty were alive today they would both be in their early sixties. What they would be or what causes they would espouse I have no idea. But take the younger philosophers and thinkers: Foucault, Deleuze, Althusser . . .* I may be blind, but I just don't see how their research and theories can have any meaningful application to practical politics, at least for the time being. I have no idea whether or not they are ahead of their times or out of step with them, whether they have discovered the truth or are raving maniacs: that's really not the point. The point is, they are "elsewhere."

At the time of the '58 referendum, for example, it was perfectly normal for us to ask Sartre to write an article for the magazine, and it was just as normal for Sartre to write it. And what he wrote did not fall on deaf ears. Sartre was in Rome, I remember, and Jean-Jacques went down to talk to him about writing the piece. He sent us a torrent, as he usually did, counting on Simone de Beauvoir to edit the text. Have you ever seen one of Sartre's manuscripts? His hand-writing is small and very legible. He begins at the top of the page and he fills up all the lines — he uses lined notebook paper — but as soon as he has to cross something out, he starts a new page.

It was a very strongly and beautifully articulated piece.

* Michel Foucault, author of *Les Mots et les Choses,* and Gilles Deleuze, coauthor of *L'anti-oedipe,* are the two French philosophers who are most influential among young people. Louis Althusser, an older Marxist philosopher who teaches at the Ecole Normale Supérieure, is also very highly considered. — *Translator.*

Today, everything Sartre writes interests me in relation to his past, his career, his self-hatred . . . When he writes for the extreme-Leftist *La Cause du Peuple* it's . . . touching. He is a touching person, who can be forgiven for virtually everything because he's generous. Whenever he's been wrong, he's been generously wrong. But it's also true that, as Mauriac used to say, he's inoffensive. Mauriac could indeed be devastating. And Sartre, indeed, has become inoffensive.

In any case, he too is "elsewhere," in a realm which is not that of Foucault, as Foucault's is not Althusser's, which is not Deleuze's, which is not Lacan's, which is not . . . etc. All of which may well be a subject of great interest to many people, and in fact is of great interest to me. But it in no way falls within the pale of journalism, even of the most sophisticated sort, except perhaps to take note of its existence. I will go further: never has the intellectual ghetto been more hermetic than it has since the intellectuals tried to speak to the people.

In this confusion, as I was saying, *L'Express* generally managed to steer a steady course. What exactly does that mean? It means first of all that one should never allow one's intelligence to be intimidated by the various intellectual terrorisms that hold sway for a time and then give way to the next, or that prevail simultaneously and contradictorily, in those periods of history when basic issues are being re-examined. *L'Express* remained open to all the various currents of thought without allowing itself to succumb to any one. Further, we do not loathe modern society, under the pretense that in today's world you die from traffic accidents rather than from tuberculosis or typhoid as in times past, or because today everybody and his brother have access to places where only the happy few could once have trod.

Everything that the wave of economism has wrought since the end of the war, that is the extraordinary increase of consumer goods in all areas, has produced its fair share of positive results, even if the wave was often rough and, in particular, had some devastating effects on the French countryside. Today, the problem is how to control the economy and the process of expansion, not how to destroy them.

Ever since religion lost its sway over men, their goal has been to find happiness. Bravo! All we ask is not to be told that happiness consists of dunghills, infant mortality, oil lamps, and potato-picking by hand, or that the assembly-line process becomes pleasurable as soon as it ceases to benefit private capitalism and is made to benefit state capitalism.

No one is questioning anyone's right to believe in the collectivization of the economy, that is in state capitalism as opposed to private capitalism modified and controlled by government taxation. But I remain skeptical on the question of whether the drawbacks of state capitalism more than compensate for its advantages, at least in an industrial society. But at the very most such comparisons would have to be limited to technical discussions, even when such elements as work relationships and human relationships, or the possibility of changing them appreciably, are included.

Progress. Let's talk about progress. What is it today? What will it be in the future? Moot questions, no doubt. Will it consist of reducing the amount of productive, remunerated work-time, that is, will people be paid, as it were, both for x hours of mechanical work-time and for an ever-increasing number of hours of free-time? Or will it consist of making activities more interesting by the very fact that each person will be responsible for organizing his own free time and will himself determine his own goals?

I must confess that I myself have trouble understanding how, on the one hand, you can call for personal responsibility on all levels, believe that it is both good and necessary to help bring about "de-alienation" — it's terrible to have to resort to that vocabulary, but I too have been corrupted, contaminated — and that then on the other hand want to transfer everything to the state, every initiative, which is to say "de-responsibilize," if I may coin a term.

There, it seems to me, lies an obvious contradiction. What I have as much trouble understanding are the people who say, "I'm all for capitalism, Swedish style. That's the road to take, for an industrialized country. But how can we expect to apply it to the French?" I can only describe French politicians' attitude toward their constituents as unhealthy. Back in 1830, La Fayette also used to say that the American Republic was, of course, the ideal system of government, and how much he would have liked to be president under such a system, and there he was, at the Paris Hotel de Ville, waiting for what? . . . For the French to become mature! Thanks to which they ended up with Louis-Philippe. And then 1848, and everything that ensued. Today, there are those who think that the French are not mature enough to be given television programming which is responsible instead of one that makes fun of them, and there are others who think that the French aren't mature enough to understand that nationalization of some major French bank will not insure their receiving a pension at sixty.

L'Express's political position is the same today as it was in '53. Then it asked its readers to believe that the happiness and future of the French did not reside in the conservation of its colonial empire; it asked its readers to trace and then follow the real means of progress.

The motivating factor for progress is generally and widely accepted, is it not? It's the same as it has always been since time immemorial, since the first man refused to resign himself to his fate or his condition. The ways of progress are many and open to endless discussion. I say let's discuss them. But let's not turn our backs on them under the pretense that "the

French aren't mature" . . . There is one route which *L'Express* has always faithfully and assiduously followed: the European route.

— And yet Mendès-France was not systematically pro-European!

— Unhappily, I have to admit that on this point he did not have a very clearly defined policy. In 1953, I had invited Mendès-France and former premier Antoine Pinay to lunch at my house. Also present was Hervé Alphand, who perhaps has had only one real conviction in his life, but that one was as solid as lead: Europe. And we persuaded both men — Pinay and Mendès-France — to sign a joint declaration about European unity. The text was written, both of them had signed it, the type was set, with each of their signatures at the bottom of what was scheduled to be a double-page spread of the issue that was to appear the following Saturday. Where the leak happened, I still don't know, but, the press proof of that two-page spread somehow ended up in the hands of the Communist leader Jacques Duclos, who handed it around to the members of the National Assembly, accompanied by remarks you can easily imagine. Pinay got scared and retracted his declaration. The whole thing was a fiasco.

When Mendès-France came to power the following year, his first month was fully occupied with the Indochina negotiations, of course, since he had said on taking office that he would resign if he was unsuccessful.

Did you ever hear the story about the *petits-suisses?* No? I told you I'd refrain from telling you any anecdotes, but . . . Anyway, it occurred during the delicate and agonizing negotiations at Geneva, the day when Chou En-lai lunched with Mendès-France. Among the dishes served were *petits-suisses.* Chou En-lai had probably never seen them before. In any case, he started to eat his without removing the paper. Mendès-France shot some rather frantic and eloquent glances at the people at the other tables. And, imperturbably, Mendès-France and all his luncheon guests, ate their *petits-suisses* paper and all, in order not to hurt Chou En-lai.

Following Geneva, the French parliament voted unanimously to ratify the agreement. Mendès-France is a man with great powers of concentration, but also someone who can't concentrate on two things at once. And unfortunately, there were a great many pressing items on the political agenda.

Among them was the so-called European Defense Community — known as EDC — whose purpose was to integrate into one European army the various armies of France, Germany, Italy, Holland, and Belgium. It was like a running sore in French political life, an abscess that no one dared lance. You may recall that at the time the United States backed the EDC, while the Soviet Union was against it. That meant that the French Communists were opposed to it, while the Christian-Democrats and the Socialists were all for it.

No previous government had risked its political life by bringing the matter before the French parliament. Mendès decided he was going to settle the issue once and for all. As for his personal feelings on the subject, I still think that he never had any strong convictions except that he would have liked to see Great Britain included. And that is where his circle of political intimates played a role. His close friend and intimate adviser was his private secretary, Georges Boris, who was fanatically opposed to the concept of European unity. So was Mendès' economic adviser, Simon Nora. How he became Mendès' economic adviser is a whole other story, and one worth relating for a number of reasons.

The man whom Mendès had originally decided to appoint to this post was Gabriel Ardant. A young woman who was one of our colleagues on *L'Express,* whom we had "loaned" to Mendès-France, learned of his choice and alerted Jean-Jacques. She happened to be in love with Simon Nora, whom she had met at *L'Express* and whom, in fact, she later married. Motivated by a combination of youthful zeal and friendship, Jean-Jacques mounted his white horse and wrote to Mendès-France: "If you don't take on Nora, I must conclude that you are acting contrary to your own best interests as well as the best interests of your honor and government. In which case, to my great regret, I must inform you that I shall no longer be able to work with you."

Looking back from the vantage point of the present, when Jean-Jacques and Simon Nora have become political opponents, it's difficult to imagine or describe the relationship between them as young men. And their relations with Mendès-France, whom we called by the code name of "Augustin" because of our fear of telephone taps. They were a little like two sons of the same father, inseparable, lunching together, dining together, spending their weekends and vacations together . . . Simon never ceased remaking the world over in his own image, with fifty-five minutes of brilliant theorizing followed by five minutes of raving to top it off; Jean-Jacques on the contrary, stubbornly sticking to the concrete, the factual . . . But still they were very close. It's difficult to imagine the inventiveness, the gaiety, the concrete results that emanated from their teamwork. And the mutual warmth of our friendship. What no woman could have ever accomplished politics did, which was to break up that friendship — and I can't help but be saddened by it.

In any event, in 1954 Simon Nora joined Mendès' cabinet, and the very mention of the initials EDC drove him wild. It had the same effect on him as it had on Michel Debré, who knew every article of the project by heart and who, as soon as he heard anyone timidly express a favorable opinion regarding EDC, would shout: "What! But just let me quote article 14 of paragraph 3 . . ."

Simon Nora carried around in his pocket a series of photographs showing the horribly mutilated faces of his former comrades-in-arms, killed by the Germans in the Vercors region. One day when someone from the German embassy, the first secretary as I recall, called him on the phone, Nora said to him: "I do not speak to Germans!" To which his caller responded: "I fully understand, sir. My entire family was wiped out at Auschwitz."

What was more, at the time Simon Nora was a great admirer of the methods employed in the Soviet Union. Like a great many people who had been in the Resistance, he came out of the war very close to the Communists. He exerted as much pressure as he could to have Mendès-France present the EDC to the French parliament so that it would be rejected.

Among the partisans of the European Community in Mendès-France's entourage were Gaston Defferre and François Mitterrand, but in fact neither of them had a great deal of real influence on him.

And then there was Servan-Schreiber. In this affair his guilt was one of omission, of not really putting his heart into it. It's a reproach one can rarely level at him. He was attached to the notion of a unified Europe, he never doubted the necessity of building a politically unified Europe, but in this one instance the arguments of those opposed to EDC made an impact on him. He conceded that the EDC was perhaps not the best way to begin the unification of Europe, since it was the area where sensitivities were most acute. He wanted England to participate. Like Mendès-France, he was anxious for the French parliament, which literally paralyzed French political life, to be eliminated in one way or another. But he didn't ponder his decision at any great length, and in the end lost interest in the subject so much that he went to the mountains for a vacation. But before he went, a rather extraordinary scene occurred which had historic repercussions.

Trying to find some way to resolve the situation, Jean-Jacques asked Mendès-France: "Since it's England's absence that annoys you in this whole EDC affair, would you be satisfied by its symbolic presence?" Mendès-France said that he would. At which point Jean-Jacques suggested that he go directly to Churchill and ask him pointblank.

That conversation took place on August 16 or 17, 1954. Before leaving for the six-power meeting on the EDC in Brussels, Mendès-France took a quick trip to Chartwell to see Churchill. Later, Churchill confided to his doctor, Lord Moran, the following story, which the good doctor passed on for posterity. "Mendès-France asked if he could come to Chartwell to see me. I'd like that . . . I shall say terrible things to him — of course within the limits of hospitality. I shall arrange for a guard of honour at the airfield. I shall wrap up what I am going to say in a lot of flattery. I shall tell him that the world is not going to be ruled by the French Chamber. I shall warn him that if the Chamber rejects EDC France will be alone in the world. I shall tell him bluntly that we shall go on without them. Never was such obstinacy founded on such impotence."

Mendès-France arrived at Chartwell, and you can imagine his feelings — for a veteran of the war, to be on English soil, with Winston Churchill . . . The elder statesman received him, together with Anthony Eden. The conversation started all right. But when finally Mendès-France said to Churchill, "Give me a regiment, just one British regiment, and I'll support the EDC," he was greeted with silence. A long silence. And then he saw that Churchill had fallen asleep. He was already on the verge of senility. Everyone knew it, but no one dared oust him from office.

It is impossible to say what might have happened if a Churchill in full possession of his faculties had given that regiment. Nor can I even speculate about the dangers that the

EDC might have caused us, or the repercussions it might have had in international affairs.

But I think that on the domestic front, Mendès-France underestimated the forces which the defeat of the EDC would unleash against him in the French parliament. The irreducible hatred of both the Christian-Democrats and the M.R.P. dates from that time, and at roughly the same time the Americans began to think of him as some sort of Communist harbinger, an opinion which must have been the final straw for a man whom the Communists have always feared and detested, even when they happened to vote for him.

In those days the classical line of political analysis went something like this: you could win over a goodly portion of the Communist voters to a non-Marxist Left, provided that this new Left was active, dynamic, up-to-date, and that the potential electorate had a real feeling that its interests were been represented and defended.

The fact remains, to come back to the question of European unity, that later on, as a member of the National Assembly, Mendès-France voted against the Common Market. And it's also a fact that *L'Express* refused to back him on that stand. In 1956, when Jean-Jacques was in Algeria, I had a serious altercation with Georges Boris because I had published in the magazine, simply because it expressed my deepest convictions, a pro-European article by Gaston Defferre. We had a violent, very violent, argument over it.

As you can see, therefore, I don't put faithfulness to Mendès-France's early convictions above everything else. If those convictions turn out to be stupid, if we discover later on that they were ill-founded, I prefer frankly to come out and say so! But it's a fact that Jean-Jacques has remained faithful and steadfast, as have I. Even unto the subtleties that separate us.

— How would you describe those subtleties?

— Very generally, I would say that I remain more skeptical than he about the possibilities of politics being able effectively to change the world. Like Valéry, I believe that
Ampère and electricity were much more important than
Lenin. I'm much more susceptible to things that can alter
human relations — relations of authority, the nature of
power that some people wield over others — than I am to the
efficiency of any economic plan. I'm resigned to capitalism
as the lesser evil, although I don't like it. Anyway, however
adaptable I am to any and all evolution, I react to the painful
aspects of change more than Jean-Jacques does; I would say
that he was born to welcome "future-shock" easily and fear-
lessly. I don't think he knows that the world began just a
few years before his arrival in it.

What else? I don't know. In any event, all that's not very
interesting, is it? It would only be interesting if it contained
the germs of some deep conflict . . . One never knows, but
I don't think it does. Whenever we become irritated or exasperated with each other, it's always on a superficial level.

 XIII

LET'S TALK instead of the others . . . Where are they now, twenty years later? The political agitator I mentioned, Masmoudi, is today Foreign Minister of Tunisia, very close to Bourguiba. He's one of the most intelligent and shrewdest political minds of the time. Power has neither deadened nor corrupted him.

Although they're very different in many ways, Bourguiba himself reminds me of Ho Chi Minh, one of those men who is both impassioned and wise, sincere and crafty, who at a certain time in history incarnates the soul of a people in search of its identity and bears the destiny of a whole people on his shoulders.

A little while ago I mentioned a dinner with Bourguiba and Servan-Schreiber where the two had talked politics, the dinner Mauriac wrote about in his column. I was there that evening too. It was as I recall October 1954. Bourguiba had been taken from the island to which the French had deported him and brought to a villa just outside Paris, where he was placed under house arrest. It was there we went to see him. He was living in real poverty. The French had kept him imprisoned for twelve years, and among other things the long term had ruined his teeth.

Since Mendès-France, who was then Premier, had given him his word and promised domestic autonomy for Tunisia, Bourguiba had put his authority and prestige with his people on the line and publicly stated that he believed that word would be kept. But three months had gone by, and Bourguiba knew a thing or two about how previous French statesmen had failed to keep their word, so he was concerned about whether Mendès-France might not also be paralyzed politically.

In Tunisia itself, all the French who occupied the key administrative positions of colonial government wouldn't even hear of the notion of domestic autonomy. What was more, the Arab terrorists were stepping up their attacks, which provided grounds for political repression. And meanwhile, as all this was going on, Bourguiba was going stir crazy under the house arrest, to which he had agreed, suffering the martyrdom of doing nothing.

Although he has enormous self-control, his deep blue eyes were literally flashing — and if that sounds like the usual cliché, I can verify that for once I really saw it. Stubbornly, Jean-Jacques continued to defend what Mendès was doing. And then at one point Bourguiba shouted: "I'm warning you, all this will end up in bloodshed, bloodshed!"

I saw Mauriac withdrawing into himself, as only he knew how to. Bloodshed! This upper-bourgeois gentleman from Bordeaux, this exquisitely well-bred Nobel-Prize winner — what in the world was he doing here in this sinister house, seated in front of a plate of cold spaghetti, while across from him a Tunisian was ranting and raving? . . .

Late at night, in the car taking us back to Paris, we all sat without saying a word. And then, as always, Mauriac wrote what had to be written, gave expression to what each of us was thinking: that in North Africa, France was in the process of either winning everything or losing everything. There was no half way. And of course Mendès-France kept his word. But what he won, others later on took over and undid, at the tremendous cost we all know.

Maybe that's the legacy of Mendès-France: the man who kept his word. And he keeps it because he doesn't make a commitment simply to win votes, saying to himself, "Later on, we'll see . . ." What is especially admirable in the man is the fact that he is willing to wager on the intelligence of the person he's talking to — and on that of the voter — rather than playing on his credulity.

— You carefully refrain from offering the interpretation of that attitude that has often been given: the failure syndrome.

— What does that mean, "failure syndrome," in everyday language? Actually, let's not try to define it. What people mean, when they say it, is that the person they're referring to is unconsciously looking for failure rather than success and that he therefore creates conditions conducive to failure for any of a number of reasons: either some deep-rooted desire to punish himself, or to be able to complain later on about what a terrible victim of fate he was, etc., etc. That's it, no?

Let's not go into any kitchen psychoanalysis. But simply judging from the facts, from what we as observers can see, Mendès-France's political efforts certainly don't fall into that category, do they? I would even say they reveal the opposite. His entire career seems to suggest that he cannot bear the notion, the perspective, of failure. For him, failure seems to be something that endangers his inner economy, upsets his psychological balance. Therefore, whenever he does get involved, when he does act, he acts superbly. But it is the involvement which is made difficult, which is deferred, feared at the same time it is desired, which he may ultimately be forced into by outside circumstances, by someone, some group, on whom, if the commitment fails, he can lay the blame. Blame vis-à-vis himself, of course: it is not a question of finding a scapegoat. It's a matter of there being some third party readily available to spare him, in his heart of hearts, from being in danger.

Who is Mendès-France?

He's the cloth merchant's son who was a brilliant student and who, at the age of twenty, had already published a monograph on "the Poincaré experiment." His broken nose stems from fistfights in the Latin Quarter against Rightist students. He got involved in politics while he was still very young: he was elected to the Assembly at the age of twenty-five. In 1938, at the age of thirty-one, he was an undersecretary of State in the Treasury Department in Léon Blum's government. During the war he escaped from a French prison and joined the air corps. He turned down offers to join the government-in-exile, preferring to remain in combat, until De Gaulle persuaded him to join the provisional government in Algiers.

When he resigned from De Gaulle's postwar government in 1946, it was because De Gaulle chose not to follow his advice and impose some very harsh financial measures which the times required. None of that bespeaks a man tempted by failure. Mendès-France, moreover, is fully aware of his capabilities, and deeply desired power.

But what happens when he is on the verge of attaining it? There exists a little-known text which is highly revealing: it is the transcription, recorded in 1953, of conversations he had with the then President of the Republic, Vincent Auriol, when Auriol was holding discussions with Mendès about his forming a new government. Unbeknownst to his visitors, Auriol had a hidden tape recorder in his office. Thus it was that the following text, which was discovered among his personal archives, has come down to us:

Thursday, May 29, 1953

Received Mendès-France.

V.A.: I charge you with forming a new government, after you have determined whether you can accept the office.

P.M.-F.: For years I've been working toward the goal of moving France in a new direction, and if I do say so myself I've done so with courage [. . .] I have the impression that up till now you have not known how to use to best account what it is I have to offer [. . .] I don't want to form a government like all the others that have ended up in crises. I would therefore like to go to work under the best conditions possible [. . .]

V.A.: It will be too late.

P.M.-F.: Well then, if it's too late, it won't be my fault [. . .] Can't you really give me a few days? This way, you'll break my back before I start.

V.A.: That's the third time you've used that expression [. . .]

P.M.-F.: I'm trying to tell you that I'll be a candidate when the time is ripe.

A further conversation:

Friday, May 30, 1953

P.M.-F.: I accept, with a great deal of emotion I accept. It's done, it's done . . . I haven't seen one person worth his salt who thinks it's a good thing.

V.A.: In that case, don't accept!

P.M.-F.: You've forced me into such a situation that I can no longer refuse to accept.

Later, President Auriol noted:

"Mendès-France thinks I'm sending him to the slaughter. It's not out of fear, but he has a deep-seated desire to win, and that I understand. By any standards, he may well be letting the propitious moment pass him by. He already has. But still he has to try . . . I lost my temper and said to him: 'You're too erratic, there's no doubt about it. For the past hour I've been wasting my time.' "

During the first few months he was Premier, the Americans baptized him "superman." And never has the term been more appropriately applied. But this "superman" always needs someone to "send him to the slaughter." At least that's how I see him, from my analysis and observation of a number of seemingly insignificant facts. This behavior remains the same in other circumstances of his life and might be only one of a hundred character traits, a hundred weaknesses which make a strong man all the more touching and attractive, traits I have on more than one occasion affectionately teased him about, telling him that he is just too unbearable at times, insincere in his relations with other people.

But unless I'm mistaken, it's this same characteristic that in January 1956 kept him from coming out and saying to Guy Mollet: I'm the only one who in the present situation must assume the post of Premier. But he chose not to, with all the dramatic results that ensued, not only as far as Algeria was concerned, but in many other areas as well: his image, his influence and prestige, his aptitude for leadership were annihilated, broken for all the years to come, and with them went the whole non-Communist Left. It was this same characteristic that made him flounder — in my opinion — in May of '68 and, above all, yes above all, in April 1969.

It took me a long time to figure it out. And who knows, maybe it's a fabrication of my own mind . . . If anyone is able to come up with a more plausible explanation for such a baffling attitude, I'd be the first to accept it. But as for Mendès being prone to self-defeat . . . no, I don't think so.

Why are we dwelling on the subject? Because we are all the same. We spend our time imbuing a person with absolute qualities and then when he doesn't live up to them we go around saying how wrongly we judged the poor man. Everyone is disappointing when measured by absolute standards, including you and me. People who love us or who loved us "absolutely" have one day said to themselves, are perhaps saying to themselves at this very moment, "Really . . . Coming from him, I must say I'm disappointed . . ."

— Twenty years later, your feelings toward Mendès-France are . . .

— Unchanged. I'm steadfast in my feelings.

— Then let's say your judgment?

— I have no desire to make any judgments. Besides, I've never invested any politicians with superhuman qualities — nor have I with persons, as a matter of fact. I'm not much given to kissing the archbishop's ring. Intellectually and from the standpoint of personal courage, Mendès-France is a great man. But those qualities never prevented anyone from having blocks and neuroses. I can observe them — including my own — with interest, and when men in potential positions of power are involved, I can try to evaluate their positive and negative qualities, both as individuals and as public servants. As for the others . . . Let's not be so ridiculous as to start handing out gold stars . . .

— How do you explain that he didn't foresee that the Algerian War was coming?

— What? In November 1954? Who saw it coming? No one. Of course there were some people, and I was one of them, who realized that Algeria, because of its very population density, was a colony that risked becoming far more serious a problem than either Tunisia or Morocco. But to say that I foresaw the course of events . . . Mendès-France was harassed to death. He was the object of violent attacks in the Assembly, from those who received their anti-Communist incomes from sources subsidized by John Foster Dulles, from those who hatched the famous affair of the "leaked docu-

ments" against his Minister of the Interior, François Mitterrand . . .

Today, that affair is gone and forgotten. In an era when
Nixon does a thriving business with Mr. Brezhnev and
embraces Mao Tse-tung — both of which please me no
end — it's a bit difficult to describe the climate that reigned
in those days. But when you have lived through it . . .

The handful of Frenchmen who made a living from anti-
Communism had hatched a plot to discredit the French government and at the same time render it suspect to the Americans. Allegedly, there had been a number of leaks regarding
certain aspects of French defense secrets, documents that had
been purportedly passed on to the Communists. By whom?
None other than François Mitterrand. Actually, the documents were false, forged by a police informer and exploited
by a former police prefect who had never forgiven the
Mendès-France government, and especially his Minister of the
Interior François Mitterrand, for having ousted him from his
functions.

It was Mitterrand who bore the brunt of that attack. I saw
a lot of him at the time, and to say he suffered political
martyrdom is a gross understatement. Politics was a very
dirty business . . . and still is. Just think back to 1968–
1969: remember those fake photographs of the late President
Pompidou's wife in compromising situations. A sorry attempt,
but at least one can say that this kind of moral assassination
is a step forward from out-and-out assassination.

It should be noted that, in Mendès-France's period, that is
under the Fourth Republic, the system was completely in-
adequate for any sustained or serious governmental action, in
any crisis situation. It was in a way an absolute democracy,
the same kind of government still in effect in Italy, where
everyone does exactly as he pleases. Without the problem of
decolonization it might have lasted . . . After all, the

Fourth Republic also spawned the Monnet Plan, that five-year economic plan that enabled France to rebuild after the war.

Under the Fifth Republic, we've had another kind of government. So far no one has done anything. The French historian Lavisse once noted, speaking of the power of the people in France under no matter what regime, that the country is run if not by a coterie then at the most by a consortium of people who have come to power by some initial accident and are busily trying to stave off some ultimate accident . . . It's rather terrifying, this method of doing nothing while waiting for everything to fall apart, and acting as though there were a chance it might not. In any event, that's another story altogether — the next one on the agenda.

In 1954, Mendès-France was stepping on too many toes — from the vintners and distillers to the wealthy colonists and those whose incomes were paid by John Foster Dulles' America — not to be eliminated quickly. After he had served his purpose.

— Do you mean that France was no longer in a frame of mind to accept him, except insofar as he was able to lance the existing abscesses?

— I don't know. It wasn't the French who overthrew him, nor their elected representatives, although it was the French parliament's vote that caused his government to fall. His fall was brought about by a combination of several men. Just what they represented in depth I'm not quite sure . . . Perhaps simply that eternal collusion between the Rightist interests and the Communist Party, that objective collusion which prevents France from having any Leftist government except by some accident which is quickly repaired.

What Mendès-France's brief administration taught me, in any case, was that any man who comes to power in France has three months before him in which to act shockingly, in the real sense of the term. To produce shocks. Make waves. A hundred days, no more, no less. That is perhaps not the case in other systems of government, but it's true in France. In the United States, for example, the first hundred days of the Kennedy administration were filled with such sinister affairs as the Bay of Pigs and the crisis in Laos. The American President, actually, has a freer hand during his second term in office, if he gets re-elected. In Germany, Willy Brandt marked time during his first hundred days. But as time went on he seemed to grow stronger and stronger politically — until he was brought down by a political scandal. In France, though, it's in the beginning of your term that you must make your moves. Afterward, all the elements of opposition form or reform around you. And if the newly elected leader is still around after these elements regroup, he has to strike out in several directions at once.

— And after that experience, you didn't become a die-hard pessimist?

— No, my pessimism derived rather from the field of battle. The government fell in February 1955. The elections were scheduled for the following year. It was a question of winning them.

— But today, looking back, don't you tend to be pessimistic about a government that operates in this way?

— From the way you word the question, I gather that what you're expressing is your own feelings about it! As far as pessimism and optimism are concerned, it's really a matter of glandular or molecular make-up, something of the kind. We all learned that in school from the story of Jean who laughs and Jean who cries. I don't think that I'm a particularly optimistic person; I'm stubborn, which is different. When I sink my teeth into something, I don't let go. I'm not sure what it's called. A bulldog quality?

— Don't you ever think you're wrong?

— Who do you take me for, Simone de Beauvoir? On the contrary, I'm always afraid of being wrong. But we were talking about politics. What does it mean to be wrong in politics? Not to have picked the winner? When someone wants to gain political power, or wield some portion thereof, it is obviously vital to be on the winning side. At least from time to time! Everything else belongs to literature. And it's also vital to be on the winning side if your career or business depends on the state.

All of that is foreign to me: both the noble ambition of wielding power and the need to hobnob with people in positions of power simply because of their positions. If they are my friends for other reasons and from other circumstances in life and come to power, I can adjust to the situation — though poorly. I'm not talking about purely professional relations, naturally, but about personal ones. Therefore, I don't see why I ought to worry about backing the "winner"; if that had been my concern, I would have backed the Gaullists for the past fifteen years. But as the saying goes, they're not my cup of tea. It's another matter altogether to be mistaken about men, about what they are and what they will do in any given situation. There my average is good.

And it's still another thing to be mistaken in the analysis you make of any situation or of any tissue of relationships. There my average is at least honorable, for reasons I think we've already mentioned. I don't have the ability to portray things the way I would like them to be. That's a powerful brake that has often embarrassed me and kept me from acting. But it also keeps me from both dramatizing and embroidering. My natural tendency, in fact, is to underdramatize, to think that it's raining less hard down in the street than it seems from looking out the window.

— In May 1958, for example, did you see things clearly?

— No, of course I didn't, if by that you mean that I clearly foresaw what was going to happen.

Between the 1956 elections and the moment in 1958 when the Fourth Republic crumbled and the coup d'état being hatched in Algiers brought De Gaulle back to power, I had every opportunity to understand that with every passing day the situation in Algeria was growing worse.

In January 1957 Servan-Schreiber came back from Algeria with the concrete experience of what that war which was being waged under the name of "pacification" was all about. He related it in his book *Lieutenant en Algérie,* which resulted in his being indicted for endangering the security of the state. And there was, as a result of that indictment, the explosive affair of General Bollardière. Do you remember it?

Bollardière was in charge of the sector to which Servan-Schreiber had been assigned. He wrote a letter to Jean-Jacques in which he backed him up for breaking "the conspiracy of silence" about the methods being employed in Algeria. And he gave Jean-Jacques permission to make his letter public. What he was referring to, of course, was torture — the torture which he, Bollardière, had outlawed. As a result of that letter, he was ousted from his Algeria command. Torture was authorized. It was truth that had been outlawed.

Bollardière was really an extraordinary man, I can assure you. One of those men who, on days when doubts of various kinds assail you, reconcile you with the human race. A career army man, the son of an army officer, Catholic, a native of Brittany, a member of the Foreign Legion, a parachutist; and he was a man who had the courage to put everything on the line. Everything. Not only his military career, which he ruined when he denounced the use of torture and which he later left, but his own past, his youth, the warfare he loved, the intoxicating effect of victory in battle. Everything. He is perhaps the only man I know who has managed to make what he does accord completely with what he says, who really lives his moral convictions.

In 1957, it was his startling revelation that forced the government to set up a "Study Commission on the Question of Torture." The then Prime Minister, Guy Mollet, had the audacity to assert, at the time of its creation, that if there were any cases of torture, "you could count them on the fingers of one hand."

Over the two-year period prior to De Gaulle's return to power, we also witnessed the impressive spectacle of all the governors of Algeria falling apart one after the other. No, they were no longer called "governors." What was it they called them? Yes: "Resident-Ministers in Algeria." Poor wretches! Wasn't there one politician in all France sufficiently immune to the poison of power to resist what was happening to the representatives of the French government in Algeria?

If they had sent Gaston Defferre, the mayor of Marseille, he might have been strong enough to hold out against the assembled forces there, because when you've been the lord and mayor of a big city and have learned how to handle yourself and your affairs with feudal authority, you're not liable to have your head turned by a motorcade, soldiers parading in review, or screaming crowds acclaiming you. What these well-meaning "Resident-Ministers" used to do was emerge onto the balcony, shout "Long Live French Algeria," listen to the acclaim of the assembled throng, and think they were loved by the whole of Algeria. Loved indeed! How many times was it that Robert Lacoste announced that the war in Algeria was entering its "final quarter hour" . . . and the worst thing was that he may have believed it! He was as well suited for that position as I am to be pope. Defferre, though, would have resisted: he would not have been duped by the illusion of a victory through military might, as he would have been deaf to the blandishments of the French in Algeria, those who controlled the press and owned all the money . . . But he had made it clear that he would be tough with them. So it was Lacoste who was chosen rather than Defferre.

There were . . . But let's not recite once again the litany of shame and lies that was elevated to national policy. Who wants to remember it? I certainly don't. Situations of this kind do have one positive aspect, however, in that they divide the world into two camps and force you to choose one, thus making everything more simple. Especially for the Left, for whom it's ideal. With torture and colonialism on one side, they know they have to be on the other. It's so much more simple, isn't it, than having a hard and fast opinion about the issue of floating currency exchanges or whether the Concorde should be built or not . . . And then May 13, 1958, arrived, and with it the uprising in Algiers hatched by the followers of De Gaulle who wanted to force the French President to call the general back from his retirement in Colombey. They seized control of the government headquarters in Algiers. A Committee of Public Safety was set up, presided over by the military leaders who, although they had no heart for it, ended up adding their voices to the cries of "Long Live De Gaulle!" . . . Meanwhile, back in France, panic was the order of the day: people expected to see the army oust the government . . .

For several days I, like everyone else, thought there was a real possibility of a military putsch, and I was worried about the danger to a certain number of people, who would be on the army's priority arrest-list. Quite literally in danger of facing firing squads. Why not? The climate was ripe for it. Mendès-France had received numerous threats, serious threats, against his life. His face was a familiar one in France, therefore recognizable. I found him a hideout with a friend who could be trusted. On our way there, we got caught in a traffic jam. People in neighboring cars began staring, obviously recognizing our passenger. He remained impassive. Mendès is not someone who, in such a situation, says: "Let's get down and hide." He looked left and right. And from behind the windows of the cars on all sides, people smiled back. And yet the vilification campaign against him had been incredible . . .

One night about two or three in the morning my telephone rang. It was the friend I mentioned to you earlier, Lucien Rachet, who had called to tell me that the parachutists were on their way from Algeria, that I was high on the list of those who were to be arrested, and that, out of friendship, he wanted to help me from getting caught.

It was intoxication pure and simple, a tactic intended to persuade the people to call on De Gaulle to form a new government by popular demand rather than having him called by the handful of politicians who would use him to protect them from the madness of the army.

But that night anything seemed possible. I got dressed, I took a gun and slipped it into my pocket against any eventuality, and I left my house for the only place where, at that hour of the morning, I could decently go: my sister's. At that time I lived in an apartment overlooking the Bois du Ranelagh. My sister lived on the other side of the Woods, no more than fifteen or twenty minutes away on foot.

It was a warm night. Streets are lovely when you take them by surprise while they're sleeping. And suddenly that solitary, silent walk, with a gun in my pocket, on my way to find a hiding place, took me right back to the Occupation. It was incredible! Incredible to start that whole comedy over again!

One day a year earlier I had been at the hairdresser's and had said: "Don't cut my hair. I'm going to let it grow long. With what's going on in Algeria, I'm going to wind up in prison again one of these days. It will be easier to have long hair." I had only been half-serious.

My sister, with all the poise of a seasoned veteran, welcomed me, offered me a chair, and didn't even ask me what I was doing there at that hour. The following morning, there were no more parachutists in Paris than there is snow in hell. Romanticism had scored zero. I felt humiliated at having been taken in.

And then on May 28 there was that lugubrious parade in Paris, where 100,000 people conscientiously marched — and I was among them — to protest the abdication of the government and the President of the Republic in favor of De Gaulle. "To defend the Republic . . ." The problem was, there was nothing left to defend: the government had already destroyed itself and its edifice with its own hands. The Fourth Republic had already ceased to exist. All that remained were two forces: De Gaulle and the army, each of which fully intended to utilize the other. The question was, which one would win out?

In that climate of frenzy and uncertainty, I remember that I was fairly calm, very calm in fact, completely against De Gaulle's return to power over the prostrate bodies of the military, but somehow not upset or alarmed. And yet things could have turned out badly. It was Trotsky who, as I recall, said: "The annoying problem with army revolts is that the army is armed." That's exactly the situation we found ourselves in. On the other, more positive side, it's also true that soldiers are accustomed to following orders. There's always someone with one more stripe or star.

The people around me were far less sanguine than I. They foresaw the worst, which to their minds meant a Hindenburg or, at best, a Naguib. There were good reasons for thinking that, but . . .

My own feeling was that, given the situation, De Gaulle was without doubt in the best position to end the war in Algeria. There are many moments in history where a man of the Right is necessary to impose some Leftist policy, as there are moments when only a military man can seem to turn defeat into victory. But what I saw as most disturbing was that periodic tendency on the part of the French to turn their fate over to a Great Man sent to them by Providence. Disturbing and alarming. And I thought that it was necessary at any cost to publicly resist that spirit of resignation.

Looking back from the vantage point of the present, I'm pleased that we at *L'Express* adopted that attitude, despite the rigor we attached to it. It was a difficult and dangerous attitude, one in direct contradiction with prevailing public sentiment. And it was also clear that De Gaulle had come to power with the full intention of staying there . . . He hadn't fretted out there in Colombey for twelve years, eating his heart out for having been ousted from power through a simple miscalculation — thinking in 1946 that within a week they'd be back knocking on his door asking him to return — to let himself be ousted a second time, or to simply save the situation and then quietly return to his retreat.

I voted "no" in the referendums. Out of principle. I just can't work up any real enthusiasm for changes of constitution. Since the French Revolution of 1789, we've had twelve different political regimes — two empires, three kings, five republics, and one marshal at the head of government — and we've had fourteen different constitutions, not counting the revisions.

De Gaulle proposed that the French President be elected by popular vote rather than by the French parliament. Whether or not that's good or bad is a point that can be debated till the end of time. The argument over institutions, which the French so love, is for me the subject which represents the sterility of our judicial system. You can change the constitution as often as you like: if the people don't like it, don't want it to work, it won't work.

There are several aspects of the present system that I find open to criticism, or dangerous. The most obvious one is that the system is neither presidential nor parliamentarian. And it's also terribly long: seven years is a very long time to give any President, assuming it's he who determines the country's policies. We all remember, and I believe agree with, Lamartine's pointed remark that moderate institutions are tiresome, that people grow bored under such regimes. It's not healthy to let the French remain bored for too long, without any prospect of being able to air their views and opinions, their claims and demands by voting. True, they can do it at the time of the legislative elections which are held every five years. But if the results turn out to be contradictory to the results of the presidential elections, what then? What does the President do? To succeed in voting for a man every seven years and against his policies every five years is probably what is called being Cartesian!

The present system worked in 1969, when a great many people were saying that the day De Gaulle vanished from the political scene chaos would ensue. But that experience does not suffice to conclude that France has become really democratic and civilized in its political habits. What would Pompidou have done if, for instance, in the second-round run-off elections in 1973 the French had confirmed the hostility they had shown in the first round? The question remains theoretical, since both in that election and in the most recent 1974 presidential election the conservatives won by the thinnest of margins.

The proof would be conclusive if a candidate who won an election with Communist backing and votes came to office as peacefully as Pompidou did in 1969. Or if the law of alternation came into play, as it does in the United States between Democrats and Republicans. Otherwise, if the system ends up constantly returning a conservative president to the Élysées Palace, it is obviously an imposture. But who is responsible for the imposture? Would you personally like to have a Communist Minister of the Interior? I wouldn't. And what is more, is there any member of the Central Committee of the Communist Party in France who really wants to see a Communist Minister of the Interior? They're not so dumb. Or maybe they are . . . Maybe they haven't learned anything, or remembered anything from history; maybe they don't know that the first wave of Communists who come to power will ineluctably be liquidated by the second wave, and I mean liquidated in the way these gentlemen carry out such business. Out of love for humanity and the proletariat, of course. But perhaps each Communist leader thinks to himself that when that day comes he'll be the Stalin of the operation and not the Trotsky. The Kadar and not the Nagy. The Boumedienne and not the Ben Bella . . .

As for us as individuals, the whole thing is to come along at the right time in history, isn't it? What can anyone dream of more delightful than being a French bourgeois between 1872 and 1913, for example? Or a Russian revolutionary between 1917 and Lenin's death? What more satisfying than to be a Jew in Israel in the '50s? What more remunerative than to be a collaborator in France between 1940–1945?

And, to carry on the analogy, what better than to be a Gaullist under De Gaulle? I'm referring to the second term, of course, not to 1940. De Gaulle didn't care a whit about money, but he always knew that other men did not share his indifference on that score. A Frenchman in London, André Labarthe, who was anti-De Gaulle, although De Gaulle did everything in his power to try and persuade Labarthe to join him, told this story about him: "Come. Join us," De Gaulle urged. "We're going to win. And when we do you'll have glory, money, women . . ."

In 1945 a few did have all that, in fact. In 1958 and the years following, the glory was slightly tarnished . . . But as for the money and women, the friends of the regime did very well indeed, to say the least. Not everyone, though — there were even some honest ones! Did De Gaulle know about it? Of course he did. He made a few remarks, which for reasons of libel cannot be repeated, that show very clearly he knew just what was going on . . . In particular about one notorious knave to whom the entire government and its hangers-on catered with incredible solicitude . . .

No matter. I don't want to pretend that venality and corruption began in 1958. Until 1962, in fact, I think that this tight little group behaved itself relatively discreetly, huddled there under its big umbrella that the wind from Algeria might blow away at any moment.

✣ XIV

THOSE YEARS . . . how endless they were! Endless and dreary. The kind of danger to which we were exposed was stupid. I'm not talking about the issues of the magazine seized, or the indictments to which we'd all sadly grown accustomed. And they went on under De Gaulle, because the tortures were still going on and as long as they were we had no choice but to keep writing about them. No, I'm talking about the physical dangers, when the assassinations began.

For months unpaid guards patrolled the roof of the building which housed the magazine. There were people who showed incredible courage and devotion . . . Some set up teams which spelled one another, keeping an around-the-clock guard of the apartments of those among us who had been openly threatened. During the day, they set up a guard system at the office. No one could enter the office without leaving his identity papers at the front desk. An alarm system had been installed. What most concerned us was the blindly thrown bomb that would kill or maim at random.

At our homes, plastic bombs had wrought havoc. The other tenants were up in arms about it . . . against us. At the magazine, what terrified me most was the thought that one of the young secretaries or receptionists might be killed or wounded. The journalists who had stayed with us had made an open choice: in 1958 we had given all who wanted it the right to leave the magazine if their consciences so dictated. But the others . . . It was a sad danger, without anything exalting about it, as is always the case when you're on the defensive. But we had no choice! We had to do what we could to save our honor, proclaim that not every French-man had been anesthetized, browbeaten to the point of total inertia, that we were not all accomplices to what was going on in Algeria. It may surprise you, but the press was not united in thinking this way, far from it.

I have had more than ample time to reflect, since then, on the relationship between morality and politics . . . and on many other things as well. All the more so because for me 1960 marked the end of something: the end of a long cycle of a privileged existence because something had been given to me that many people never find throughout their lives and which, for want of a better expression, I'll call "unity."

We all live more or less divided, torn between conflicting feelings and desires. Between what we should do and what we'd like to do, home and work, interests and convictions, sometimes between two women or between two men, between dream and reality, and Lord knows what else — I could go on forever. We live within the framework of an eternal, and more or less exhausting, give and take. And within it we feel, as some people put it, fragmented and broken up.

Through a remarkable set of circumstances, I lived through a long period of coherence, when the various elements of my life all came together: loves, friendships, family life, profes-sional life, pleasures, duties, passions, involvement — all fitted together under circumstances that may not have been satisfactory to anyone else but suited me, with all my little personal neuroses.

I was never unaware of how fragile that unity, that rare equilibrium, was. I savored it all the more intensely. And perhaps for this same reason I also kept it isolated from anything that was dependent on me, made it into a kind of "work." And yet it broke. And I broke with it, was broken and dismantled. Shattered and destroyed.

— What do you mean "broken"? Can you be a little more specific?

— It's hard. It's not that I'm afraid of the words; it's only that I don't quite know how to talk about those things that belong to me personally . . .

In brief: to live just for the sake of living has never held any interest for me. I want to live well, in relationship to criteria which I myself have set and which may or may not be meaningful criteria for others. But there came a time when I began to live badly, with respect to these criteria, that is, I was in a state of inner tumult, inner disorder, brought about by the end of a love affair.

I failed to understand why something that might well have been hard, even painful — but nonetheless something people do get over — had taken on such proportions. Today I know what it is, because in the interim I've become an adult, assuming there are any such creatures. Let's say that I've at least turned the corner toward adulthood.

I know that the cruelest part of the suffering you experience when someone leaves you stems from the fact that it gives rise to a feeling of inadequacy — quite different from the feeling of loss you feel when someone you love dies. In the former instance, the other person isn't dead. He's there. And what's more, often he's happy . . . If you can convert your feelings into anger, or hate, you're saved. I'm a wonderful woman, or an admirable man, and yet this vile creature I thought I loved prefers some asinine creature to me, some scheming adventurer — the situation is perfectly viable. You can even turn it to good account by plotting some kind of revenge. Unfortunately — or rather fortunately — that kind of salvation wasn't right for me.

Unhappily, what struck me as my inadequacy in the situation also reawakened all the long-buried ghosts, all the scars of my childhood. It wasn't a woman's wound that had been opened in this case, but a boomerang returning from a long way back. Everything that I had patiently overcome, everything that I had repressed, covered over, forgotten for all those long years, everything that had made me different, resurfaced as so many reasons for my rejection. The familiar "You're not like the others . . . ," which so often had sounded like a compliment to my ears, suddenly turned sour. As though I had been a black woman, for example . . . It was the same kind of mechanism at work.

I didn't understand all that at the time. But I did realize that I had been affected to the very depths of my being. And that I was beginning the long, long walk through the valley of hell.

At that point I drew a series of thirty vertical lines on my office wall. Thirty. And I said to myself: "I'm going to cross out one every day. If by the time I've crossed out the thirtieth I haven't got hold of myself, I'm going to commit suicide." It seemed better to put an end to these years, which had been beautiful, in some esthetic way. Esthetics also has its place in the scheme of things.

I crossed out the thirty lines. And I told one of my friends of the decision I had made. I was struck by the fact that he wasn't able to come up with anything but the usual clichés; he couldn't give me any compelling reason why I shouldn't put my plan into effect. We were in the country, on a broad expanse of lawn. The weather was lovely. Inside the house, people were expecting us for lunch . . . But despite the idyllic setting, he saw that I was locked inside a prison which, while probably imaginary, was one from which there was no escape.

I knew one young woman who had conveyed this same feeling to me. Her name was Evelyne Rey. She was an actress, had been involved with Sartre, and had had a part in his play, *Les Séquestrés d'Altona.* Beautiful, intelligent, sensitive: a wonderful person. And a few years ago she committed suicide. I knew her very well, and was very fond of her. I saw her two or three days before she killed herself . . . I knew that she would, and that nothing I or anyone could say to her would stop her. I knew that one night someone would do something — however insignificant — and precipitate her suicide.

Someone did it to me; it doesn't matter what the incident was. And I teetered and went over the edge. I organized everything very well. In general, I'm a well-organized person. But when death doesn't want you, all the arrangements in the world are worthless. Death didn't show up at Samarra . . .

What followed was terrible. And endless. Someone who really loved me then would have understood that it would have been better to let me die. But that's asking too much of love.

Years went by, during which I was a walking ruin, blackened and burned out like a forest after a fire has swept through it. It took years for me to find another way of living, years before I was able to re-establish a suitable relationship with myself.

I'm not one of those who believe that suffering ennobles. On the contrary, I think it debases, especially when it keeps your intelligence at bay. And if there is one area where intelligence is powerless, it's in the realm of phantasms, those birds one has in one's head . . . There is no better method of learning true humility and the limits of freedom than the work which consists of exorcising those birds, which goes under the name of psychoanalysis. Intelligence is an art of accomplishment. You can derive all kinds of pleasure from it, like practicing the piano or painting. But when you have learned, at your own expense, that intelligence is not what's guiding you, you've really learned a lot . . . about others. It's not intelligence that rules the world, and that holds true just as much for intelligent people as for those who are stupid. And that was something I hadn't known before, not really. I had always deep down wanted to believe in the supremacy of reason.

At the same time as I was discovering my own impotence, the opportunity was equally propitious, during the years under De Gaulle while the Algerian War was dragging on, to observe it in others. To see what I might call "a-intelligence" at work. That is, passions. Interests can always find some common meeting ground; passions never.

De Gaulle's passion was power; therefore, he would remain in power. The Algerians' passion was independence; therefore they would somehow wrest it away from those trying to keep it from them, even at the cost of hundreds of thousands of dead. They didn't need Lenin to tell them that great historical problems can only be resolved through force. The army's passion was a certain notion it had of honor; therefore, it would revolt. As for the passion of the French living in Algeria . . . Even the most liberal among them never for a moment thought that they would have to leave their beloved land. Therefore, they would stick with the army.

The only unknown factor in the equation was the real relationship between De Gaulle and the army. But here mainland France played a part. It was behind De Gaulle and against the army. One had only to sit back and watch this absurd and deadly game endlessly unfold.

There were a few distractions, though, during those years. Khrushchev in Paris . . . John F. Kennedy in the White House. When in 1957 we published the then young senator's picture on the cover of *L'Express* and reprinted his speech on Algeria, one French politician said to us: "You really honored him too highly by putting his picture on your cover. He's just a rich young nobody with high ambitions. He hasn't any future . . ."

Six years later, in Washington, I saw all the heads of state in the world kneel before his bier. The Pax Americana ruled over both land and sea. After the fiasco of the Bay of Pigs, Kennedy had constructed and placed in their underground silos four or five times more intercontinental ballistic missiles than the Russians had. It was an America at the peak of its wealth and power that confronted the Russian threat at the time of the so-called Cuban missile crisis, that eyeball-to-eyeball encounter that led to a dialogue between the United States and the Soviet Union. There's no denying that Kennedy was largely responsible for getting America bogged down in Vietnam, and in so doing, for the country's loss of something essential, something it will never find again, something that, at least for the time being, broke its vital spirit. But we were unaware of all that at the time, and we saw that John F. Kennedy had discovered "the great secret of those who enter public office, which is to seize men's imaginations."*

And I, a French newspaperwoman, therefore hardened and skeptical, went and laid flowers on his grave. He's buried near Washington, a beautiful, really inspired site, on the side

* The quote is from the seventeenth-century French politician and writer, Cardinal de Retz. — *Translator.*

of a hill in Arlington Cemetery. During the first few days after he was buried there, there were so many visitors they wore the grass away. I can't tell you what made me go there and stand for a long moment in an icy wind watching the little blue flame flickering over his grave.

That was his wife's idea. She lighted it so that it might "symbolize my everlasting devotion to him and to his ideals." I wonder if that flame is still burning. What's Mrs. Onassis doing there in Greece, where those who oppose the regime are jailed and tortured? Defending John Kennedy's ideals? . . .

I'm sorry. What I just said is stupid. I'm as much a victim as the next person of that curious need the whole world seems to have to see the young widow remain forever faithful to the hero struck down tragically by an assassin's bullet. This amazing little Greek millionaire, who suddenly placed a jeweled crown where the halo had once been, broke our little doll for us, the doll that said "Jack" when you squeezed it.

It's not a tragedy. It's a comedy. And what right do we have anyway to stick our nose into her business, to ask that Jacqueline Onassis remain forever faithful "to the ideals" of John F. Kennedy when we forgive most of those who pretend to have them? Just because her former husband is dead, what right do we have to prevent her from living her own life any way she wants to? . . . It's an absolutely medieval reaction. Especially its view of women's place in the world. To love one, and only one man, from adolescence till death ye do part? What did we expect, a widow who would be forever inconsolable? Or is it that this dream of eternal fidelity relates to some deep feeling of insecurity within us, which would help explain why so many people experienced it vicariously in the person of the woman probably least suited to incarnate it, the person the least inclined to be self-effacing, to losing herself in any man, be he alive or dead . . . All you have to do is see how she mounts a horse to realize that she's not easy, that she has a mind of her own.

There was one person who wasn't wrong about her, and that was De Gaulle. He made the remark to Malraux, who passed it along. "She'll wind up on the yacht of some munitions manufacturer." That didn't keep De Gaulle from being fond of her. The day Kennedy was buried, a Monday, he flew to Washington and paid her a private visit at the White House to tell her with his own lips how deeply the French felt about her husband. She wanted to show him her gratitude. There was a vase in the room filled with flowers. She took a daisy from it and handed it to him. Our ambassador in Washington, Hervé Alphand, told me the next day how moved De Gaulle was by the gesture, which he described when he got back to the embassy, still holding the daisy she had given him.

No sooner had the news of the assassination reached France than I jumped in a plane to cover the event for *L'Express*. I arrived just in time to see, on television, a man named Jack Ruby shoot Lee Harvey Oswald. No, I don't know anything more about it than you. But I read everything on the subject, everything. The official version is incredible. I've always wondered whether the Americans chose to believe it out of credulousness, or because they preferred not to face what might come out if the truth were known.

For several days, the television screens of the country were a merry-go-round of funeral pictures and dirges that kept turning, turning, till it became sickening. Mourning doesn't become America. Neither do worry, shame, and sorrow. There is in America — at least there was, and I think there still is — a kind of life force which orders it to act rather than sigh or moan. But the country nonetheless bore its mourning, and the shame of the murderous violence abroad within its borders, with extraordinary dignity.

America has had four Presidents murdered, suffered several corrupt Presidents, a civil war, two World Wars, one particularly ineffectual President — Hoover — who left office with a legacy of the '29 crash and 12,000,000 people out of work. And yet it has never really questioned the bases of its institutions. We French, on the other hand, as I mentioned to you a while ago, have had twelve different regimes. In the States, at this moment of crisis, the system once again functioned without a hitch.

This holds true even today. If because of Watergate Nixon were to leave the White House before the end of his second term, whether through impeachment or resignation, you may be sure that, once again, the institutions would continue to function. And yet the shock to the system would probably be greater even than Kennedy's assassination. Different, but greater. For in this melting pot, which America still is, the major unifying factor is the rule of law. This explains in great part why the country is so appalled when it discovers that the head of the country has, apparently, been lying and cheating: it is a betrayal of that sacred office.

But believe me, America will not "fall" because of Watergate or the crisis of the presidency, because there is a strength in the United States that we in Europe constantly tend to underestimate. All we see are her scars and her wounds, for the simple reason that, unlike most countries, America doesn't try to hide them; but we forget her basic health. Strength: that is the term that comes to mind when I think of the States, strength for both the best and the worst.

Following the Kennedy burial, there was an amazing reception at the State Department, that building that looks like it was built as a setting for Kafka. There was no formal receiv-

ing line, in the French sense of the term. In France, the
Foreign Minister would have remained stationed by the door,
with his wife, while a uniformed attendant would have
solemnly announced each new arrival. Here there was nothing of the sort. It was like a rather intimate party where
everyone knew everyone else, shook hands, and moved from
one knot of people to another. Only "everyone" had names
such as Prince Philip, Ludwig Erhard, King Beaudouin of Belgium, Alexander Douglas Home, Mikoyan, etc. De Gaulle
and John Kenneth Galbraith, who stood fully as tall as he,
"the world belonging to tall men."

It was one of the strange gatherings of heads of state — a
few years later there was a similar assembly at Notre Dame,
for De Gaulle's funeral — where one is always tempted to
ask oneself what would happen if they were all wiped out
with one fell swoop. The question, of course, is how much
such men personally affected the course of history.

Earlier, I had heard from an unimpeachable source that
John Kennedy had been deeply disappointed by his visit to
Paris in '61. He was very sure of his personal charm and of
his political arguments, of his enormous power of persuasion
that at least tempted friend and foe alike to consider the possibility of sitting down and "reasoning together." Actually,
if you reduced his policy to its essentials, it could be resumed
in two major points: (1) cerate an Atlantic Community between a Europe, enlarged to include Great Britain, and the
United States and (2) open conversations with the Soviet
Union. In other words, it was a policy radically opposed to
that of De Gaulle.

De Gaulle knew that the security that the United States
provided for France could in no way be jeopardized. He had
unreservedly backed Kennedy during the two key crises of
his administration, Berlin and the Cuban missile crisis. But
why, from De Gaulle's viewpoint, should he give up the

political and moral advantages to be derived from running his own show in order to meld his country into some new Atlantic Alliance? Why should he yield on the point of letting England into the European Community?

He therefore stubbornly maintained his own positions. And, beneath the formal courtesy of his welcome, Kennedy had thought he detected an unyielding mixture of spite, scorn, and hatred for the United States. But who at the time would ever have thought that of the two men, De Gaulle and Kennedy, it would be the young President who would be the first to disappear from the political scene?

I am hard put to say just what that meant as to the evolution of the United States and, consequently, the world. Sometimes one is tempted to think: nothing.

If you judge Nixon's policies with respect to the Soviet Union and China as good, you also have to conclude that they are the same policies Kennedy would have wanted. And, when all is said and done, would Kennedy have been able to extricate himself from Vietnam any better than Nixon has done? . . .

But facts are only part of the whole story. There is the image projected, the spirit imparted, the manner. We saw the same thing in France with De Gaulle. It's difficult to measure the full impact that the hatred of Nixon, among a portion of European public opinion, will have on the domestic policies of various European countries. But you may be sure that it will be exploited to the hilt. Isn't it already difficult in France to say that you like America?

Kennedy was much loved outside the United States. There is no question but that the man had a seductive personal charm, that enigmatic quality we sometimes refer to as charisma. Anyone who knew him at all felt it. The day following Kennedy's death, I had a brief conversation with Arthur Schlesinger, Jr., at the White House. He spoke very soberly, but also very movingly, of the very special quality that John Kennedy possessed and projected.

Jean-Jacques Servan-Schreiber, whom Kennedy received secretly at the White House — secretly in order not to create any undue diplomatic complications — preferred Robert, whom he knew well, to John. I didn't like Robert very much. It was a subject of comical discussion between Jean-Jacques and me. I told him that I would never place my confidence in any man who had given his wife eleven children.

Apparently she likes having a large family and is a happy person. Or was. But I saw her as rather a pathetic character. I remember one time in particular: it was April of '68, in New York, where Robert announced his candidacy following Johnson's bombshell revelation that he would not run for a second term. The press conference took place in the morning, in a room that was too small. There were a number of tables in the room, on which were scattered dirty cups. A rostrum had been hastily erected. Robert spoke, then answered questions with that arrogant air he had, that air of an old little-boy who was hiding a slingshot behind his back and who might, at any moment, bring it out and shoot you between the eyes . . . For some reason his wife Ethel was there, seated in a rickety chair just below the rostrum, facing the public. I remember that she was wearing a red Courrèges coat that fit her poorly. And I said to myself: "Why did he have to drag her here? . . . What a curious custom these American politicians have of showing off their wives and dogs to enhance their public image . . ." I wrote that at the time. And a few weeks later, after Robert had been killed, I regretted it. Perhaps she was there with him that day simply because she was afraid, afraid of what might happen to him. In any case, I remember that she looked tired and worn out.

Still, the custom in the United States is for the political candidate to campaign with his spouse by his side, presumably to show how considerate he is of his wife and, by extension, of women in general. The French are beginning to imitate the Americans on this, and I firmly believe that what these men are really expressing in so doing is quite the opposite.

When you are really considerate of your wife, you don't force her to act out the part of the good housewife and mother, the woman who knows how to stretch her dollar at the supermarket, who is swimming happily through a sea of marital bliss . . . not that the little lady doesn't have a head of her own, mind you . . . That depiction of the "model woman" is really dismaying. In Sweden, the Prime Minister's wife, if I remember correctly, is a professor, who continues to exercise her profession. In fact, it would be frowned on if she did not.

A feminist? I've already told you I'm not, at least not in the general acceptance of the term. What I mean is that I don't for one moment believe that over the centuries some universal plot has been hatched by men to keep women in a state of servitude.

I enjoy reading Kate Millett, because she is intelligent, even brilliant. And also in her own way beguiling. One day I interviewed her in Paris for *L'Express*. It was a very amusing interview. I had pressed two of my male colleagues from the magazine into service in order to ask her "male questions." Both of them spoke English very well. They arrived literally terrorized at the idea of meeting that militant castrator, and therefore very aggressive. And then they saw a young, shapely brunette come into the room, a woman who though not really pretty was pleasant to look at, with a charming smile and a soft voice that responded to their questions with considerable humor. After two hours of conversation, she had completely disarmed them, and later, back at the office, they went around saying to one and all: "Kate Millett isn't at all what we thought she would be!" And yet, on the basic issues they had discussed with her she had not given in one iota from her stated positions. But she's a woman of wit, made all the more winning by the fact that you sense a vulnerability about her.

Men's plot against women . . . I must say she failed to convince me. If such were the case I would say: "All right, if indeed they fomented it and pulled it off, it's because they were right: women really didn't come up to their level."

Why not rather recognize the fact that the history of humanity is a very long one during which the division of labor between men and women was, like many other things, dictated by profound necessity — slavery, for example. In Engels' *Anti-Duhring* there are some extraordinary pages on the necessity of slavery for the birth of civilization . . . Yes, Engels.

And then we come to a time in history when machines begin to replace men, when it suffices to have three children for three to survive, when women no longer die in childbirth and infant mortality virtually disappears . . . habits have deep roots, which endow one class with privileges over another, or one sex over the other, and they go on as though they were quite natural, despite the cultural changes that have occurred. When mores are no longer founded on the law of civilization but on habit, then comes the revolt. This is the situation today with women: conditions have changed, the old mores are still lingering on, and women are rebelling.

And they're right to do so. Today, women can produce just as well as men in virtually any area . . . Besides, the work to which they are condemned is the most frustrating and unproductive in the world. In the past, women used to bake their own bread, weave their own material, make their own clothes, their food, their light — in the form of homemade candles . . . Today, they buy what they need for themselves and their families. What human being can derive satisfaction in life simply from buying?

Therefore, this revolt is part and parcel of the evolution of human affairs, and is right. But when it expresses itself as hatred of men, it's stupid. The best way to hurt a man, if you hate him, is to be the object of his desire, not to hustle him into the kitchen to do the dishes. One sometimes has the impression that American women have a kind of dishwashing fixation.

Generally speaking, what bothers and bores me about the American feminist movement is its "missionary" aspect. All missionaries are my enemies, even when their cause is good. The world probably needs them, and I respect them for their courage, but only on the condition of not being compelled to endure them, as one endures mass, without having the right to laugh or saying you don't agree with what they preach.

I agree that the place of women in the world — and especially in the United States — is detestable. Believe it or not, it is worse in the States from a salary standpoint than it is in France, that is, the disparity between men and women in the States is greater than it is in France, at least in the so-called top professions. The percentage of women doctors, judges, engineers, etc., is considerably higher in France than it is in the States, where it is ridiculously low.

On the question of contraception, however, the United States is ahead of France, where public information on the subject is still forbidden. It's also far ahead on the matter of abortion, since the Supreme Court has now legalized it — something I strongly doubt will happen in France for many years to come.

The United States is different on the following essential point of relations between men and women. Obviously, it's absurd to generalize, especially in an area where anyone can find ten examples to prove you wrong. But I really think there are no more than two countries where men love women. One is France and the other Russia. I admit I haven't visited every country in the world, but I have traveled to a great many . . . If you can name me a third . . .

When I say "love" women, I mean love their company and their conversation, I mean a country where men listen to what women have to say, take into account their judgments and opinions, etc. All of which does not imply, of course, that there are no misogynists in France; there are, as there are cads and boors, homosexuals, and delinquents. Nor am I am implying that either of the two countries is a paradise for women; far from it. But I do believe they are "less bad" than the others from that viewpoint. In this same way, the Russians also love women. The English and Americans do not. I think they're bored by them. And women are probably bored by men, too.

All this said, and despite everything you hear, Russian women also complain a good deal about their husbands who come home and put their feet on the table while they, who have also spent the day outside the home working, prepare the dinner. But the fact remains that in Russia almost all the women do work outside the home, do earn their own living and therefore escape the dependency syndrome — which makes all the difference in the world. It always comes back to that basic point.

— When did you go to the Soviet Union?

— In November or December 1960, during that troubled period I was just describing . . . It was then that I saw Khrushchev for the first time. We didn't have what I might call a real conversation, but I was very much impressed by the man, by the impact of his presence. You have to be careful with heads of state and other luminaries: it is all too easy to endow them with qualities they don't really possess but which, superficially, they seem to have been lent because of their rank or station in life. We all know stories of people who have returned from meetings with the "great" of this world and piously relate the pearls of wisdom they have culled from provisionally august lips. That day Khrushchev was in a jovial mood and wanted at all costs to persuade me to smoke a cigar. Seeing my resistance, someone whispered to me: "Go ahead and smoke it. Otherwise he's going to lose his temper!" Me make Khrushchev lose his temper! God forbid! And what if he were trying to lure me into some trap? But to smoke the cigar . . . Then why not do a belly dance for him if he demanded it?

I asked why he seemed to attach such importance to that cigar. "Because I have a new friend who just sent them to me," he answered and burst out laughing. The new friend was Fidel Castro. I took the cigar. Khrushchev turned on his heel and left. I took this cigar with me back to Paris, where one of my friends lighted it absentmindedly, completely unaware of its historic importance . . .

At the time of Khrushchev's visit to Paris, we had made an effort to reproduce a full-color photograph of him on the cover of *L'Express*. It was pretty bad, and it was clear that one day sooner or later we would have to apply ourselves and perfect the full-color process. But meanwhile, Algeria was still weighing heavily on everything, and not only on our own plans.

In January 1960, Camus was killed in an automobile accident. Since he had withdrawn from active involvement in the Algerian conflict and had, morally speaking, opted for a Red Cross uniform rather than combat dress, he had written to me but I had never seen him again. Doubtless those who were born in Algeria, those who were affected and torn asunder by that war in a different way than we were, are the only ones who can properly judge him. And anyway, in the name of what can anyone demand that people make a commitment? . . . We at least knew that, with Camus, it was not a question of cowardice, but rather a mixture of despair and love for life. I remember the damning phrase that Sartre reportedly uttered when we learned that Camus had won the Nobel Prize: "It's only fitting."

Mauriac loathed Camus, and the feeling was mutual. During the time when both of them were working at *L'Express,* they used to meet each other in the hallway, where they would exchange perfunctory greetings. Never anything more. Later, Mauriac discovered to his great surprise that Camus was the son of a cleaning woman, and he always thought of him thereafter in a somewhat different light, with more indulgence and understanding. So many people have already written about Camus that I've sometimes wondered whether he didn't have more childhood friends than all the schools in Algeria could contain over a twenty-year period, so I'll refrain from adding to the existing mass. All I want to say about Camus was that he had the most beautiful way of looking at you of anyone I've ever met. An expression that was open and yet tinged with darkness.

Time was passing, and I was filled with an ever more compelling desire to extricate myself from politics and find new roots somewhere else. Anywhere. In the earth, music, fashion, especially in medicine, that old dream . . . For a moment I thought I might really be able to realize it. I was ready to do literally anything to study medicine; I'd work thirty hours a day. But you needed a good background in mathematics to get into medical school, and I couldn't start from scratch to learn math.

I had to yield to the truth that I was no longer a young woman, with that marvelous mobility that had once been mine, that certainty of being able to do anything if I really wanted to badly enough, of being able to assimilate anything new.

It was at this time that I faced certain facts for the first time. I couldn't start to learn math from scratch. Therefore, I was no longer young. Not long afterward I came to the realization that I was "blocked" musically. When you are growing up, there comes a time when your bones are grown as much as they're going to. That's where I was with music. I could still appreciate and enjoy Webern and Stockhausen. But my son took me to a concert at the *Domaine Musical,** which he enjoyed immensely, whereas I was bored. Oddly, that's not true with rock music, which I find voluptuous if you really give yourself to it.

Everything doesn't get blocked at the same time. And as far as politics goes . . . I don't know whether one should say "happily" or "unfortunately," but the fact is that interest in politics never lessens. Mine had simply suffered an eclipse. All it took to restore it was one or two seizures of the magazine. After '58, one would have thought that that indignity would at least have ceased. But it hadn't. *L'Express* was seized a dozen times between '58 and '62.

Each time it was the same script that was followed. In those days the magazine went to press on Wednesday to go on sale the following day. On Wednesday evening a telephone call would come informing us that this or that minister had objected to a passage in this or that article. All the copies were confiscated by the police, which is highly illegal. According to French law, the police are supposed to keep two or three copies as evidence for the courts that you indeed committed a crime in writing whatever the authorities objected to. But there is nothing that legally allows for an entire printing

* In France, a concert series dedicated to promoting avant-garde music. — *Translator.*

of a magazine to be seized. That doesn't stop them. They seized it anyway. So what he had to do was reprint the issue Wednesday night, with big white holes indicating the censored passages.

When you think about it, though, why would the seizures have ceased, since the tortures were still going on, and it was always against them that we were up in arms? But it was obvious that De Gaulle didn't give a damn about the tortures. Political mishaps.

As Mauriac used to say: "I don't mind not going any longer to see the classic tragedies being massacred on the stages of our subsidized theaters. Politics is quite enough to satisfy my taste for being shocked by historical characters." That was at the time of the Algiers insurrection, after General Massu had been replaced. The Lagaillarde show was marked by this superb remark by De Gaulle: "In the Fifth Republic there is no February 6th.* Monsieur Lagaillarde, and Monsieur Pinay as well [the latter had just resigned as Minister of Finances], are in the wrong Republic!"

Let's be fair: as far as superb one-liners are concerned, we had more than our share under De Gaulle. What happened next? Or before? With the passage of time, it gets a little confusing to follow the precise chronology of insurrections, historic speeches, the generals' shifting allegiances, the barricades . . .

Looking back, what importance did it all have? The only interesting question is whether things might have ended differently. And there I find it impossible to say. Theoretically, yes. In reality, I doubt it. I loathed that period, from one end to the other — including the demonstrations in which I dutifully participated — because all of it was unnecessary. At least for France. And all the more so for the French Algeri-

* The day in 1956 when Guy Mollet was pelted with tomatoes in Algiers. — *Translator.*

ans. What more could they lose! Perhaps it was historically indispensable for the birth of Algerian awareness . . . But what a frightful mess!

And all that, which took eight years of our lives, will be given twenty lines in the history textbooks of tomorrow.

— Will De Gaulle have twenty lines?

— No. One. "Saved the honor of France on June 18, 1940."

— That's the entire balance sheet, in your opinion?

— That's not a bad balance sheet! Who in the autumn of his years wouldn't settle for as much?

XV

DE GAULLE'S BALANCE SHEET doesn't really interest me very much. That's accounting. His story, yes. That obsessive and yet sublime identification by one man with his country, that compulsion to seize fate, those love affairs with a person named France — cruel, versatile, unfaithful the moment she had been won, rebellious the moment she was subdued; ungrateful the moment she had been cured of her bawdy acts with the Mollets and Pinays of this world; and, finally, betraying him with a Pompidou, before his very eyes . . . And he watches, he remains silent, and he dies . . . It's Tristan discovering that Isolde is sleeping with the gamekeeper.

His genius for the word, with which for years he replaced the weight and power that France no longer really had . . . One could admire him for this one sentence about Pétain, uttered at the charnel house of Douaumont at the fiftieth anniversary of Verdun: "If in the late winter of his life, and in the midst of momentous events, the wear and tear of old age led Marshal Pétain to unfortunate lapses, the glory that twenty years earlier . . ." etc.

Is it possible to phrase it any better than that? How I love words, and appreciate people who know how to weigh them, how to weave them into a meaningful whole. One kind of poverty that frightens me is the one I envisage whereby I would suddenly be stripped of words, with only the following left behind in my memory: "It's lovely weather . . ." "I'm cold . . ." "Pass me the salt . . ." "What time is it?" I remember one day when I was in prison, a cellmate of mine had reached the end of her rope; the solitude and inactivity had got to her, and so to distract her I began to recite poetry the way you sing to calm children, any verses I could think of. When I came to a particular refrain she liked she repeated it over ánd over, the way you suck a piece of delicious candy. And afterward she wanted more.

De Gaulle was a prince of words.

And then there was his exit — one could argue endlessly about whether or not he really wanted to lose the April 1969 referendum. As though Charles De Gaulle, alone, was immune from ambivalence! He too wanted to be loved, and wanted people to keep telling him so. Who has ever managed to escape that? Not even Stalin, who foundered into paranoia, which might best be translated by: "No one loves me . . . even though I'm God . . ."

You have to admit that politics is the ideal terrain for paranoia. When you are a manufacturer of stovepipes, it's rather difficult to convince yourself that they're the most extraordinary stovepipes in the world, and if your business isn't booming it's because the people who buy stovepipes are plotting together against you. And if the day ever comes when the stovepipe manufacturer begins to think that way, it's virtually impossible for people not to become immediately aware of it.

In the field of politics, on the contrary, paranoia can develop to its heart's content, either on the party level or on the level of an individual. "I'm right, I have a clear vision of things, and my opponents are plotting to do me in . . ." is commonplace at best. Such a statement won't win any militants to a cause. A pinch of paranoia, in any case, is just what is called for in a situation of struggle. Boxers say that you have to hate your opponent to win, hate him purely and simply. In politics, if you are able to see your opponents' point of view, whereas they are incapable of seeing or understanding yours, the best thing to do is to change professions. That, by the way, is why I think I'll never really go into politics, why I've resisted the temptation all along: because the reasons why the others think or act the way they do interests me too much.

I was saying that De Gaulle needed constantly renewed proof that people loved him. Perhaps the peculiar conjunction of circumstances that were his destiny prevented him from ever having the unanimous backing of the country. On two different occasions he was the war leader of a France divided against itself.

Which reminds me of the story of Maurice de Nassau, the man who saved Holland ten times. One day he was in the town of Gorcum, where he was told that those who had helped him take Barneveld now regretted it and when they talked about him referred to him as "the tyrant." He found it hard to believe. But when, at noon that day, a market day, he walked through the center of the village waving left and right to the townspeople, no one returned his greetings, and be realized it was true that the people had ceased to love him. Then he began to lose weight, until he wasted away to nothing and, very shortly thereafter, he died. Perhaps he had a predisposition to melancholy. But power is always melancholic, since it is solitary.

Today there are various means of verifying the truth before you start losing weight: there are elections, which are pleasure pure and simple, since to win them proves beyond any shadow of doubt that the people prefer you; there are public-opinion polls; there are referendums.

De Gaulle verified the real situation. And we are all very stupid — I am, in any case — to have thought that he wouldn't know how to exit gracefully from history before he was overtaken and sunk by old age, since he was, more than anything else, the personification of pride. His relationships with God . . . now there's something we would love to know and never will. And yet it would be far more interesting than knowing what his relationships were with his Premier, Monsieur Couve de Murville.

The fact remains that his exit was superb.

Hitler, to take another example, tried to kill Germany rather than leave it to anyone else. Does the analogy shock you? It's De Gaulle himself who made it, in the very same context that I am using it. Go back and read what he wrote in *Le Salut* . . . I can't quote it from memory; it's better to look it up and cite it verbatim.

Here's how it goes: "That man who came up from nothing, offered himself to Germany at a time when she was casting around for a new lover. She gave herself to the unknown passerby who represented adventure, who promised domination, and whose impassioned voice aroused her secret instincts . . . If Hitler was strong, he was also and always clever. He knew how to entice, to caress. Germany, seduced to the very depths of her being, followed her Führer with all her heart and soul."

Is it possible to describe any more clearly than that how one conceives of the relationships between a man and a nation? Is it possible to describe any better the real sense of the quest for power, and the thirst one is trying to slake in seeking it?

Metaphors don't spring to mind when one is writing unless there is good reason. Lover, domination, caress . . . To that degree, it's almost too perfect. And that is nothing next to the text which he deliberately inserted, in 1959, as an epigraph to *Le Salut:* Paul Claudel's *Ode,* in the form of a dialogue between France and De Gaulle. Listen to how it pleases De Gaulle to have France speak:

> "But tell me that this relationship which has finally been established between us won't end!
>
> "I don't care about the rest, but you, ask me that thing which is naught but everything!
>
> "They thought they were making fun of me by saying I was a a woman! They'll see the kind of woman I am, they'll see what it means to have a soul in one's body!
>
> "They've asked me often enough for my body; and you ask me for my soul."

To which the General replies:

> "Woman, hold thy tongue!"

You can laugh, get angry, or be otherwise moved if you are one of those who feel they are of a mind to say to any President of France: "But tell me that this relationship which has finally been established between us . . ."

Any intense relationship with power is an avatar of sexuality. But that is fairly obvious. The day in April of '69 when the general said: "Woman, give me your answer . . . ," things turned sour. It had to happen sooner or later. The point is, there was no longer any woman at all — assuming that the image was adequate to start with — but only those people who are very embarrassing for those who govern, namely the governed, with their ever-increasing tendency to stick their noses into places that concern them. Strangest of all, of that whole group of leaders, De Gaulle was perhaps the only one to realize that fact. But it was too late.

For three years, from 1962–1965, he possessed total

power. To do what? It is unlikely that anyone ever again in the history of France will hold such power, giving him the possibility of doing whatever he wants to, without coercion. The fact is — and therein lies the rub — he didn't use it to dynamite some of our bottlenecks, he didn't use it to unify Europe politically, in the final analysis he didn't use it at all! . . .

In 1963, for the first time half of the eligible voters had passed the critical age of forty-five, by which age conservative tendencies are thought to have set in. In other words, De Gaulle had at his disposal an impregnable electorate, over and above that portion of the people who, for one reason or another, felt closer to him than they did to the bourgeois politicians. He had at his disposal an electorate which could be made to swallow literally anything, as long as it came from him — and that included violent reforms of the system. And we have every reason to believe that he was fully aware of how necessary those reforms were . . . But perhaps the truth of the matter is that, even when your name is De Gaulle, you govern less absolutely than you think from the Élysée Palace.

As for Europe . . . One day Jean Monnet wrote De Gaulle saying: "You must be the first President of Europe. And the second will be Adenauer." De Gaulle invited him to come and see him. They had a long conversation. And with Jean Monnet, there is never any question of ambiguity or lack of clarity as to details. After their talk, De Gaulle told some of his cabinet members about the plan, which in his mind appeared in these terms: "After all, if Germany wants to become French . . ."

For Europe, he was probably too old. More's the pity. For in that three-year period he could have done anything, not only in France but also in Europe. But he was like the setting sun of this world.

I don't know what our next dawns will be . . . luminous or bloody. But today no golden light is any longer capable of illuminating the dusk . . . must we say, "of the West?" The never-ending obsequies of a culture, a civilization, and a few other amenities that I appreciate just as much as the next person, this perpetual funeral to which those who have read Spengler and those who have never heard of him are forever inviting us, is an alibi for impotence. For sterility. And also for fear of the void.

Too late for God, too early for the Human Being; that's simply an elegant way of saying the same thing. That something is winding down to a close is obvious, but it was in 1940 that the bell tolled. Since then, we've been in a state of suspense, waiting for something else to be born. And births are far more fascinating than deaths.

At least that's the way I see it, at the same time understanding that one can, on an individual basis, view this period with horror, for any number of reasons. One may be that you belong to a protected or privileged social class and that a certain leveling is taking place which destroys all kinds of things you hold dear, including the very barriers of protection which shield you. Or this period may horrify you because, being completely ignorant of the past, you are shocked and upset by the spectacle of poverty, the wretchedness of servile labor, the tacit complicity of the masters — whether they be those who control the economy in a country or the masters of the world, the massacres fed by the weapons we manufacture, and other abominations.

I understand both positions — one can, in fact, parodoxically adhere to both — but I cannot pretend to react to the entire situation by defeatism, since I don't feel it, even if sometimes I have doubts . . . Assuming that you don't confuse metaphysics with social structures, defeatism is not any more reasonable than optimism, and the latter has the virtue of being bracing.

If you begin to ask me about the meaning of life, the scandal of human suffering, and the absurdity of the human condition, I have no answer today, nor will I have one for a millennium hence . . . assuming that between now and then no one drops the atom bomb . . . You have to accept it, get used to it, even if you do so with the help of a pain-killer.

We belong to a strange species which needs to believe that life has a meaning. Do elephants ask themselves such a question? Yet they're alive too. They have a social structure, one which has remained the same since elephant time im-memorial; they practice the division of labor and the domina-tion of a minority over the mass of elephants, without it hav-ing led to elephantine disputes, at least so far as we have heard. And those sturdy builders, the beavers, have never made an ounce of progress in the art of construction since beavers first made their appearance on the face of the earth. No language, therefore no transmission of knowledge, there-fore no progress. But also no anguish.

We're not elephants. We are paying a very dear price for the fact that we invented the wheel and invented the bal-lerina's skirt, ever since a certain Prometheus, disgusted be-cause women were the source of life rather than he, went off to steal fire from the gods. What else is there to do but accept it and knuckle down to it? . . . But enough about the human condition. There is the daily condition of men, women, and children, about which we are not powerless to do something; or at least I refuse to believe we are.

Let's not go all the way back to the famines of the Middle Ages. We're in the process of taking a bird's-eye view of a half century, the one I've lived through. The countries that we refer to today as "underdeveloped" were not any better off fifty years ago. And the fact that the notion of a Third World has come into the conscience of the West can only be taken as a sign of progress. Humanity only poses problems for itself that it can solve. Let's say, for argument's sake, that we are passing through that disagreeable moment when the problems are being posed. And that is also probably true insofar as a number of other areas are concerned, such as ecology, the exhaustion of natural resources, etc.

To take the concrete example of France: if I compare my own situation when I was a young stenographer with that of a girl today earning the same salary, there is simply no comparison. And not only because of Social Security, which has less meaning for someone who is young than it does later on in life. Although I must say I remember once when I had a case of appendicitis . . . A month of paid vacation; I never knew what it was to have a vacation. Charter trips and organized travel; in my day that didn't even enter into your wildest dreams. Paperback books, the lithograph available at the local ten-cent store, blue jeans and the T-shirts, instant mashed potatoes, the transistor radio you can buy for next to nothing, the boyfriend who has a Citroen 2CV he bought secondhand, and off you go to the country. And the pill! It's not a better world; it's another world altogether.

Marx's analysis has not proved accurate because we have witnessed an increase both in profits and salaries. We have seen that production techniques have managed to make consumer goods widely available at cheap prices, that the standard of living in Europe has increased by 54 percent in the past ten years, that the market economy can find — and in the case of Sweden did — a corrective through taxation so that profits are to a large degree transformed into collective assets.

Is it possible to still say that "class" is defined by the position one occupies in the productive process? Nobody talks any more about the "working class," actually, but about the "workers," who can hardly be thought of as a homogeneous class, even if none of them controls the means of production.

It is less than obvious that the conflict surrounding the expropriation by the state of these means of production takes into account the real antagonisms today which, basically, are aimed at "society" more than they are against capitalism. What happens then? I'm not an economist-philosopher, any more than I'm a philosopher-economist! And although economics is my secret vice, this is not the time or place to go into it further.

But when one has wished for, as I have — and as many others have as well — a situation where the maximum number of people can have a real chance to be educated, and the possibility to enjoy a wide variety of personal pleasures, I am not any more going to cry bitter tears when that happens than I am going to be surprised when I see that mass of humanity begin to voice its gripes. On the contrary. Ultimately, the more the masses become educated and aware of intellectual concerns, the more demands they are going to make. Those demands are going to focus on a more effective participation in the formation of a collective will, the attempt to accede to positions of economic strength and power over the way people think. Look at the struggle going on today in the fields of the press and television. From where I sit, even if I wanted to I couldn't turn my back on this aspect of the situation, since I hold a fragment of power by my ability to influence people's thinking. And, unless I refuse to ponder any question seriously, I'm obliged to keep asking myself how I'm using that power.

L'Express belongs to Jean-Jacques Servan-Schreiber and two of his sisters. Not to me. I am therefore not in any position to decide tomorrow to turn it into an instrument of social disintegration, assuming I wanted to. But I do have the ability to leave it. I don't leave it, therefore I am taking part in the existence and propogation of an instrument of integration: that is uncontestable. It is within the framework of that society that the magazine's struggle to change it is situated, a struggle which can be — and surely has been by some — described as an effort to anesthetize, to enervate, in the real sense of the term, the potential revolutionaries who read us, to channel their energies from some revolutionary project by lulling them with various reformist plans. In the final analysis, therefore, according to those same people who thus judge it, it serves the ruling class.

Personally, I'm willing to admit that evaluation, on the condition that those who make it are willing to concede that no revolutionary plan for the Western societies really exists, that there isn't even the start of any new ideology and *praxis* to liberate human labor from its servile state, and that Europe is the last place in the world conducive to carrying out controlled experiments, unless a joint decision is made by Germany, England, Holland, and Belgium to attempt it simultaneously. Don't mistake the nationalization of the pharmaceutical industry called for by the Socialist-Communist program in the 1973 French elections — which I would gladly pass up — for a plan to overhaul society. I believe in integration as long as one retains one's critical faculties. If society changes as much in the next half century as it has in the past fifty years . . . and it will change.

The only things that strike me as being interesting or worthwhile today are to seize the movement of life, go along with it, accelerate it, participate in the processes of transformation, give them impetus with all the strength at your command, help understand them, therefore make them live and grow. But perhaps my attitude can be explained as emanating from where I am and what I am today.

To reiterate: I understand that people lose interest, that

they withdraw from the game, that they devote themselves to appreciating painting, for instance . . . But painting is reflection and sends you back to the world. No, make no mistake about it: you cannot lose interest.

What is happening in the United States, which Jean-François Revel was the first to feel and reveal in France, is perhaps what the revolution of the Renaissance was in the sixteenth century. Europe, after all, didn't wake up one day and say: "Hey! Today's the Renaissance!"

Whether we expect the light to come from the West or the East, what is somewhat depressing is that things aren't happening here anymore. De Gaulle probably suffered more than anyone from the diminishment, the shrinkage, the weakened condition of France — and with her all the countries of Europe — with respect to the "great powers." And what nostalgia he must have suffered thinking what he might have been in days of yore, as head of a powerful state, flouting Bismarck, dealing with the Czar! He was an anachronism. That is perhaps why he managed in a way to be ahead of his time, since he was able to remain indifferent to and transcend bourgeois values.

I think that Pompidou was much more conservative than De Gaulle. De Gaulle wasn't afraid of movement. But he didn't succeed in taking over the leadership of that movement. In May of '68, he missed the opportunity of becoming the Mao Tse-tung of the West, all things being equal.

In his destiny, and to a lesser degree in that of Winston Churchill, isn't there food for thought regarding what part chance plays in major political adventures?

Take De Gaulle. In June 1940, he did everything in his power to persuade the President of the Council, Paul Reynaud, to leave for London. Reynaud, who was a remarkably intelligent man, was curiously under the spell of a coarse woman named Madame de Portes. She decided everything.

At the height of the debacle of 1940, William Bullitt, then the American ambassador to France, showed up one morning at Reynaud's residence to transmit an urgent message to him from President Roosevelt. Paul Reynaud received him in their bedroom, saying: "You can talk openly in front of Madame, as though we were alone." The ambassador then told Reynaud that the United States was ready and willing to deliver pursuit planes to France immediately. Madame de Portes' reaction: "Oh, no, not help from those bastards!"

It was she who governed the country. Was she in the pay of the Germans? It seems unlikely. Someone would have discovered it by now. Later that year, during the exodus on the roads of France, she killed herself.

The fact remains that De Gaulle's influence was nil and hers was great, and that, therefore, Paul Reynaud did not go to London, taking the legitimate government of France with him. Otherwise, who would have spoken over the BBC from London on June 18? Paul Reynaud, of course. And the entire course of Charles De Gaulle's life would have been different. Perhaps the course of other lives as well.

At the same time, another scene of another sort, but doubtless just as decisive, was taking place, and this one involved Churchill. When Chamberlain came to the conclusion that he was not the Prime Minister England needed to lead it in time of war, he himself named his successor, as was then the tradition in the English Conservative Party. He named Lord Halifax. In order to give the government as broad and solid a base as possible, he made it clear that he would like Churchill to be part of the government as well. He summoned him and said to him: "Halifax is the best man for the job. But we need you. Will you accept the number two post?"

Out of patriotism, duty, and because of that authentic grandeur which is abnegation in the face of superior interest,

Churchill said he would. A few hours later, Lord Beaver-brook, the tycoon of the English press and a man with a touch of genius, asked Churchill to receive him as soon as possible. When he arrived he said: "I understand that you've agreed to allow Halifax to be named Prime Minister? That's impossible!" Churchill answered that that was an affair of state and not something he cared to discuss with Lord Beaver-brook. The latter refused to be swayed. Churchill observed that he had no choice. To which Beaverbrook rejoined: "It's a crime against the country. You're the only one who can mobilize Great Britain." He insisted; he argued. Finally Churchill was convinced that Beaverbrook was right, but he objected: "I've given my word. And I don't intend to go back on it."

At that point, Beaverbrook said: "Then grant me only one favor. When you are summoned with Halifax to meet with Chamberlain, and when Chamberlain asks you to confirm your acceptance, remain silent for three full minutes — a hundred and eighty seconds — before you say yes. I ask it in the name of England!" Churchill found the request prepos-terous and didn't see how it could change the situation, but out of his esteem and friendship for Lord Beaverbrook, he promised he would.

The next day, Churchill and Halifax went to Chamber-lain's office at No. 10 Downing Street. "Would you be so kind as to confirm to Lord Halifax that you agree to join his cabinet?" . . . Thirty seconds. Fifty seconds. Still he didn't speak. A minute. Still silent. A minute and a half. Still no word. Before the three minutes had elapsed Lord Halifax said: "I think it's Winston who ought to be the Prime Minister." The least one can say is that those three minutes played a major role in the history of World War II.

And then, at the end of the Churchillian epoch, the English people quietly voted for Labour and sent Winston into retirement after the war. And at the end of the De Gaullian epoch, the French people coldly forced him into a run-off in the '65 presidential elections. Churchill returned to power, but as a tired, old man. De Gaulle remained in power for four years after '65, but essentially he too was without the strength or prestige of his earlier years. And do you remember the amazement of '65! Do you remember?

I remember ours, at the magazine, when the election results began to come in, and De Gaulle's percentage of the vote kept falling, only a little after 8:00 P.M.

— You hadn't foreseen the results at all?

— No, I really hadn't. I still must have the little piece of paper that I had framed, on which Gaston Defferre, Jean-Jacques, and I all wrote our predictions over the weekend of All Souls' Day in 1965. We had all guessed that De Gaulle would win between 51 percent and 55 percent of the vote.

— Why had *L'Express* backed Gaston Defferre as a candidate for the presidency in the first place?

— Because he was, theoretically, the best possible candidate to oppose De Gaulle for the office. He could win the Socialist vote, as well as the centrist.

— And from a practical viewpoint?

— On the practical level he lacked the prime ingredient, that is, the desire to lead the fight. He's a fighter, but strangely he's modest, timid, which doubtless accounts for his occasional verbal aggressiveness, which can be incredible. In any case, he is not someone who could be called overly ambitious. He's a "doer," as the Americans put it, someone who's at his best in bringing projects to fulfillment. Enterprising, daring, courageous . . . very courageous. He was an excellent minister; and doubtless will be again. He's a great mayor. He acts, but he doesn't consider himself among the political luminaries of the world. He wants to be first in his native Marseille, but when it comes to national politics he tends to hang back. That is why, three months before the presidential elections, he gave up.

Actually, men of great ambition are rare. What is sad to see is what those young men who, at the age of twenty, were consumed with ambition, become as they approach their fifties. The percentage of waste is devastating.

— Do you think of yourself as a person of great ambition?

— No, but I have never pulled back from trying to fulfill myself.

— So Operation Defferre failed, and at the same time you thought that *L'Express* needed to be transformed.

— There was no relationship between the two — unless, as you say, a temporal one. Actually, *L'Express* was adequate to its task, in its initial format, up until the end of the Algerian War. It was an instrument of combat: simple to produce and print . . . And outside the realm of politics, it was also in the ascendance. That's not as natural as it may seem. The political Left is not necessarily receptive to what is new in the fields of literature, painting, movies — of the arts in general.

We were receptive, and that, I believe, is one of the more meaningful aspects of the magazine. The spectrum of our receptiveness went from the new novel to our effort to explain the full sense of what the computer revolution was going to do to our world in ten years; it went from the prediction of the crises that were to ensue in the universities to Godard's films and Rauschenberg's paintings; from ecology — I think we published one of the first major texts on the subject, in 1967 — to the battle for contraception.

On that front, there was no break between the old and the new *L'Express,* which still had its antennae out for new trends and movements. But in all other areas we had turned into a firebrand — which was to be expected in the atmosphere of civil war through which we were then passing. But when France emerged from the state, the magazine was no longer in tune with the times. It threatened to become the periodical of the veterans of a civil war. Jean-Jacques therefore decided, against the judgment of most of the staff, to change the physical format and layout. I'm forever amazed at those people who talk endlessly of change but who scream bloody murder when someone shifts their desk.

— And how about you? Were you for that change?

— I knew that the time had come to grow. It's never very pleasant or easy to grow. I had already been through one experience on a magazine that had evolved from a small-craftsman stage to a large enterprise. The small-craftsman aspect always remains; it's inseparable from the publication of any magazine, fortunately! But the dimensions change, if only in the size and situation of the offices, and the human relationships dependent thereon. I didn't try to block the change, however; on the contrary, I was all for it, since I judged that it was inevitable.

And besides, I figured we might well be in for a decade of monarchy tempered with elections, which would, on each occasion, give the Gaullists a working majority. The 1962 elections were enlightening. I'm not overly fond of election rallies, far from it, but I once saw, during those campaigns, the surprising spectacle of a candidate who arrived at a meeting in Normandy and said to the assembled voters: "I have nothing to say to you except that I'm for General de Gaulle. That's all." And he swept all the votes, while a man like Mendès-France was being voted out of the office he had held as representative from the Eure department for twenty-five years. It was a parliament where there was no room for a Mendès-France, but plenty of room for a captain in the gendarmerie.

It was a time when, for a while at least, you had to turn

your attention to other matters. In fact, I had started to turn my attention to myself, something that hadn't happened to me for many years, and to rediscover a way of living that took me back a long time, when I had loved to dance, take in every film that came out, hand in hand with some beloved friend; when I had driven a car very fast, driving all night to end up, at dawn, on the shores of the Mediterranean, and diving into its waters as the sun rose over the horizon.

One has to have done that in one's life, and I had done very little of it. Now I did it again, knowing that I probably wouldn't ever do it again but that, if it gave me a little pleasure, well, I had earned it. All of which did not keep me from working; I wonder if anything could keep me from working?

Jean-Jacques proposed that we try to build a new *L'Express,* become a major magazine. Why not? I lacked a goal, and that was one.

With a few exceptions, the employes of *L'Express* were recalcitrant. A few left.

I suppose that Jean Daniel* would have left *L'Express* anyway. He's very much aware of his own worth, which is considerable. And he wasn't a man to put up forever with not being the number one person on any paper.

On that score, I'm always astonished at the way people judge the movement from one periodical to another in France. Someone moves to a new job? He's a traitor. It's all they can do to shake his hand when he leaves. And, seen from the outside, the public tends to bury a newspaper or magazine whenever an important editor leaves it. In the States, when an editor of *Time* magazine leaves for a new post, the magazine publishes a little notice, saying in so many words: "We are proud to announce that Mr. X has been

* A former editor of *L'Express,* now editor of the rival newsweekly, *Le Nouvel Observateur. — Translator.*

named to a new post with ABC Magazine. He, and those of our former colleagues now with other staffs, are proof that *Time* does its job well. It will not be long before most of the American press will be staffed by former colleagues of ours who have learned their trade at *Time* . . .," etc.

I would gladly do the same thing at *L'Express.* Anyway, Jean Daniel left, taking three or four others with him, to found *Le Nouvel Observateur,* which had been bought by the industrialist, Claude Perdriel. As far as I know, their collaboration has been highly successful, as I've already suggested.

At *L'Express,* the influx of capital required to transform it into its new format was considerable. The risk, therefore, was great. If it had failed, Jean-Jacques would have been up to his ears in debts for years, and everything his father had derived from the sale of his share of *Les Echos* would have gone down the drain. It was consequently a gamble, but a reasonable one. Anyone with eyes could see that France, emerging from the final stages of decolonization, was going to take the plunge into the industrial society, behind Germany and, of course, the United States. You can think whatever you like about industrial societies, you can love them or hate them; you can prefer the pastoral life. But the fact is we no longer have any choice, which was already the case in '62. We had to fashion a magazine to fit that society at a given moment in time.

During the preceding ten years, there had been a very important development as far as the press was concerned, and that was the growth of television — outside of the uses to which it was put by De Gaulle for political purposes. Do you know the story about De Gaulle and TV? The first time he talked on television, in '58, he read his text. Within the hour, Marcel Bleustein, the advertising executive, called De Gaulle to ask for an appointment. De Gaulle was fond of him and gave him one almost immediately. Bleustein simply said to him: "General, when you come to visit me in my home, I don't feel like seeing you in profile, wearing your glasses, reading. When you're on television, you're visiting me in my home." De Gaulle gave no reaction, but from that time on he never read on television again. He wrote out his texts, which he then learned by heart.

Television, which was then monopolized by the party in power, nonetheless grew rapidly in the space of a few short years, even if, in number of channels and hours of programming, it still lags far behind countries like Japan or the United States. In both those countries, television begins early in the morning. Here, at least, hell doesn't begin until lunch time! But there are nonetheless three radio networks which do begin broadcasting at dawn, and which have assumed considerable importance. What had happened was that we had reached a point where we were being bombarded by news programs which were largely incoherent and which, in the long run, completely annihilated any personal reflection, not to mention understanding, of the events described. Thus the initial service that needed to be rendered the public was to evolve some order out of this general chaos, sort out the important from the trivial, give some structure to the news. No one can assimilate the amount of information broadcast daily without going half insane. It's a question of quantity of news being the opposite of disseminating meaningful news.

— Do you think that in creating this second *L'Express* you did something as innovative as you did with the first?

— Yes and no. No, because from a format and layout point of view, it was analagous to those of *Time* magazine in the States, and to *Der Spiegel* in Germany, which had imitated *Time* after the war.

L'Express was innovative in France where others had tried and failed. For it was not enough to change your format and replace one type of printing — letterpress — by another —

offset. It was a whole journalistic technique that had to be reinvented, assimilated, and adapted for France. Short articles — those that most newspapermen write in six pages — can almost always be reduced to three, concision, getting to the heart of an article as soon as possible, the lead sentences, and many other things besides . . .

Imposing that new technique, even on those who were ready and willing to learn it, was very difficult. Those first few months of the "new" *L'Express* left me reeling. Fourteen-hour days, and at the end of the tenth week, the near certainty that we were heading straight for disaster. A pure nightmare.

And then we took off. But what an effort! Sometimes, when I happen to pause in front of a mirror and look at my face, at every line and wrinkle there, I can almost name the date and place of each one. There's a saying that our faces are the maps of our lives. Mine is, in addition, the map of a magazine.

Anyway, it's better than having a face which bears the traces of alcohol, drugs, overeating, jealousy, boredom, whatever . . . It's a dear old face. I've never devoted much time to it, and it's done its best to resist everything I've inflicted on it.

One day when I was eighteen years old I went to see a famous fortune teller whose name was Fraya. She had an enormous salon. When I entered it she cried out: "Oh! I see, I see!" I waited for some marvelous revelation. Then she went on: "I see that you'll remain young for a long, long time . . ." When you're eighteen, that's not the kind of prophecy you're looking for to sustain you. I left deeply disappointed.

Still, it's a bore to grow old. It's unesthetic. People ought to die beautiful.

— Why do you talk about death so often?

— Do I talk about it a lot? I don't know. Maybe because

death has struck so often, and so close, to me. So many of my friends. Young people, I mean . . . It's like a circle of shadows around me. But you have to keep from becoming their prisoner. It's the living you have to worry about. On that score, I do as much as I can.

❧ XVI

— HERE IT IS 1965, and you're at the head of a renovated *L'Express*. You said it broke through?

— It didn't break through; it literally exploded. Its rate of growth exceeded every prediction. I wasn't at the head of the magazine, as you put it. It had become a business, a relatively large, heavy business which required all kinds of complex commercial strategy. I was only in charge of the editorial end. I spent so much time and effort going over other people's articles that I had hardly any left to write myself. It was only at the end of 1966 that I began to write a regular editorial.

— And yet I remember that you followed the presidential campaign on television. I remember your articles about it . . .

— Yes, because I had a shock. Everyone did, in fact. When one party has had a monopoly on television, when only its members have had the right to speak, and only its propaganda has been aired on its channels, even if you know better you tend to forget that anyone thinks differently. If De Gaulle hadn't been so sure of himself, and, it must be added in all fairness, if the notion of dictatorship had not been so foreign to him, he would never have allowed the candidates opposing him to appear on the magic screen.

Suddenly, and for the first time, television was allowing the opposition to be seen and heard. Up till then these gentlemen had been described by the Gaullists as a bunch of lumberjacks. And all of a sudden the public was discovering that these gentlemen who were polite, decent-looking, and as capable of speaking for fifteen minutes without notes as De Gaulle himself, were not Gaullists. It was discovering that another political viewpoint, another platform, could be presented peacefully and rationally . . .

When that portion of the French electorate generally referred to as the center realized that salient fact, De Gaulle's magic was shaken once and for all. And it must be noted that the "center" is a decisive swing vote.

— Who shook it? Mitterrand?

— I don't think so. In 1965, Mitterrand's political profile was disturbing to many, first of all because he was against De Gaulle, but also because he was the candidate of the Left, including the Communists. He was the man through whom the Communists might come to power. And his early television appearances in the midsixties did nothing to dissipate that visceral reaction he so often arouses in people. But he has worked hard to eliminate that irritating quality, and I think that in the recent presidential campaign he tended to go over much better. Mitterrand is a man of great patience, and no one I know works harder to overcome apparent shortcomings.

But what a heavy past he was then dragging behind him politically! We've already talked about the affair of the "leaks." And then there was the Observatory affair, which was even more important. Do you remember it?

— It rings a faint bell. I remember some kind of scandal.

— It was in October of '59. Mitterrand was driving home.

He lived opposite the Observatory Gardens, and just as he arrived, his car was fired on. He wasn't touched. It was thought that he had escaped an ambush, as there were a goodly number at the time. And then several days later, a somewhat dubious character named Pesquet revealed that the so-called armed attack had been staged with Mitterrand's complicity.

Today, we more or less know what really happened. Pesquet presumably had been paid to kill Mitterrand, and instead informed him, convincing him that the only way to avoid really being assassinated was to involve himself in the fake attempt that Pesquet would pretend to carry out. At least that's the version generally accepted. At the time, though, there was a big scandal, and Mitterrand was indicted.

I saw him one evening break down and cry. It seemed that his career was ruined. We gave him what we could, that is we opened the pages of *L'Express* to him so that he could at least say what he had to say. I remember that he wrote: "What shall I say to those who love me and esteem me, except to ask them to believe in me." It wasn't the easiest thing in the world to do. The pressures were incredible. Keep away from Mitterrand, people from all quarters were whispering, or you'll go down with him.

My daughter, who was then a little girl, still remembers having seen him one evening when he came to dinner at the house. She remembers that he looked so different from the way he usually did that she realized that something very serious had happened.

Years went by. It was said that if the prosecution was never followed up with all the vigor one might have feared, it was because Mitterrand, on his side, had a dangerous file on one of De Gaulle's ministers, a file he had had in his hands while he was Minister of Justice.

Nonetheless, hardly a month passed without there being

some mention somewhere of the Observatory affair. How can people get involved in politics, I would like to know? What is that passion that tears them away from enjoying life and its attendant pleasures and propels them unflaggingly into that inexpiable struggle, the moment their ambitions exceed mediocrity? . . .

Be that as it may, in 1965 I was afraid, afraid for him, and what he represented, afraid to see the rumor build once again. But how could I tell him that? There may be some people who find it easier to talk to and communicate with Mitterrand than I do, despite all the years we've known each other and all the battles we've fought and the untold hours we've spent together. There is something unfathomable in him which holds me back, some secret spring which eludes me . . . I haven't given up hoping that I'll discover it some day, especially if he continues writing . . . When you know how to read, writing ultimately reveals everything.

Meanwhile, in October of '65, I asked Defferre to express the fears we had, and tell Mitterrand that Pesquet was talking too much.

But Mitterrand took the bull by the horns. It was a good gamble.

Much later, only a few months ago, when I was reading an article Mitterrand wrote about a book by Pierre Viansson-Ponté, I found a sentence I noted, because it was very revealing. Speaking of someone else, Mitterrand remarked that the movement toward power can be accelerated "when, before the obstacle reputed to be unsurmountable, there enters into play that element called pride, that terrible desire to be oneself, to prove oneself before proving to others that anything is possible if you make up your mind to attain it." He had, therefore, made up his mind.

Since then, I have in fact revised my opinion on the attitude one should take with respect to slander. Ultimately, it's the same as with blackmail. You should never give in an inch. It's purely a question of courage.

— Mitterrand had courage.

— He has a great deal of courage, but I never questioned that about him. I can even say that he has an attraction for teetering on the cliff's edge that can be dangerous. But in 1965 I didn't think courage was enough. As it turned out, it was. It's a lesson to remember.

— You said: "It was a good gamble." But he lost!

— Lost what? He had nothing to lose, and he wound up with a very impressive percentage of the final votes in that election, and almost 50 percent in 1974. After the 1965 elections, he suddenly found himself propelled into a position of leadership of the Left, a position he had earned himself. Even with all the ups and downs that followed, it's nonetheless thanks to that gamble that he became head of the Socialist Party, worked out an electoral alliance with the Communists, and came within a fraction of winning the presidency in 1974. That was what he really wanted: to become the President of France . . .

— All that didn't modify your analysis?

— My analysis . . . Let's rather say statements of fact. Like everyone in 1965, I came to the realization that the presence of Communists in any coalition acts as a repellant to that portion of the electorate without which there can be no Leftist majority. Is that a factor that we will always have to contend with? Is that repugnance something that will lessen as time passes and more and more younger people reach voting age? Will the Communists, by dint of disguising themselves as sheep, end up by being taken for sheep? But in that case what will distinguish them from the social-democrats and even from the tough-minded Socialists whose goal is in essence to attain socialism without resorting to Socialist methods?

All I know is that Communism has never assumed and maintained power other than by force, and that it has never, anywhere in the world, allowed free elections even when it has been in power long enough to feel sure that the majority of the people were in favor of it. And that leads me to wonder about this system which is supposed to assure the people's happiness, and yet doesn't dare ask the people if it would like some changes in the system or the methods.

And what if all the world's ills did not stem from capital? What if Marx, who was the heir of the eighteenth-century rationalists, had known Freud and suspected that, as far as the dictatorship of the proletariat was concerned, the truth is that any group of human beings who holds power has only one thought in mind: to keep it — and that includes those who set themselves up as representatives of the people?

Power is never "good." I don't care whose power it is. And yet at the same time power is necessary for any collectivity. So the question comes down to this: how do you limit that power without stripping it of its efficacy. That is a question to which I have no answer.

I do note, however, that capitalism has a great capacity to adapt. There's something very mysterious about the evolution of human history. No one decided from one day to the next that societies would become capitalist — and yet they did. It was Lenin, I believe, who remarked that the problem with Russia in 1917 was not an excess of capitalism but an insufficiency.

Many people did decide to set out to set up socialist societies, but up to now they have never succeeded in attaining their original goals.

— Do you believe in Mitterrand's socialism?

— In his convictions? I believe that he is sincerely, in a true Christian sense, on the side of the weak and the downtrodden, the poor and the humble; I believe that he *feels* misfortune and is not simply content to talk about it; I think that in his heart of hearts he is a "sharer," but that at the same time he has no idea of the complexity of the economic mechanisms which obtain in industrial societies. Mitterrand is a lawyer. Give him a judicial case, and he can not only assimilate it with great speed, but he can argue it in court quite wonderfully. He has a great talent for expressing himself and, what is rare, he writes as well as he speaks. That does not imply either a profound knowledge of, or especially, a deep concern for, what he is arguing. He says to himself: "Once I'm in power, we'll see." Actually, I can see him as being relentless. The whole question is: relentless toward whom?

Don't misunderstand me. I would not mind living in a socialist society; nor would I find anything wrong with being paid a lower salary, in such a society, than a skilled worker, since my profession is more interesting than his. But what am I saying! In 1918, Gorki paid a 35,000 rouble fine for having published in his magazine a story that the authorities did not approve of, and since 1918 no periodical that is independent of the authorities has ever appeared in Russia — or in any other people's republic, in fact. Therefore, I would not be a journalist any longer, since I am not by nature cut out to be an apologist . . .

I could be what? A fashion designer, a cook, a hairdresser, a chauffeur, a number of things. A pianist in a nightclub, if indeed nightclubs still existed. But what I hope I never have to live through is a civil war, no matter what form it might take. People being denounced and informed on, executions, prisons jam-packed, hate elevated into an official doctrine . . . My love of progress and my adaptive ability stop short of any such situation. Like that reactionary humanist Rosa Luxemburg, I believe that freedom is always the freedom of the person who has a different viewpoint from your own.

And that is a concept I hold dear. And Mitterrand does, too, of that you can be quite sure.

Let us not be apocalyptic. What I fear much more than what Monsieur Marchais and the Communist Party would do if they came to power, or became part of the ruling coalition, is what those who have been in power have failed to do.

It's not enough to cite what happened in Prague. On this point, Mitterrand's logic appears irrefutable: he says that the world is divided in two and we belong to the American camp, a fact of which we're well aware. The Americans, who did not lift a finger when the Russians entered Prague, would never allow the Red Army to enter France. Therefore, the Red Army will never enter France. Therefore, there's no point in worrying about it. Prague is a most regrettable situation. But it's not our problem.

— Is that the way you reacted to the events in Prague?

— No, I reacted to them very strongly and wrote about it accordingly. But I'm not a politician locked into some strategical concept. I have every right to react emotionally to a certain event or to harbor my emotions, without worrying about the effect my reaction might produce. Prague happened during the summer of '68, right? Shortly after the May strikes and student riots in France, when we were sick and tired of hearing how terrible the consumer society was. It was impossible not to draw the parallel . . . And at the same time I hate this parallel which seems to reduce the field of possibilities for any industrialized country to only two: Prague, or the society we live in, where the elderly starve to death and the high government officials cheat on their taxes.

— And Dubček's experiment might have led to a new possibility, so that one's choice might not be limited to the two you just mentioned? Do you think that if the Russians had allowed him to go ahead and put his ideas into action . . .

— Let's say there are times when we need to believe so. Actually, what was interesting was that we were dealing with a relatively industrialized country, one whose standard of living and level of education was roughly the same as those of France in 1939, a country that had been a parliamentarian democracy. It is easy to see why the Soviet Union could not tolerate such an experiment in one of its satellite countries. The reasons have been reiterated a hundred times.

— Do you think there was anything symbolic about the fact that Prague and the events of May in France occurred so close in time?

— Frankly, no. Maybe it has something to do with sunspots, or magnetic storms or other phenomena of that sort about which I know nothing, but it does seem that they do in some way affect human behavior. Plus the incontrovertible fact that a new generation was coming of age throughout the world, a generation whose memory was not encumbered by World War II.

To be sure, there's a strange coincidence between the fact that the events of Prague in '68 were concretely set in motion by poverty, by lack of food and services: that renowned university where for heaven knows how long there was no heat or light and where finally the students got fed up to the point where they revolted. The French students, on the other hand, were up in arms against the plethora of food and services, against the so-called consumer society.

But, after all, that's merely the sign that our society is more advanced, and therefore, its causes of explosion are different. Still, it's like a law of physics. The explosion occurs as a result of a compression that goes on too long. That was also the case in France.

— How did you react to the events of May '68?

— It's difficult to say anything new or fresh on a subject that has been so talked and written about, by me as well as so many others. I don't really feel I can come back to the subject; it makes me feel that I'm putting an old record on again.

— But what about your personal involvement? Were you surprised by it?

— Surprised . . . I can't hear that word without thinking of the story involving the French lexicographer Littré. One day Littré was in bed with the family maid when the bedroom door opened and Madame Littré came in. "Oh, Monsieur! I'm surprised!" She said. To which Littré replied: "No, Madam, you're astonished. We're the ones who are surprised."

Did the events of May '68 take me by surprise? . . . No. The student explosion didn't surprise me in the least, perhaps because I had been following what had been going on abroad, in Germany and the United States. L'Express in general, and I in particular, had been following these events very closely. At the time, I was one of no more than fifty people in France who had not only heard of Marcuse, but had actually read him. I was also one of the fifty who had read the situationists' texts, including Raoul Vaneigem's book Le Traite de savior vivre a l'usage des jeunes générations [The Manual of Good Manners for Young People]. It's a book that was published well before 1968 in which you find virtually everything that later flowered in graffiti on the walls of France — and much more. Besides, I had two children who were students, and even in their branch of medical studies, which doubtless was not the seat of the greatest number of aberrations, it was still obvious that something was wrong, something was no longer working. Finally, ten years before I had got deeply involved in the explanation of French youth and its attitudes in a study we undertook at L'Express which we called "The New Wave." Later I turned it into a book based on thousands of letters by young people, a book which bore the same title

("Really a terrible title," was the comment at the publishers. "Can't you find a better one?").

A factor that did not appear statistically important — that is always the weakness of public opinion polls — emerged clearly in some letters. In particular, the worry and anxiety of some young people at the prospect of having to become part of our society, which is the other side of the coin from those who refuse to join it.

Since there are many and various articles to support my claim, I can safely say that I was one of the first to foresee the malaise that was one day going to take hold of a generation which had no idea of what it was like to be deprived. Perhaps the fact that I knew the United States rather well also helped me to see clearly. In any case, I knew there would come a time when the rising generation would start asking questions about the meaning of diligence, of exertion, of work — in short, of life itself.

Like all those who have had to raise children, I had given a good deal of thought to the question of how you instill respect for things you don't respect yourself. No one knows the proper way of bringing up children. I don't claim to. But did a generation of automaton-parents, as it were, producing the attitudes and mouthing the words which they themselves no longer believed, think for a moment that they were going to produce robot-children who would quietly insert themselves into the work-machines?

I would dare to assert today that I had been one of the first to see the early wisps of smoke of the impending fire, except that, as I have said, I have proof of my contention in pieces I wrote over the years.

On another level, I can still empathize with a person who feels horrified at the idea of "adapting." I say that knowing full well that I am, or I hope I am, more or less an adult in my thinking. The question is: to adapt to life or to disengage oneself from it. And at what point does the happy adaptation become base resignation?

The explosion in 1968 on the part of the workers derived from the amount of the minimum guaranteed-salary scale that had been granted. Seated there on his pile of gold, De Gaulle could see a long way, all the way to the United States, but he couldn't see directly beneath him. And his Prime Minister, in dealing with the miners' strike in 1963, had shown that he too had no feeling for labor.

Therefore, that explosion came as no surprise either. What made the event unique was the conjunction of the two — workers and students. Personally, I judge it to be of immense importance — perhaps the most important event in our history, from a sociological viewpoint, since the Paris Commune.

At the time of the May events, I felt an instinctive sympathy rather than panic. I went to a number of places to see with my own eyes what was going on: to the barricades, the Sorbonne, to the Odéon theater. I was fascinated by the verbal flood. An admirable illusion of communication, isn't it? I speak, therefore you're listening. But whether anyone was really listening to anyone else was really unimportant. Everyone was talking, and this multi-voice monologue in which suddenly repressed thoughts and words were set free resulted in the expression of all kinds of things that had never been said, and after which nothing would be the same as it was "before."

At L'Express people went a little crazy, as they did everywhere, no more, in fact, probably less. A few revealed themselves to be aficionados of the barricades: there was a feeling of rapture, of ecstasy in the air, but above all there was the basic problem of how to get the magazine out, and, after it was printed, how to distribute it, under conditions that can only be described as "unprecedented." The printers were only working for the daily press, a discrimination that was peculiar to say the least. To print offset, the way the magazine was normally printed, would have meant going abroad, and that was out of the question. Reverting to letterpress, we managed to print three issues of the magazine and ferry them into Paris by air. None of the issues bore any advertising, of course. Then we shipped them by truck into the major provincial cities. We lost several thousand dollars on the operation, but we decided that our presence on the scene was essential. I personally delivered several packages of the last issue of the magazine to the Parisian newstand vendors, and when the vendors went on strike, all the employees of the magazine took to the streets, hawking it themselves.

I saw Daniel Cohn-Bendit steam into my office one day, wild and sweet and full of laughter, looking for all the world like a young boxer, all ruffled and red. In masterly fashion, he took me for a hundred dollars — plus several reams of paper — and did it with great aplomb.

I was somewhat uneasy to know that my son was frolicking on the barricades. But then, I wouldn't have been happy knowing he wasn't there either.

— Weren't you worried or concerned about being in the dark?

— Generally speaking, I tend to be curious about the unknown, to be drawn to it. I could even say that I was not overly unhappy to see the edifice, whose bases were being shaken to its very foundations, tottering. All those whose power was being questioned had been too stupid, too egotistical, too blind, too excessive in everything they had done. And, too, there were those moments of real joy at seeing the number of people so sure of their own importance, their power, the glitter of their high stations, all of a sudden being questioned, discussed, re-evaluated. Knocked off their pedestals from within.

I had frightfully ordinary reactions. It was a funny sight,

wasn't it, with on the one hand those who announced the end of the Roman Empire because their son had said "shit" to them and those who were groveling at the feet of anyone under twenty? It's strange, that deep-seated fear of death which impels some people, as they grow older, either to throw up their hands and say that the world isn't what it's cracked up to be and that they will therefore leave it without regret, or to throw in their lot with young people, literally rub up against them as though, hopefully, they might be contagious . . . I have to admit that seeing Sartre at the feet of Cohn-Bendit made my heart sink, the way it does when I see a middle-aged woman in a miniskirt.

One evening, I can't place it in time exactly, Jean-Jacques and I happened to find ourselves in front of the building that houses the magazine. He looked it up and down, then placed his hand on the wall and murmured: "We haven't done too bad a job. A pity it's over." That's as far as his regrets went, or at least as far as he expressed them. As for me, I didn't even feel like expressing any.

In the high-rise building where I live, the accumulation of uncollected garbage was the most eloquent evidence of the kind of decomposition that was taking place. After a while, the smell had permeated everything, and in it there was something truly symbolic: a society that was no longer capable of making its garbage disappear, a society that stank.

There's a saying that goes: there's nothing more difficult than catching a black cat in the dark, especially when there isn't any cat. That, no doubt, is what is called an elusive situation. But was there or wasn't there a cat? The question still remains unanswered.

I knew that May was over, in its secondary phase, the day when among the graffiti which had covered the walls of our elevators and which, up to then, had been either Surrealist or obscene, there appeared a drawing which seemed to belong to time immemorial: a heart pierced by an arrow . . . Thus, in the spring of the year, the nightingale's song announces that the world is still turning on its diurnal axis.

As for the rest . . . It's too late to rely on one's impressions, too soon to reflect with proper perspective. I'm still far from fully understanding the real meaning of May '68.

To change life . . . Translated, that means to "enjoy." Nothing more. And what is keeping us from enjoying? Father, mother, society . . . and there we are back at the same old station: society which prohibits, restrains, demands, imposes rules and regulations that we absorb to such a degree that we obey them even when no one is looking to make sure we do. Do you pick your nose when you're alone?

There is really only one completely revolutionary project, and that is the anarchists': to destroy the existing order, do away with the rules and regulations, lift the restrictions. Everything else consists of replacing one order by another, one power by another, one set of rules by another.

Pierre Tkatchev, the Russian anarchist, the man who declared that if you really wanted to make over the world the way to start was to get rid of everyone over twenty, described in about 1870 the future joys of the revolution that needed to be made in Russia, in the following terms: "The peasant will be happy and well off. From dawn till dusk, his table will be covered with meats, patés, and wines. He will eat to his heart's content, will work when the spirit moves him, and will take orders from no one. Do you want to eat? Eat. You want to sleep? Sleep. You want to . . ." What a beautiful life it would be, right?

It found its echoes in such slogans of May '68 as, "It is forbidden to forbid" or "Enjoy to your heart's content." Frightful promises, those of the anarchistic utopia, where all the desires of the tiny child are united.

By definition, there will never be any anarchistic society, since there is an irreducible contradiction in the two terms. Nonetheless, that powerful will to happiness which has expressed itself, which at times takes the form of a parody of a return to nature — you don't wash, you don't shave, you don't pick things up, you don't work, you go to the beach, you feed your face, and you fuck — that overpowering demand is something which every last one of us, even those who deny it most vehemently, have felt and heard within us.

Is it possible that we cannot return to nature, that we'll to the woods no more? Is it impossible to undo, by even a degree or two, the iron corset imposed by that which distinguishes us from the animal state? Is it out of the question for the renunciation of pleasure that society demands to be reversed? And if it, what will we resort to to endure so many difficult demands? Drugs?

I don't know. But I can tell you that I who am incapable of remaining inactive for an hour without feeling guilty, who am the very incarnation of society's restraint and my own self-restraint, the product of rules which, though they may not be those by which everyone lives, are nonetheless just as implacable, strongly feel the suffocation today's children are trying to escape. That desire they feel to share happiness, their need to change the rules of the game.

How can it be done? . . . I have no program to suggest. Let's talk about it again in ten years; we may have a clearer idea.

Today's youth seems to have discovered in Marcuse what Freud wrote in that little but extraordinary book entitled *Civilization and its Discontents*. One of the most comical quirks of fate of our time is that which has befallen Marcuse, who has become a kind of Garbo of philosophy. I'm afraid this old gentleman, who when all is said and done is the last

Hegelian philosopher, a Hegelian who would seem to have read Galbraith, has lost all sense of humor about it, and humor was a quality he once had in generous quantity.

I once had a long conversation with him during one of his trips to France. It was in 1968, I believe, and he was still completely flabbergasted by his sudden though tardy celebrity. And I must say that this sarcastic giant managed to amaze me. Not by his theories, which I knew very well, but because every question I asked him was answered by his wife. And when, to her great regret, she let him answer for himself, he turned to her to make sure she approved of what he was saying. I was with two of my colleagues from the magazine. At one point one of them slipped me a note on which was written: "Now I understand why Marcuse is militating against oppression! . . ."

What do you say we call a halt. It's not that we're short of further subjects of discussion, but I feel the press of time, and besides, perhaps from this point on we're too close to events to comment on them in any meaningful way.

We had come up to 1968, '69 — even 1971 as far as L'Express was concerned and 1974 as far as politics. In either case, these years are too green; their events are too much in a state of flux for me to comment on them in any meaningful way.

The past . . . I know that, when I reread what we have said about it, I'll think to myself: "How could I have forgotten that evening in Moscow at Rostropovich's? How could I have skimmed over Roger Vailland so briefly? Why didn't I describe Kissinger in his White House office, expansive and open? And the Shah of Iran in his reception room in Teheran, arrogant? Castro in Cuba? And what I saw in Tokyo and Hong Kong? And my impressions of Angkor Wat? Etc., etc."

But I've never kept a notebook, and never will. I have

all I can do to publish a magazine; to keep my own journal to boot would be more than I could cope with!

— All right, let's take up where we left off ten years from now. Where will you be?

— I have no idea. Nor do I have the slightest desire to know. Life isn't tomorrow, it's today, this moment we're experiencing right now, when that plant there in front of the window has just unfurled a new leaf. Smooth, fragile, and tender like my newest grandson, this one coming through the door, just learning to walk. *"Salut, Jérémie! Salut, mon garçon!"*

Life is this minute when I'm beginning to grow impatient because I feel they're waiting for me at the magazine where some decision or other has to be made, and you're here, and you're keeping me from making it . . . Life is my joy and my hope, not tomorrow but today.